Inventing Africa

INVENTING AFRICA

History, Archaeology and Ideas

Robin Derricourt

PlutoPress
www.plutobooks.com

First published 2011 by Pluto Press
345 Archway Road, London N6 5AA and
175 Fifth Avenue, New York, NY 10010

www.plutobooks.com

Distributed in the United States of America exclusively by
Palgrave Macmillan, a division of St. Martin's Press LLC,
175 Fifth Avenue, New York, NY 10010

British Library Cataloguing in Publication Data
A catalogue record for this book is available from the British Library

ISBN   978 0 7453 3106 5   Hardback
ISBN   978 0 7453 3105 8   Paperback

Library of Congress Cataloging in Publication Data applied for

This book is printed on paper suitable for recycling and made from fully managed
and sustained forest sources. Logging, pulping and manufacturing processes are
expected to conform to the environmental standards of the country of origin.

10   9   8   7   6   5   4   3   2   1

Designed and produced for Pluto Press by
Chase Publishing Services Ltd, 33 Livonia Road, Sidmouth, EX10 9JB, England
Typeset from disk by Stanford DTP Services, Northampton, England
Simultaneously printed digitally by CPI Antony Rowe, Chippenham, UK
and Edwards Bros in the USA

Contents

Preface:
The construction of African pasts

This book explores narratives of Africa's past, especially of its deep past, and how they have been created, used and misused. All such narratives are products of place and time, limited by context and intent as much as by available knowledge. In presenting a critical account of such narratives, I note the dangers of oversimplifying the history of a vast and diverse continent, for perceptions and images of the past influence perceptions of the present and expectations for the future. While there are influences and connections between the examples presented in this book, the chapters can be read in the order of the reader's choice.

The African continent, with a billion people today in over 50 states (and some dependent territories), covers over 30 million square kilometres across environmental zones from extreme desert to dense tropical rain forest, supporting every kind of economic activity, religious belief, cultural sensibility and political structure. Yet 'Africa' has been the victim of generalising statements, simplifying histories and prehistories, stereotyping and imaginings from ancient times until today. The yearning to describe all or parts of the vast continent in simplified terms may be strongest in outsiders to the continent, but those living within Africa have also contributed. Africa has its own equivalents of Orientalism, which was defined by Edward Said as 'a way of coming to terms with the Orient that is based on the Orient's special place in European Western Experience'.

As with the better-known debates about Orientalism, generalising images of something described as 'Africa' or 'Africans' have dangers and implications that have run through history and continue today. It is easy to categorise as racist the views we see in the ancient world, or in the world of the Atlantic slave trade, or in the colonial era, or in societies receiving a major African diaspora. But the same issues of the danger of generalised frameworks apply today, both within and outside the African continent. They may be negative images of a still-dependent Africa whose social and economic challenges require outside intervention and aid. Or they may be images of a continent with a romantic wilderness of landscape, flora, fauna and still-traditional societies. All simplified models and images have their impacts, and understanding the range of 'Africanisms' can warn us about these.

The area described as 'Africa' has changed through time. The zones occupied by humans have grown, as described in our first introductory chapter, expanding from our hominid ancestors in the savannah regions to the settlement only recently of some offshore islands. There has always been an Africa of 'the Other'. Since the worlds of earlier civilisations, those parts of the continent that lay beyond immediate neighbours or influence were lumped into an Africa – under different names like Punt, Aithiopia, Bilad al-Sudan – that was characterised by images either negative, or mythical, or both.

Islamic influence across and south of the Sahara limited European contact and trade, but a fascination with the legendary Prester John and the kingdom of Ethiopia built the idea of a new Christian ally for Europe. With the expansion of European coastal trade to West Africa, Africans were seen as trading partners, but when slave trading came to overtake the trade in precious metals and produce, a new attitude to African people took hold in Europe. The end of the slave trade saw the emergence of paternalism then colonialism, followed by new kinds of dependency in the relations between Africa and the west, which are surveyed in the introductory chapter.

The remainder of the book looks at some of the narratives of Africa and its past that emerged during and after the colonial era. In Chapter 2 we present some of the ideas of an ancient and lost mythic and mystic Africa that fascinated readers, mainly Europeans outside and within Africa, from the mid-nineteenth century. The literary inventions of Rider Haggard, crediting ancient Mediterranean and Arabian civilisations with the stone ruins of southern Africa, started with rumours and travellers' stories but came to influence the actual historical interpretation of those ruins, with implications that continued into modern politics. The search for a 'Lost City' in the Kalahari Desert was an echo of such a narrative. And Zulu writer Credo Mutwa would create for the second half of the twentieth century believable myths about the African past that survived the transitions of power, to be taken up afresh by New Age adherents.

The twentieth century saw the replacement of imagined and fallacious constructions of the African past by scientific research, which started to give Africa its full place in human history and history its fuller place in African identity. But Chapter 3 shows this transition was not straightforward. The most important contribution to Africa's prehistory, the 1925 announcement by Raymond Dart of the Taung fossil as the earliest African ancestor of humankind, was from a writer and researcher whose writing was equally dedicated to extending the 'mystic Africa' stories of alien races invading and building and mining. The enigma of Raymond Dart is of a scientist whose work straddled the old imaginings of the African past and the new discoveries.

In Chapter 4 we describe some of the other pioneers of the study of early human ancestors. The role played in the nineteenth century by European explorers of Africa, inspired by commerce or missionary zeal or fame or nationalism, was paralleled by the fossil-hunting explorers of the twentieth century. Powerful egos, rival nationalisms, variable fortunes played their role in this story, one of the few scientific endeavours where 'discovery' meant just that, with the human story changed by the blow of a pick-axe. Interpretations of finds, including naming rights to the new fossil hominids, reflected the importance acquired by the adventurer-scientist. Aspects of the lives of Robert Broom, Louis, Mary and Richard Leakey, and Donald Johanson illustrate these themes.

If arguments about the name and nature of early human ancestors dominated the last decades of the twentieth century, new debates and arguments have emerged over the African origins of anatomically modern humans and of modern human behaviour, and these are discussed in Chapter 5. Grand sweep narratives were created to account for the emergence of societies that could be recognised both physically and mentally as of modern human type, with preferences reflecting different disciplinary backgrounds. The geography might suggest one story, with another from the distribution of archaeo-logical remains of stone tool-making, and the distribution of early skeletal material had to be tied to this. Then geneticists' studies of mitochondrial DNA came to challenge earlier assumptions and clarify a story of biological spread, but whose chronology had to fit the accounts derived from other sources. These debates are still very active, and this chapter reviews some of the diverse views in the debate.

We discuss in Chapter 6 another strand of the accounts and interpretations of the African past: that of the influence of Ancient Egypt. Writers have tended to think of pharaonic Egypt either as part of the ancient Mediterranean, or of the ancient Near East, or of the African continent, and battles over its identity have continued. Sir Grafton Elliot Smith in the early twentieth century developed his 'hyperdiffusionist' model under which Egypt was credited for the unique invention of numerous skills and inventions that spread elsewhere in the world, though mainly out of, rather than into, the African continent. Radical Senegalese scholar Cheikh Anta Diop, writing from the 1950s, redefined Ancient Egypt as a black African state, extending its influence to create European civilisation across the Mediterranean, while also having a long-term influence on the other black societies of Africa.

Such a model of 'Afrocentrism' would be taken up with enthusiasm by groups within the African diaspora. In the United States especially, the image of a powerful (black) civilisation on the African continent would inspire the new Black Studies movement. Into the debate came the work of British academic Martin Bernal, whose *Black Athena*, published from the 1980s onwards, created a generation of debate about the African roots of Egypt, and the Egyptian (and Semitic) roots of European civilisation.

The work of Basil Davidson, from the 1950s into this century, has been dominant in providing an image of the African past in Africa, Britain, North America and beyond. In Chapter 7 we review the life and work of this important and skilled writer. His books generated a wide awareness of past African civilisation – states with dramatic art, architecture, cities and trade. Such writing not only informed readers unaware of African history but inspired a generation of both Africans and others in the African diaspora, especially since it coincided with the growth of Black Studies in the US. But a critical account of Davidson's work must note the impact of his major books' selectivity within Africa's history. The whole spread of Davidson's writing, concerned as much with the African present and future as its past, reveals his growing discomfort with the transition from not yet decolonised nations, celebrating their continent's history, to new societies where the power and nature of the state had a more troubling nature.

In the final chapter, we touch on some aspects of the most recent uses and abuses of images and grand sweep narratives of Africa, to reinforce the dangers that simplification can bring. We give examples of ways in which decolonising movements and post-independence ruling groups have both used and ignored history. One recurrent theme is ethnic identities and 'tribalism'. These moved from being convenient historical labels, and convenient concepts for administrators, to major barriers to democracy or the unity of states. The nature of tribalism re-emerged as a concern by those who created or interpreted it.

Outsiders' perspectives on the nature of Africa, especially sub-Saharan Africa, have changed and developed. A contrast can be drawn between the view that celebrates and idealises the innocent, primitive and simple world of an imagined continent, and the 'Afropessimist' despair felt by some about the economic and political problems of many African states. Campaigners in the west have continued to use a generic Africa to appeal for funds, or for support for policy changes by governments. In this they echo the appeals from the nineteenth century by western churches, to send missionaries to bring Christianity and the benefits of western values (and commerce) to heathen lands beset by slave traders.

The view of 'primitive Africa', with a natural wilderness and remnant traditional societies, has both negative and positive aspects. It provided the basis for a racism that justified colonialisms, whether paternalist or with the aggressive violence made famous in Joseph Conrad's *Heart of Darkness*. It provided an inspiration for Modernism in western art with the rediscovery of tropical African carving. It is represented in the descriptions of a simple pure society of Bushmen (San) revealed by Laurens van der Post, whose writings later proved to be in part at least fabrication and derived. But in the modern world the approach has returned as ecotourism, as enthusiasm for those selected parts of Africa to reflect a supposedly pure wilderness, and for those communities (San, Maasai, Tuareg) who are supposed to live a simpler life than African townspeople.

The examples I discuss in this book show some of the limits and the dangers of generalising narratives about a complex continent. In looking at some of the ways in which interpretations, models and ideas have been used in some of the grand narratives applied to Africa, this book aims in a modest way to defend the peoples whose lives are on the continent called Africa from the threats that broad sweep generalisations may bring.

My interest in these topics comes from a confluence of different backgrounds and experiences. I was fortunate to have begun my career as a professional archaeologist, researching and writing in archaeology as well as in African history, in north-east, south and central Africa. This took me into the field to research areas not previously subject to detailed analysis, and taught me the value of studying what came from different sources: oral history, written records and the archaeologist's study of environment, economy and material culture. This was the beginning of a period of radical challenges within African history. It was also one in which, in archaeology, we were beginning to question the so-called scientific objectivity of archaeology, and to recognise that the answers we gave reflected the questions we asked, which came from our own context, not those of the period and place being studied.

I have been further fortunate in a second career as a publisher of books created by historians and other academics. I held editorial responsibilities for two of the main international publishing programmes in African Studies and one of the main archaeology lists in the English language. Publishers see the ways in which knowledge is created, in which ideas cyclically emerge, take hold and fade (or are ignored or repressed). Publishers contribute to this cycle but they do not control it; they seek to anticipate trends in ideas and interests. They witness the response of writers, researchers, readers to such changes, and they give consideration to different classes of readers – national, life stage, disciplinary, ideological.

The journey to this book has been informed by numerous friends and colleagues – as well as contacts in professional work, including some mentioned in this book. I have received valuable suggestions on the structure and argument, including those from the publisher and publisher's readers. None of those who have contributed to the formulation of the ideas in this book share responsibility or blame for its arguments, errors or omissions. I have been appreciative of the online and physical resources provided by libraries, particularly those of two institutions who have provided me with formal affiliation: as a Visiting Fellow in the School of History and Philosophy at the University of New South Wales, and as a Visiting Scholar at the McDonald Institute of Archaeological Research at the University of Cambridge.

1
The changing shape and perception of 'Africa'

There is no single Africa, with consistent boundaries through time. Africa has been perceived with different geographical limits, a different concept, both by past and recent societies. As the Kenyan writer and scholar Ali Mazrui noted, 'It took European conceptualisation and cartography to turn Africa into a continent.'[1] And settlement of Africa by humans has not always occupied the whole area we describe today.

Edward Said's critique of Orientalism showed how western culture brought together varied cultures and societies and then selectively attributed certain characteristics to this imagined oriental world. Studies have appeared of certain aspects of 'Africanisms' – images of Africa created in literature and philosophy, in history or in museums of art and ethnography.[2] The cases we review here are concerned primarily with constructions of the African past including the deep past.

Often the term Africa, or its equivalent in earlier societies, has been restricted to describe a 'them', the other, outside of 'our' world. Throughout history terms have been used both by outsiders and by peoples settled in Africa itself to group together vast and diverse areas of the African continent (adding, selectively, specific offshore islands). The boundaries of Africa, when seen as 'the other', have been fluid from the earliest literary contexts of ancient Egypt into modern times. Depending on context, everyone draws a different boundary around the Africa of their own choosing.[3]

Today most people, when they refer to 'Africa', think they know the area to which they are referring, yet these may be quite varied. The boundaries of 'Africa' are fluid with different uses, a fact that is of particular importance in dialogues about African society or identity, African development or underdevelopment, political relations with Africa, African literature or culture. Politicians, journalists and scholars alike sometimes apply the term 'African' to mean the area to the south of the countries that border the Mediterranean, which are considered part of the Middle East; Africa

1

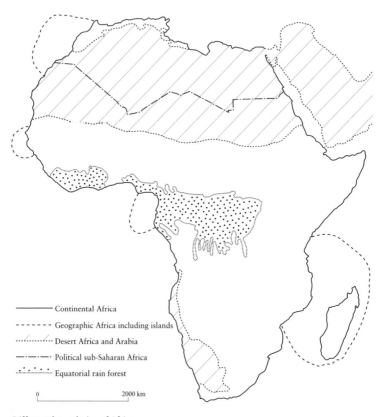

Continental Africa
Geographic Africa including islands
Desert Africa and Arabia
Political sub-Saharan Africa
Equatorial rain forest

0   2000 km

Different boundaries of Africa.

as shorthand for sub-Saharan Africa. But this tendency to separate a supposed real, black, African sub-Saharan Africa from a northern, less black, more Mediterranean or Middle Eastern Africa is contrary not only to political realities past and present, but also to genetics.[4]

The definition of Africa has been flexible in modern times, not just by the inclusion of Atlantic and Indian Ocean islands in different political definitions. European and American scholars and their institutions have recognised separate fields of 'Middle Eastern Studies' and 'African Studies'. The first frequently includes all the Arabic-speaking countries of Africa's Mediterranean littoral, with occasional extensions further south. 'African Studies' is often, if inconsistently, defined more narrowly as sub-Saharan Africa. While a wish to be inclusive may allow associations to broaden their geographical coverage, formal structures of research funding may be narrower.[5]

A special example of classificatory ambiguity comes from South Africa. Through most of the twentieth century the dominant white cultures of South Africa, in different contexts, could see 'Africa' as the area to the north, the countries in which black culture dominated. Thus 'African literature' or 'African art' were clearly different from, and exclusive of, the creative production of white South Africans. But by extension, the terms were sometime applied to include the work of the black (but usually not the coloured) community in South Africa.[6]

The continent's land boundary with Western Asia has been a flexible one, and less significant than internal environmental boundaries. Politically Sinai belongs today with Egypt, an African country, though for 15 years from 1967 to 1982 it was part of Israel, an Asian country. In the distant past Sinai represented a border zone, not a border, between continental land masses. The water boundary that today separates Africa from Asia dates, of course, only from the completion of the Suez Canal in 1869.[7] The great scholar of contemporary Africa, Ali Mazrui, has suggested that on cultural and historical grounds the Arabian peninsula could more logically be classed as part of Africa than as part of Asia.[8]

The term 'Africa' as a modern political division of the world is today most commonly applied to the land mass from Cape Town to one side or other of Sinai, together with a number of islands large and small in the Indian Ocean and the Atlantic Ocean (including a dozen island states or island possessions of European states). So geographically, some islands around Africa have long been part of the African cultural zone; others like Madagascar as much part of the Asian (or Indian Ocean) cultural zone, while some Atlantic islands can be considered effectively part of Europe. Mediterranean islands, equidistant between the European and African land masses, are usually seen as part of the European continent from which much of their cultural heritage derives.

CHANGING SPACE OF HUMAN SETTLEMENT

The long sweep of prehistory and history has seen changes to the areas of land and maritime Africa occupied by humans and their hominin ancestors.

The story of their settlement in Africa is one of gradual expansion, from origins in the open grassland areas of eastern and southern Africa, then a spread into and across the arid regions of northern Africa during their less harsh periods. The last area of the African mainland to see human settlement was the equatorial rainforest, ironically the environment most suited to humankind's closest living great ape relatives. And movement to settle Africa's offshore islands was late, sometimes very late.

The early *Australopithecus* hominins were restricted to the grasslands and relatively open woodlands of southern and eastern Africa. The boundaries created by the arid deserts to the north and south-west, and the dense equatorial forests of western Africa, delineate the area they could occupy, but the paucity of fossil remains make it difficult to map the specific limits of their territory.

Around 2.5 million years ago there was a global shift from warm and wet to cool and dry climates. The grasslands and open woodlands spread at the expense of dense forests, and the hominin species diversified, specialising to suit different environments, and including the first member of our *Homo* genus, *Homo habilis*, by 2 million years ago.[9] This species developed the first stone tools, allowing greater control over economic resources. Stone tools have greater survival than bones in the archaeological record so we can be confident that this species remained limited in settlement area bounded by forest, desert and maritime boundaries.

The successor *Homo erectus* emerged between 2.0 and 1.7 million years ago. It seemed better adapted to heat and was able to expand both into the increased areas of African grasslands and into more arid open environments.[10] Hunter-gatherer bands probably covered larger territories and were able to follow prey over longer distances. The development of Acheulian hand-axe technology allows archaeology to plot their distribution in what can seem almost continuous land use in the regions of settlement. This was the species that passed through arid North Africa to cross Sinai into Eurasia. Indeed the boundaries of Africa and Eurasia seem less important than between the occupied grassland and the most arid zones.

The expansion of the Acheulian hand-axe makers into much of Africa was limited by the dense tropical forest region of equatorial Africa, the last continental ecological zone to resist human settlement. To a foraging economy, ease of acquiring food is least difficult in temperate grassland, more challenging in tropical savannah, next in the desert regions, and most difficult in any of the forest zones. However, there was settlement in the equatorial region by modern humans around 40,000 years ago, with appropriately specialised stone tool kits.[11]

The desert areas of northern and north-eastern Africa experienced significant fluctuations in climate from 115,000 years ago, which marks the start of the last glacial period of earth's history. In the periods of greater rainfall the desert shrank, and many parts of today's deserts were occupied by hunter-gatherer communities. The long-established land link of Sinai is such that in later prehistory, North Africa and the southern Levant could be considered a single geographical area. But periods of extreme aridity expanded the deserts and made them unsuitable for human occupation.[12] We see a cycle of human occupation in the areas of today's arid regions, with absorption of hunter-gather communities in their wetter periods, and the expulsion of these communities into and through the Levant and Arabia as the rainfall reduced and the desert zones expanded again.[13]

Until human groups had learnt to construct water craft, migration routes out of the African continent were limited to the narrow strip linking to the Sinai peninsula. At current sea levels this strip was some 145km from north to south, of which only some 70km are currently dry land. The first movement 'out of Africa' was across this land boundary at around 1.8 million years ago.[14] While some scientists have pointed to the proximity of the African land mass to Arabia (at the Bab el-Mandab) and Europe (at Gibraltar, and even Sicily), these were impenetrable water boundaries until the spread of our own species.[15]

After the emergence of modern humans around 200,000 years ago came developments in cognition and human social behaviour. But it was probably not until around 60,000 years ago that water-borne technology (and the social structures and pressures that underlay it) allowed a sustainable human population to cross the Bab el-Mandab strait across the Red Sea into Arabia and thence into Asia and again by water to reach Australia.

COASTAL ISLANDS

The archaeology of Africa's diverse coastal islands is patchy, but suggests that movement to settle the islands off the shore of the African continent was relatively late in the sequence of human settlement.[16]

Evidence for earlier water crossings in the Mediterranean is very limited, and relates mainly to the Greek islands of the Ionian Sea. The settlement of most Mediterranean islands post-dated the introduction of agriculture.[17] However, in 2010 evidence was announced for Palaeolithic material in south-west Crete dated before 130,000 years ago; if accepted, this would be the earliest clear evidence for human water crossings.[18]

The more distant islands of the Atlantic were uninhabited at Spanish or Portuguese contact in the fifteenth and sixteenth centuries (Madeira may have been sighted by sixth-century BC Carthaginian and first-century AD Roman vessels blown off course). Only the Canary Islands, 100km west of Morocco, show early settlement – occupied by migrants from North Africa by at least 500 BC.[19]

Much more important is Bioko (Fernando Po), 32km west of Cameroon, and part of Equatorial Guinea. It is thought to have had occupation from West Africa by the first millennium BC and possibly as early as 10,000 years ago.[20]

The Red Sea between Egypt and Arabia has been an active maritime zone for trade since pre-pharaonic Egypt, though settlements on Egypt's Red Sea coast remained sparse. Trade was established across the Red Sea by 5,000 BC, with trade routes along the coastal strip linking to the cross-desert routes to the Nile Valley.[21]

African farming communities were exploiting the coastal resources of East Africa by boat, with at least occasional visits to the offshore islands, in the early first millennium AD, and the area was on maritime trade routes from at least this time, with sparse trade goods corroborating pre-Islamic written sources.[22] The *Periplus of the Erythrean Sea* from ca. AD 40 records the sewn as well as the dugout boats used by African communities in Rhapta. There is increasing evidence for their involvement in the coastal trade of the Greco-Roman period, which can be dated to at least 100 BC.[23]

Recent research has led to suggestions of much earlier human settlement in Zanzibar, 60km from the mainland, with cattle teeth in the fourth millennium BC and possible large stone tools suggesting human presence some 20,000 years ago. The significance of these proposals awaits further investigation and debate.[24]

Most Indian Ocean islands had first human contact not from Africa but from the seagoers of the Islamic world, with the Comoros settled from the eighth century AD. Madagascar was settled by at least 700 AD, and probably from the sixth century, with the Indian Ocean seafarers from east and north linking it to the African coast. These links helped to bring African influences and populations into the island.[25]

The South African Indian Ocean coast has few islands; Robben Island and Dassen Island, off South Africa, were uninhabited when visited by the Portuguese and Dutch in the fifteenth century and sixteenth centuries.

The classification of Africa's offshore islands with the continent has therefore been changing and cumulative throughout history.

ANCIENT EGYPTIAN PERCEPTIONS OF THE OTHER AFRICA

The first literate society on the African mainland was that of the Nile Valley. Through 3,000 years of pharaonic civilisation, ancient Egypt interacted with neighbours in south-west Asia, in the desert lands to the west, further south up the Nile, and more patchily with the lands to the south-east. Ethnicity was a primary identifier, with names and images of other peoples appearing in public inscriptions.

Ancient Egyptian records used clear and continuing terms for other peoples and other areas. Today's Egyptologists, looking down at a world map, have tended to seek to put external boundaries around these: an approach that may apply to powerful states bordering other powerful states, but has less reality when applied to diffuse communities whose interest to Egypt lay in their closest border of interaction.

To pharaonic Egypt their land was central to the world – the Red and the Black, combining the Nile Delta with the Nile Valley, and commanding both the Eastern Desert (to the Red Sea) and the oases and limited settled areas of the Western Desert. Egyptian geography recognised and distinguished the peoples and states of south-west Asia with whom they traded, and periodically had military conflicts or alliances.

Within the African continent Egyptian civilisation stood unique and undefeated by other states, though its own royal house was at times subject to military success of outsiders. The perspective was therefore of 'us', the Egyptians, with the other groups spread outwards from the Egyptian heartland. The terminology for the others has a fair degree of consistency through the pharaonic period, and is recognised not just in ethnic names (and the areas implied by these) but in artistic representation, with characteristics of physique and manner of dress. These may be stylised means of representation, not necessarily reflecting dress forms contemporary with each representation. There is no recognition in Egyptian tradition of an African continent separated from South-east Asia by Sinai and the Red Sea, nor is there a single term for those others who occupied the lands west and south of the Egyptian Nile Valley. Thus these groups have a boundary with Egypt, but not necessarily a boundary beyond.

To the west of Egypt are the groups usually translated as the Libyans, but described (in later times interchangeably) as Tjehenu and Tjemehu. These seem generic names for all those peoples living beyond the western boundary of the Egyptian polity. New ethnic names were added in the New Kingdom, with Libyan groups from further west described as Libu (from which the Greeks derived their term Libya) and Meshwesh. These are mainly nomadic people, coming out of the western ('Libyan') desert, mainly to trade but at times to raid,[26] with conflicts enough for Pharaonic inscriptions boasting of Egypt's military success against the Libyans. Rulers of Libyan origin were the pharaohs in the 22nd and 23rd dynasties (ca. 945–715 BC). Gradually the generalised sparse populations grouped as 'them', Libyans spreading thinly west, had come to rule 'us'.

To the south of Egypt areas in the Nile Valley were known as Ta Nehesy (Lower Nubia), and further south as Kush, in middle Nubia. Beyond lay the area called Irem in the New Kingdom.[27] These locations reflected the Egyptian concept of land and settlement as Nilotic: these were the people whose land bounded the Nile and extended sufficiently into the riverine hinterland as economic necessity required.

The name Punt occurs often in Egyptian writing, but the area to which it refers is unclear. It could be reached by boats south along the Red Sea and was a source for exotic products including myrrh, ebony wood and African savannah animals. This has led most scholars to locate it in the Horn of Africa, either Somalia or further north in the coast from Port Sudan to Eritrea.[28] There is an alternative strong argument to locate it in southern Arabia since elsewhere it is said to be accessible via Sinai, with Arabians acting as intermediaries for trading African products.[29] Both interpretations take the modern geographer's idea of space, looking down at the map instead of outwards. From Egypt's point of view, far-distant trading locations down the Red Sea might have been called Punt irrespective of which side of the sea – African or Arabian – they lay, and the generic use of the name Punt in many contexts would allow it to be a blurring of the continental divide. Punt is seen as a land neither to be feared (as another state) nor despised (as primitive nomads), a vagueness that again supports the lack of firm location. The name is not known in non-Egyptian written sources. Punt exists 'in a void'. It remains possible that Egypt used this name for the non-threatening world that extended probably both sides of the Red Sea, including an undefined extent of Africa that lay south-east of the more readily mastered upper Nile Valley.

Rarely do other parts of Africa intrude into Egyptian society. There are images that appear negroid in physiognomy at the Theban tomb of Amenmose, who served Amenhotep III (ca. 1391–1353 BC). There are black men accompanying fair-skinned, bearded 'great men of Punt'.[30] Savannah African animals are in the reliefs of the Egyptian expedition to Punt in Hatshepsut's temple at Deir el-Bahri.

In the 6th dynasty Harkhuf brought back from the southern land of Yam (probably Irem) exotic goods including a dwarf or pygmy 'from the land of the horizon-dwellers' – somewhere beyond the known world. But this could not be given an ethnic name, could not be depicted regularly in the symbolic friezes showing tribute from foreign races to the Egyptian king, so for effective purposes this further Africa did not exist for the ancient Egyptians. Of course, this question affects the question of ancient Egypt's possible influence on sub-Saharan African societies. If later Egypt showed an interest in Africa, this would be indicated by Herodotus' story that Pharaoh Necho II (610–595 BC) commissioned Phoenician sailors on an expedition that circumnavigated Africa,[31] but by then Egypt was confronting a world in which maritime powers – which Egypt had never been directly – were beginning to show their strength.

Apart from this, Egyptian perspectives on the continent in which they lay were linear – outwards from the Nile Valley. Everywhere to the south-east, beyond the Nile Valley, was Punt and beyond was neither known nor of major interest. This challenges the claims of Afrocentrists and others, discussed in Chapter 6, who see close relations between Egypt and other parts of Africa. Indeed, it has been suggested that pharaonic Egypt developed an increasingly discriminatory and racist approach to other Africans, especially from the late New Kingdom onwards as the Egyptian rulers sought to distance themselves from their continental context.[32]

THE CLASSICAL WORLD'S PERCEPTION OF THE AFRICAN CONTINENT

The classical world of Greece and Rome had different and evolving perceptions of the African continent.[33] These distinguished especially between areas in the hinterland of the Mediterranean coast (only a small part of which was named 'Africa'), the Nile Valley, and the substantial areas to the south, to which the term 'Aethiopia' was applied. The Greek *Aithiops* seems to be derived from *aithes* (burnt) and *opsis* (face).

The Mediterranean formed the centre of the civilised world in classical perception, and all of the Mediterranean littoral was to become part of the Roman Empire. But as in most of history, before conquest came individual settlers; before settlers were traders; and before direct trade came the penetration of trade goods through others. The 'knowledge' of parts of Africa would therefore be quite different for different groups of people. But the Sahara itself acted as a barrier to discourage Roman exploration south; only the Nile and the Red Sea route to East Africa gave both incentive and potential to reach further parts of Africa. Thus the term 'Aethiopia' (Greek *Aithiopia*) for sub-Saharan Africa, and the ethnic grouping 'Aethiopians' (*Aithiopes*) could be used for a generalised grouping of all who lived south of the area of interest, who were neither a threat to the Mediterranean cultures nor of value as trading partners. Because of the classical geographers' view that the land masses of the world were surrounded by ocean, the African land mass did, by default, have a southern, western and eastern boundary. The eastern boundary was known through trade, the western boundary much less (excluding rare expeditions such as Hanno's of the fifth century BC) and the southern coast not at all.

The area was of intellectual interest, both in real science and in literary allusion. Aethiopia served as a symbolic area even more than did Punt in ancient Egyptian culture. So in Homer's *Iliad* Zeus and other gods go off as far as was possible, to banquet among the Aethiopians. In much usage of the classical world there seems a difference between a 'worthy' Ethiopia – the civilised societies of Meroë and Axum – and the remainder, a savage Ethiopia.[34]

The Greeks used the term 'Libya' to apply to a broad area west of Egypt, and its boundaries with Aethiopia are blurred. Herodotus' *Histories* give a framework of the greater geography of the African continent through the eyes of the mid-fifth century BC.[35] He details many different ethnic groups on the Mediterranean littoral and its hinterland, and into the desert to the south. Elsewhere in the *Histories* Aethiopians are frequently mentioned – they do not need definition – but their occurrence emphasises the interpretation of this as a generic grouping. Thus they have exotic customs, but they are also one among many ethnic groups used in the Persians' army, and Meroe is described as a capital city of the Aethiopians.

Herodotus himself travelled only as far south as Elephantine in Egypt. Following a sixth-century expedition to the Greek Euthymenes to the River Senegal,[36] Herodotus' contemporary the Phoenician Hanno sailed down the west coast of Africa, beyond Senegal and possibly as far as Cameroon. The Achaemenid Sataspes was said by Herodotus to have travelled some way along the west coast of Africa in the early fifth century BC. Scipio sent historian

Polybius down the west coast of Africa, also probably to the Senegal River, in the mid-second century BC. But few other expeditions were inspired. In the first century BC Strabo described Africa as a triangular landform, but this was by assumption, not exploration.

The east coast of Africa did develop as a major trading route,[37] as best described in the first-century AD *Periplus of the Erythrean Sea*, which details trading posts down to the East African coast. By the second century AD, Ptolemy's *Geography* could have descriptions as far as Cape Verde in West Africa.

But these were trading sites. Occupation by peoples from the classical world stayed at the North African coast. The precedent was of course the Phoenician settlement of Carthage ca. 814 BC, with which Rome established a trade agreement in the fifth century. Meanwhile Greek fishing colonies had settled in Cyrenaica. But the later conflict between Rome and Carthage led to Scipio's invasion in 204 BC and defeat of Hannibal at the Battle of Zama in 202.

Romans used the names 'African' for a broader range of people than those in 'Africa', a term initially applied to the Tunisia region.[38] Areas north of the Sahara beyond the Carthaginian domain were called Numidia and Mauretania, the Gaetules were in the western desert and Garamantes further east. With the Romanisation of North Africa, those in the Maghreb outside their domain were commonly called Mauri (Moors). The Sahara 'was the limitless reserve of nomadic enemies to all that the settled societies of the Mediterranean stood for'.[39]

The colonies of Africa bore different names. After the Third Punic War in 146 BC the Province of Africa was created; and Roman interest in Africa expanded intermittently from then. The original province was known as Africa Vetus when Julius Caesar made part of Numidia into Africa Nova, and in 27 BC the two colonies were united into the Africa colony under Augustus. The fullest extent of Roman colonies was under the Severan emperors (AD 197–235), but the term Africa still represented the colony in Tunisia: from west to east were Mauritania, Numidia, Africa, Cyrenaica and Egypt. The Roman Empire in Africa had the longest frontier of the empire, but the trade routes controlled by Rome were mainly eastwards, leading especially from the Nile Valley to the Red Sea.[40] Only after the Christianisation of the empire would Africa extend over a larger area: the Diocese of Africa covered the Roman provinces of north-east Africa.

Thus 'Aethiopia' was a catch-all term for Africa beyond the area of settlement, threat or direct trade. And it remained symbolic: 'In later Roman literature, Ethiopia is a quasi-mythical fantasy land of strange sights and topsy-turvy customs.'[41]

In late antiquity, too, the name 'India' could be applied to the area of modern Ethiopia, to further confuse matters. This may reflect the perception, present in ancient Greece and in medieval Europe, that Ethiopia had a land bridge to Asia and thus formed part of 'India', while the Nile could be regarded as the true geographical boundary of Asia and Africa.[42]

ISLAMIC PERCEPTION OF AFRICA

Pre-Islamic Arabs were trading with the east coast of Africa and in contact with the black African communities of the lands opposite Arabia.[43] Indeed the first muezzin appointed by the Prophet Muhammad was a freed Ethiopian slave, Bilal ibn Rabah. The early Islamic perception of Africa began by emulating much of the same pattern as in classical times: distinguishing the communities of the Maghreb and the deserts to the south from a substantial area between the Atlantic and the loop of the Niger, which fell into the description 'Bilad al-Sudan' (Land of the Blacks).[44] This term came to be used primarily for the lateral band of Africa that came under influence from Islam, but by definition that was the only area of Africa known to the Islamic communities of North Africa. The name Takrur expanded from that of a specific community to be used for the western part of the Bilad al-Sudan from the fourteenth century onwards.[45] The primary distinctions in early Islamic world view related to religious faith more than ethnicity: Dar al-Islam and Dar al-Kufr (the abode of unbelievers).

The Arab Muslim conquest of Egypt in 639–41 and of the west Mediterranean coast of Africa in 647–8 brought into the Islamic world the former Roman provinces. The name Ifriqiya (Africa) applied to the region centred on the original Africa Vetus of Rome: Tunisia, extending into western Libya and eastern Algeria. In modern times the term was used as a term for the whole continent of Africa.[46]

The conquest of North Africa was not in itself an enforced conversion, nor was the early spread of Islam to the south. While some of the indigenous Berber people did convert others did not, but Berber nomads acted as intermediaries trading across the Sahara with the settled farmers of the Bilad al-Sudan. Islam followed trade, and it was the influence of trade and then of individual clerics,[47] not conquering armies, that brought Islam to the African communities of the Sudanic belt from the eighth century onwards. Trade was, however, augmented by raids: the governor of Ifriqiya raided south in 734–40 for gold and slaves.

There was thus increased awareness of the different communities: al-Fazari in the eighth century described the medieval kingdom called Ghana, and the eleventh-century geographer al-Bakri could write of the people of Gao, Takrur and Ghana. By the fourteenth century Ibn Battuta was to travel overland and write in greater detail of both West Africa – noting the eastward flow of the Niger – and the East African coast known through energetic maritime trade. The trade potential from the Bilad al-Sudan was substantial: not least gold and slaves, but medieval Islamic influence sat largely in the area that formed the trading zone on the northern edge of the Sudan.

East Africa was long known to the traders from the Arab world. When Muslim geographers came to write overviews of the world's geography they could draw on this knowledge or travel with traders, and visit Islamic settlements on the coast. In the eleventh century al-Biruni could describe the coast as far as Sofala and report it as far as the Mozambique Channel.[48] Here, as elsewhere in Africa, awareness, both direct and indirect and augmented by trade, led to a lower barrier between Islamic Africa and its continental neighbours.

It would take the aggressive expansion of Islam in the modern era from 1750, and more informally from the colonial era, to reach the present stage where perhaps half of the people of the African continent profess Islam, and a quarter of all Muslims live in Africa.[49]

EUROPEAN IMAGES AND PRESTER JOHN

Medieval Europe's knowledge of African geography relied on Classical and Islamic sources, and had no awareness of the size of the continent until the rounding of the Cape in the late fifteenth century. Europe's knowledge of Africa[50] was thus not only limited but intermediated by Muslim perceptions and communications. Few travellers from medieval or Renaissance Europe could boast of a first-hand knowledge of the African interior, because access to the lands of Africa was controlled by the Muslim world.[51] Important to the Muslim traders was of course the gold from West Africa,[52] which fed into the medieval European economy. European traders were at times allowed into North Africa, and on only rare occasions individuals were permitted to follow the land routes south established by Muslim traders into parts of the interior. European knowledge of the African interior therefore came from Muslim travellers and their writings.[53] It is claimed that 'medieval knowledge of Africa, especially of the coasts, extended to well within tropical latitudes',[54] but with severe limitations on accuracy.

Nor could Europeans access the maritime trading settlements on the east coast. It was therefore to the west coast of Africa that the maritime nations of Europe began to pay their attention, with fourteenth-century maritime expeditions exploring the African coast,[55] followed by the fifteenth-century colonisation of the Canary Islands by Spain, and of Madeira and Cape Verde by Portugal. Initially maritime efforts further south focused on access routes round the Cape of Good Hope. Bartolomeu Dias – who had sailed on a 1481 expedition to modern Ghana – rounded the Cape of Good Hope in 1488, and in 1498 Vasco da Gama touched ports of the East African coast on his expedition to India. Knowledge of the intermediate coast was patchy[56] and of the interior much more indirect.

There was, however, direct contact with the Ethiopian church (long represented in Jerusalem), and evidence of awareness of the Ethiopian Church by the Catholic Church in the thirteenth century. But details of the Ethiopian kingdom were unknown, and could lead to speculation about a greater Christian penetration into the African interior than was the case. To western Europeans the importance of a Christian kingdom in Africa lay in its potential as an ally in the conflict with Muslim dominance. Italians visited the Ethiopian court from at least the early fifteenth century, and probably earlier.

By the fourteenth century Portuguese and other western Christians had come to relocate and associate the legendary eastern Christian king 'Prester John' with the kingdom of Ethiopia, and thus to create an exotic image in Africa as a potential equal and ally.

Prester John had long been thought of as a rich and powerful ruler over a distant Christian land separated from the western Christian kingdoms by non-believers. The story of Prester John had early located him in India, long believed to have been the subject of an apostolic mission by Saint Thomas. A Central Asiatic context for Prester John emerged during the Crusades, and to twelfth-century Europe his was a magical kingdom, which may have been beyond Persia, or on the borders of China, or in India – 'India' being itself a loose geographical term, which could at times encompass adjacent areas of the African continent.[57] One source for the story is in a report, to the Pope, shortly after a major defeat in the Crusades at Edessa in 1145, of the victory against Muslims in the East by a central Asiatic potentate.[58] Prester John's main value, then and later, was as a potential Christian ally of the Crusaders attacking the Islamic world from the east, and a number of expeditions were sent east to try and make contact with this powerful ruler.

Having failed to locate him in the east, by the fourteenth century the Portuguese and others associated him with the Christian kingdom of Ethiopia, whose ruler bore the conveniently confusing title *žān.* This identification was to cause puzzlement and embarrassment when Ethiopian emissaries and western representatives were to meet more formally. A man named Jorge claimed to be an emissary from Ethiopia in 1452.[59] Subsequent exploration of West Africa led to accounts of an inland king called Ogané – perhaps the Oni of Ife in Nigeria – who for a period was considered to be Prester John.[60] Portuguese emissaries were sent to the Ethiopian kingdom: Pero de Covilhã in 1487 and João Gomes in 1507, but they remained there so brought no information on the 'kingdom of Prester John' back to Europe. Around 1510 an Armenian emissary from Ethiopia, known as Mateus, was despatched to the Portuguese court and inspired a failed attempt to respond with a mission to the Ethiopian king. In 1520 a successful mission from Portugal was sent, meeting with 'Prester John' (the emperor Lebna Dengel Dawit) at his peripatetic court in October that year, returning in 1526 and reported in the lengthy work of Father Francisco Álvares.[61] This factual account of the court and kingdom of Emperor Lebna Dengel reduced the magic and mystery of the Ethiopian Kingdom, with its detailed report to the Portuguese court and broader readership. Yet Álvares routinely refers to the emperor by the term 'the Prester John', though it was noted at the time 'the Moors and Abyssinians call him Emperor and not Prester John'.[62]

On an official level this was the first European mission to visit and return from the court of 'Prester John' and describe it as a real, material kingdom. But at the court were not only the Portuguese from earlier missions, but Catalans, Germans, Greeks, Italians, Spanish – resident there and locally married after escaping from Muslim captivity. Indeed the empire of the supposed 'Prester John' was not an unknown mystery but an active player in the *realpolitik* of early modern world.[63]

TRADE AND SLAVERY

By the sixteenth century maps could show a more complete image of the African continent with a plausible outline of its shape. Desceliers' map of 1550[64] combined the classical and Muslim images of the African interior with the new seafaring knowledge, including a

Nile with origins in two lakes and a Niger (although west flowing) River, within a clearly recognisable African continental outline. Oduardo (Duarte) Lopez's visit to Luanda in 1578 was followed by the publication of the *Report of the Kingdom of Congo*[65] in Portuguese and quickly translated into English.

When Africa was primarily (if indirectly) a source of gold from wealthy organised kingdoms trading through the northern Islamic world, there was no need for them to be seen as inferior by their European trading partners. The kingdoms and societies of West Africa with whom Europeans could trade directly evoked much admiration and pride that successful trade could be developed between powerful societies of Europe and Africa, and European readers were entertained with descriptions of West African towns and powerful rulers.[66] Correspondence between European powers and certain African rulers – especially those who had professed Christianity – was maintained with the civility of equal status, alliances were made, and African embassies were received with appropriate civility in European courts, so that rank took precedence over race where required.[67] A climate of mutual exchange benefited western Europe and West Africa.

European images of Africa (seen through Portuguese eyes) were ambiguous and changing. Although the motivation to explore the West African coast was primarily to trade gold, bypassing the Muslim North African intermediaries, this was soon matched then overtaken by a trade in slaves. Establishing coastal trading posts southward along the coast, the Portuguese found African chiefs more than ready to trade humans for European exchange goods, and the expanding demand for slaves transformed the trading economies along the coast and hinterland.

The trade of slaves was initially into Europe before it became a trans-Atlantic commerce of vast scale. From the 1440s Portuguese landed black slaves for sale to Portuguese households. A Spanish slave trade to Europe followed – by the 1550s the Spanish were carrying up to 2,000 slaves annually, with over 100,000 slaves estimated to live in Spain.[68] With the drying up of routes for eastern slaves that followed the Ottoman conquest of Constantinople in 1453, Italy became a major market for black African slaves.[69]

As West Africa grew as a source of slaves and European wealth, Europeans had to develop a concept of Africa and Africans in a different mould to mesh with the Christian conscience. In Renaissance Europe, people from different parts of sub-Saharan Africa, as well as their descendants, were grouped as 'blacks' (*negre*, *negro*) and at times Africans (*africano*).[70] Italy, whose contact with Africa was more indirect, would use the term Moor (*mori*) both for black people and for North Africans. The area and the physical type were linked, though some, especially Spanish and Portuguese of the sixteenth century, would use the term Guinea for a broad sweep of West Africa. The prejudice against those now seen as natural slaves extended to Elizabethan England where blacks were not formal slaves but a servant class[71] – to the English sub-Saharan Africa was the 'land of Negroes'. The links with the Ethiopian church remained, with Ethiopian communities and churches in Rome and Nicosia.

Earlier cultures had lumped together areas south of the familiar world with a single term, reflecting its relationship as the 'other', the outsiders. So early modern Europe, despite its greater geographical awareness of the size of the continent, came to consider all those who were neither Christians nor Islamic Moors as people whose relationship to European civilisation was dominated by a role as slave traders and slaves.

These three transformations went hand in hand. European interest in West and equatorial Africa became changed from mineral wealth to human slaves, with a trans-Atlantic slave trade that moved perhaps 10 million, perhaps 17 million people to the Americas, as well as vast numbers of 'incidental' deaths.[72] The economies of the coastal African communities were transformed by the size and wealth of the demand for slaves: a demand that was met not just by trading criminals and prisoners of war and domestic slaves but by African rulers raiding their hinterland specifically to capture slaves to sell. And to reflect this relationship and justify it in a Christian ethic, the peoples and societies of Africa had to be reclassified by European societies as less than human; they lost individuality, history, culture and humanity in the ideology of the nations involved in the Atlantic slave trade over four centuries.

BEFORE AND AFTER COLONIALISM

The willingness of coastal African communities to meet the demand for slaves and other produce, together with the impact on Europeans' health of tropical African climates (until quinine could tame malaria), kept much official European settlement perched on the West African coast until the nineteenth century. The larger settlement of Europeans at the Cape in South Africa was an exception, not the norm, and only the pressures of the Napoleonic War brought Britain there.

Following their seventeenth-century establishment of Caribbean settlements, Britain became the largest transporter of slaves across the Atlantic from the late seventeenth century onwards – 60 per cent of all trans-Atlantic slaves were transported between 1721 and 1820[73] – and, after the banning of the British and United States slave trade took effect in 1808, the British became the most enthusiastic blockader of slave ships in the nineteenth century. The slave trade reduced but did not cease.

Through much of the nineteenth century European powers were not anxious to extend their control of Africa deep into the interior. The era of exploration began selectively. British exploration maintained certain themes: 12 of 17 book-length accounts by British explorers in West Africa in the period 1841–60 were concerned with the lower course of the Niger.[74] The image of the African interior from the writings of adventurers and explorers could show and warn about the exoticism of the continent's peoples, and selectively feed western readers' self-confidence in their superiority to barbarous tribes. More significantly, Christian missionaries needed to maintain the twin images of primitive barbarism and Islamic aggression to attract support for their early endeavours to convert Christian souls in the African continent.

European powers were drawn into creating African colonies by multiple factors, including domestic pressures and mercantile opportunities, not least as preventative measures to ensure rival European powers did not secure all the hinterland of important coastal regions.

The image of 'the Negro's place in nature', first created to complement the role of Africans as slaves, was transformed to present them as the beneficiaries of colonialism. The benefits might be peace between warring tribes, or protection against remnant slave trading in the Arab-dominated east coast; they might be improvements in rights of citizens or the saving of souls by Christian missions. 'The image of Africa was largely created in Europe to suit European needs – sometimes material needs, more often intellectual needs.'[75]

The Great War brought the African colonies – some relatively new in their colonial or 'protectorate' status[76] – further into the global political framework, whether through their economic supplies, as sources of manpower or even (as in the British and German East African territories) as theatres of war. In the new post-war world new images emerged of the colonial role and of the nature of the Africa societies. The emphasis moved to creating new forms of administration, to economic growth, and to the expansion of white mining, commercial and (in selective regions) farming enterprises.

All this required the growth of education and training, which in turn helped define the ideology of what would be developed and taught. Pride in pre-colonial pasts and pre-colonial identities was treading on dangerous ground, useful only selectively. Different colonial nations took widely different views on what the new education should feature, but the emphasis was often on seeking to ensure the most educated elite identified with the European colonial power, or with a European-based church, and with their values and perspectives.

In this interwar period there were debates on the most appropriate presentation of the past: whether an emphasis on tribal and regional heritage would strengthen the colonial structure, or loyalty to the colonial administration required more emphasis on the benefits of the colonial era. British 'colonial education policy hoped to create loyal Africans who knew their place in gendered colonial and racial hierarchies'.[77] Progressive educationalists in British Africa did argue for a broader curriculum. But a leading British educationalist who travelled in Africa and advised enthusiastically on the expansion educational development reflected the perception of the time:

> A fact of primary importance in African education is that outside of Egypt there is nowhere any indigenous history. There is tribal memory, of course ... but there is no history in our sense. ... The absence of indigenous history in Africa has had two effects. It has prevented the growth of a self-conscious culture, and it has lowered the status of the African in the eyes of the outside world.[78]

He proceeded to advance the view that the developments that had take place in Africa were attributable to outsiders: Muslims, Europeans and further back the supposed ancient builders of Great Zimbabwe. 'A primary aim of history teaching in Africa is to put the African into the stream of history from which he has been absent for so long.'[79]

It took the Second World War and its aftermath to raise with the European powers the spectre of decolonisation, either as an eventual, though presumed long-term, probability, or as something to be resisted forcefully. Ideas of the African future began to be debated widely within Africa and outside, and part of this was debate over the nature and significance of the African pasts. As time progressed, and decolonisation happened by process, inevitability or forceful struggle, the whole colonial period could be seen to be just a short interval in Africa's long trajectory.

The following chapters of this book examine the creation and impact of some of the ideas of Africa's deep past that were advanced between the beginnings of the colonial era and today.

2
Mythic and mystic Africa

Africa inspired ideas of an exotic imaginary past that came to be believed as a real history. To the ancient classical world, the Islamic world, to a lesser extent medieval and early modern Europe, and importantly the colonising European nation, it was important to have realistic knowledge of the parts of the African continent with which they had contact; contact in trade, political relations or military encounter. Beyond that 'real' world the imagination could develop without practical implication.

Thus from antiquity Africa, and especially the African interior, have become the location for stories of exotic, mystical and romantic places, peoples, events. Some have been told as fictional creations, some as if true stories, and the blurring of these genres has been a blight on African history.

This ambiguity was addressed by Herodotus in the fifth century BC; he records both his own observations, and stories he has been told, noting that he cannot vouchsafe for their truthfulness and in some cases leaving it to the reader to decide. After such a renunciation of responsibility he is able to weave stories of a magical Africa into his narrative.[1] Some but not all strange items hold truth: the presence of gold, and elephants, and ebony with very tall, good-looking and long-living men up the interior Nile. The tales told of the different tribes across Africa west of the Nile have broad credibility, while detailing some exotic customs, and avoid the most lurid and extreme attributions. Later classical writers could add more exotic attributions to unknown Africa.

The myths that surrounded the 'Prester John' of European imagery mixed fact and fantasy. But as Europeans encountered more of the reality of Africa, they sought at times to credit it with an exotic past.

GOLD, OPHIR AND LOST CIVILISATIONS OF SOUTHERN AFRICA

In the later part of the nineteenth century, as European colonial powers imposed their rule on the African continent, the idea of

'The Temple of Truth' from H. Rider Haggard, *She*, 1887.

past non-African presence in interior Africa became an active theme in fiction and in historical interpretation, and has remained so in much popular imagery until today.[2] This was a strong line of argument in the European interpretation of the pre-European past in southern Africa, where European settlement was greatest. But when applied to specific sites or categories of finds, the detail became obscured: there was agreement that black Africans could not have been those responsible for stone-walled ruins and abandoned gold mines, but sometimes a deliberate vagueness on the who and when of alternative explanations.

The material riches obtainable from the African interior were long known to the Arabs trading on the East African coast, and to the Portuguese who settled at Sofala and elsewhere in the sixteenth century. The Portuguese learnt of the African interior through the Arab traders. They wrote of the black African kingdom of Mwene Mutapa (Monomotapa), the stone walls of its buildings called Zimbabwe(s) ('Zunbanhy', 'Symbaoe') and the gold from this area of the interior.[3] They also recorded speculation of exotic, ancient origins for some of this stone building, and in 1609 João dos Santos suggested that King Solomon's Ophir may lie within this central African region, or that its resources were exploited for the Sabaean monarch of the Bible, the Queen of Sheba. These romantic ideas gained widespread currency in Europe.

The Transvaal of Southern Africa was visited from the British colonies to the south in the early nineteenth century and settled by emigrant Boers in the 1830s and 1840s. Europeans, travelling in the African interior, encountered large contemporary settlements but also the stone walls from abandoned locations. The missionary John Campbell visited the Tswana town of Kaditshwene in 1820 and described this community of 15,000 people living in stone-walled enclosures. He noted the similarity of current stone wall settlements to the stone of 'ancient ruins'.[4] And many other travellers reported current, recently abandoned or earlier stone-walled settlements in and beyond the Transvaal.

In the imperative of seeking mineral wealth Europeans also encountered the sites of African mines, abandoned after they had been worked out by the available technology. Reports of these 'discoveries' inspired historical conjecture and more powerfully some creative fiction.

The mystic, the exotic, the alien peoples. Ironically, it seems that fiction preceded claims for historical truth, and that fiction inspired historical interpretation, which was itself highly fanciful. Some of this was tied to the search for the Ophir of the Old Testament, although the numerous biblical references to Ophir and its wealth make it very possible that 'Ophir' was a generic reference to sources of trade goods rather than a specific, but as yet untraced, single settlement. The biblical riches were 'gold of Ophir' just as later traders sought 'spices of the Indies'.

A German missionary in the Transvaal, Alexander Merensky, heard reports of ruins to the north but was unable to reach them.

Inspired by such stories, Hugh Mulleneux Walmsley published in 1869 a novel entitled *The Ruined Cities of Zulu Land*,[5] which linked the ancient Egyptians and the rich Ophir of King Solomon's times to the African stone ruins. Here were the Phoenician crews of Pharaoh Necho's expedition mentioned by Herodotus, from the seventh century BC. They discovered Ophir, which was then exploited for gold, cedar-wood and precious stone, and they married into the local tribes, leading eventually to the much-admired Zulu nation. Ophir lay north of the Ndebele kingdom of Mzilikazi, in the Zambesi Valley; European adventurers with Mzilikazi's permission passed through to find the great walled ruins and their wealth. There were massive ruins of pyramidal form, constructions of stone without mortar, plant and animal carvings (birds carved in stone had been mentioned earlier in the piece). But this becomes a subsidiary plot to the novel's adventures that include shipwreck and piracy and even the Indian Mutiny.

A study of some 500 British works of fiction and non-fiction about Africa[6] notes that fiction has long influenced, and continues to influence, outsiders' perceptions of Africa. It was observed that

> there are two Africas, different and incompatible: the Africa of anthropology and that of popular 'literary' conception. ... Four centuries of [British] writing about Africa have produced a literature that describes not Africa but the British response to it.[7]

This study notes how from the mid-nineteenth century works of fiction were influenced by, but also had to compete with, travellers' factual tales. The core emphasis was often the British character, and the African central characters if in heroic mould were often light-skinned and less negro in appearance.[8] By the turn of the century novels sought pure escapism and attempted to echo the adventures of earlier exploration.

Young German geologist Carl Mauch was inspired by Merensky to explore further north in 1871 in search of the fabled ruins of Ophir, and was guided by a German trader, Adam Render, to the unoccupied ruins of Great Zimbabwe in the south of what was later Southern Rhodesia. Staying in the area for nine months, Mauch planned and described the details, finding important artefacts during his visit. His enthusiasm to attribute the creation of the site to Phoenicians was encouraged by identifying wood from the valley's Elliptical Building as cedar wood, despite the improbability of outsiders transporting their own wood for construction such a distance.[9] Scholarship was unimpressed by his claims that the Hill Ruin was a copy of King Solomon's temple and the Elliptical Building was a copy of the palace where the Queen of Sheba stayed in Jerusalem.[10]

In 1873 the *Illustrated London News*[11] reported Mauch's visit to Great Zimbabwe and the claims for its ruins as ancient Ophir in the northern goldfields. Interestingly, the article dismisses the identification of architectural moulding, suggesting it was of geological origin, and throwing 'the cold shade of doubt over this pretty romance'. And an early amateur archaeologist, Andrew Anderson, after visiting the ruins in the later 1870s, concluded they could not be linked to the Sabaeans (Sheba) but did assume a non-African origin.[12]

But in formal and accessible publication, the genre of romantic fiction preceded that of romantic history. To take two landmark publications, Henry Rider Haggard's fantasy adventure novel *King Solomon's Mines* was published in 1886, and the first part of the same author's *She* in the same year, while Theodore Bent's account of his explorations and exotic interpretations, *Ruined Cities of Mashonaland*, was issued only six years later, and Hall and Neal's influential *The Ancient Ruins of Rhodesia* not until ten years after that, in 1902.

Rider Haggard went to Natal in 1875, a young man of 19 with an interest in spiritualism and the mystical, and while in South Africa he heard the embellished stories of ancient inland ruins. After a brief visit in 1880, he returned to live in England from 1882. His imaginative romance and adventure fiction was thus written from a British base. Encouraged by the success of Stevenson's adventure yarn *Treasure Island*, published in 1883, Haggard wrote *King Solomon's Mines*, which on publication in 1885 proved an instant popular success. In this work he imagined an abandoned diamond mine in the area of the later Northern Rhodesia (Zambia), occupied by the Kukuana (an alias for the Ndebele, who actually lived in Southern Rhodesia).[13] The implication is that the mine had once provided riches to the Kingdom of Solomon, though operated by Phoenician entrepreneurs. There are also mentions of ancient Egyptian symbols – carved 'sculptures' (reliefs) on the side of a tunnel showing figures in mail with chariots and a battle scene with captives being marched off. Haggard's main fascination at this time was with Zulu tradition,[14] not the ancient world, so the inconsistencies in the historical background merely add to the mystery. Armour and an ancient axe are brought out as gifts. A wide road ('Solomon's Great Road') winds across the plateau to the mine, 50 feet wide and cut out of the solid rock. At the mine three statues are identified with Phoenician deities. None of this bears too much analysis; the diamonds for which this effort was devoted seem to have been left near the mine for the modern adventurers to find.

Such an image has inspired, consciously or subconsciously, much of European perception of the southern African past, on Great Zimbabwe and other ancient stone building, on ancient mining and trading. But Haggard himself claimed that when he wrote the book he had not heard of Great Zimbabwe nor ancient workings,[15] and that all in the book was 'the fruit of imagination, conceived I suppose from chance words spoken long ago that lay dormant in the mind'. He mentioned elsewhere that the book's contents were 'stimulated by vague rumours I had heard while in South Africa'.[16] On ancient mine workings this is not entirely convincing, for early in *King Solomon's Mines* Allan Quatermain speaks of seeing gold workings in the Lydenburg area of Transvaal, though also with a 'great wide wagon road cut out of the solid rock'. Early prospectors for gold were already using the numerous ancient workings in the Transvaal and especially in Rhodesia.[17] Despite Haggard's fictional inventions – one review regretted that 'sceptical theories should be gratuitously scattered broadcast in his pages'[18] – the massive sales influenced a whole generation of readers with an image of Africa's ancient past and exotic present.

Encouraged by the success of *King Solomon's Mines*, Haggard wrote *She* in six weeks during February and March 1886.[19] It was published in serialised form in 1886–7, coming out as a book just as the serialisation was ending. *She* thus reflected the same priority of imagination over history. A journey inland of the East African coast, in the north of modern Mozambique, brings the heroes to the ruined inland stone-walled settlement of Kôr. This city, with its passages and tunnels and reliefs, had been built by a truly ancient 'great race' (possibly ancestors to the ancient Egyptians, though their writing was compared to Chinese) more than 6,000 years ago, until its occupants were destroyed by a plague. In later occupation of the area over 2,000 years ago Ayesha was queen of a community of pre-Islamic Arabian origin; she wooed and then killed a visitor fleeing from late pharaonic Egypt. She gained immortality, and her yellow-skinned subjects continued to speak an archaic form of Arabic, which could be understood by the visiting scholars from England.

Arabian am I by my birth, even 'al Arab al Ariba' (an Arab of the Arabs), and of the race of our father Yárab, the son of Kâhtan, for in that fair and ancient city Ozal was I born, in the province of Yaman the Happy. ... Thy talk doth lack the music of the sweet tongue of the tribes of Hamyar which I was wont to hear. Some of the words too seemed changed, even as among these Amahagger, who have debased and defiled its purity, so that I must speak with them in what is to me another tongue.

Popular response was positive, though literary reviews were more critical. The *Pall Mall Gazette*[20] noted:

there is a Dark Continent in which the imagination can expatiate at ease. Ancient and titanic civilizations on the one hand, and picturesque barbarisms on the other, supply hints which may well quicken even a sluggish fantasy.

Meanwhile, perhaps inspired by Haggard's success, the explorer of Africa and friend of Richard Burton, Verney Lovett Cameron, published a lesser novel, *The Queen's Land*, on a race of Africans descended from the Queen of Sheba.[21] A whole genre of literature had been born around the 'lost race' idea, continuing until the 1920s and beyond.

To make possible understanding and communication between the exotic discovered societies in Africa and the modern adventurers Haggard needed to give them a common language. For *King Solomon's Mines* this is a version of Zulu. For *She* Haggard needed the language of an ancient community that was still spoken, which ruled out Phoenicians or ancient Egyptians; the lurking anti-Semitism of the era, reflected in Haggard's work, would rule out languages of the Jewish world so Arabic was a reasonable choice. At the end of the nineteenth century many British held the Arabs, especially the non-urbanised Arabs, in some awe.[22] The Sudanese Mahdi, Muhammad Ahmad ibn as Sayyid Abd Allah, had defeated General Gordon in the Sudan just 12 months before *She* was written.

The setting in an African ruined city of Kôr would remind many later readers of stone-walled settlements such as Great Zimbabwe. Haggard was not to visit Great Zimbabwe until his return visit to Africa in 1914. Amusingly, perhaps alarmingly, the then curator of Great Zimbabwe ruins, R.N. Hall, identified the fictional Kôr with the site under his care, and berated Haggard for getting details of the site wrong, to which Haggard responded that his site 'was a land where the ruins were built by the Fairies of Imagination'.[23] As with his earlier book he claimed: 'When I wrote *She*, I had only heard in the vaguest way of the Zimbabwe ruins.' However, he was happy to accept the beliefs of Hall and others in the exotic alien (and probably Phoenician) origins of the site and associated mining, endorsing the claims of 'my late friend' Theodore Bent. The relations between the fanciful fiction of Haggard and the fanciful history of Bent and Hall are thus complex.

In 1887 Haggard published a new novel, *Allan Quatermain*, which went further into mystic Africa with a story around a lost white feudal civilisation of Zu-Vendis in the centre of the African continent.

Of the many stone-walled ruins that lie both sides of the Zambezi, those of Great Zimbabwe in the central south-east of the country now named Zimbabwe are the most complex and unique, and therefore have attracted most interest from archaeologists and historians. After indirect reports by the Portuguese in the sixteenth century, awareness of the ruins was brought to a wider world after the visit of Mauch in 1871. He favoured Phoenician origins for the buildings.

In 1888 Cecil Rhodes obtained for his British South Africa Company the Rudd concession from Lobengula, the ruler of the Ndebele, in the land that would become Rhodesia, and the following year the British Government granted the Company a charter to administer the lands north of the Limpopo. Rhodes put significant weight behind his wish to demonstrate ancient white control over the resources of the land he was to conquer by force in the years 1890–97, and to name Rhodesia.

Funded by the Company, the Oxford-educated traveller and archaeological explorer James Theodore Bent was recruited to investigate Great Zimbabwe and other ruins of the eastern parts of Rhodesia, a journey of 12 months from January 1891. Within a month of his return to England in January 1892 Bent gave a paper to the Royal Geographical Society of London, which presented his discoveries and interpretations. For the general public a lively and engaging narrative of his travels and observations was written and published later the same year, and saw successive reprints and new editions.[24]

At Great Zimbabwe itself Bent undertook a wholesale and destructive 'excavation', removing substantial remains that were clearly of African cultural origins. More unusual were the soapstone carvings, of birds or of vessels with reliefs, which he recorded from the Hill Ruin. His book described the standing ruins in detail.

Bent turned his back on suggested links to Solomon and Sheba (which would have meant specifically the mid-tenth century BC), while his previous experience in the Middle East on genuine Phoenician settlements made him doubt this link.

> One of our friends told us they reminded him forcibly of the Capitol of Rome; another ... saw in them an exact parallel to the old walls of Jerusalem. ... The names of King Solomon and the Queen of Sheba were on everybody's lips ... we never expect to hear them again without an involuntary shudder.[25]

On the claimed links with Ophir, he noted this area 'may have been the land of Ophir or it may not; it may have been the land of Punt or it may not. ... There is not enough evidence ... to build up any theory on these points.' He conceded – from the dating of the many fragments of trade goods – that Great Zimbabwe had (still) been in use as a centre for gold trade between the Africans of the Monomotapa kingdom and the medieval Arab traders of the East African coast, and considered that iron finds might also be from a pre-modern African community. Bent also described other sites: the numerous gold workings of Rhodesia, and lesser stone ruin sites, whose origins he attributed squarely to Africans copying the 'ancient' sites, rather than another external group. But after initial hesitation he rejected an African origin for the construction of the site. He searched unsuccessfully in the region for exotic burial sites but found only those of African origin.[26]

Though he has since been dismissed as a fantasist, elements of Bent's approach were logical if unproven, and later disproved. His text emphasised – accurately, in the light of present knowledge – the importance to Great Zimbabwe of the coastal Arab trade of the medieval era. The Portuguese reported what they had heard from the coastal Arabs. The medieval Arabs dominated the East African coast and traded gold from the African interior to the wider world in exchange for trade goods originating in China, India, the Arabian Gulf and elsewhere. Because the construction of Great Zimbabwe clearly showed no influences of Islamic architecture or culture, Bent's model extended the trading relationship back to the southern Arabs of the pre-Islamic period, the Sabaeans (and their Himyarite successors), where there are some architectural parallels with Great Zimbabwe. In South Arabia and adjacent Abyssinia [Ethiopia] 'we may find temples which are built of similar stone'.[27]

In his lecture soon after his return to London, Bent mentioned the many other ruins in the region, some equal to Great Zimbabwe in workmanship and others inferior. Despite finding nothing but 'Kaffir remains' adjacent to the Elliptical Building in the valley, his dating was confident. The ruins were

> not in any way connected with any known African race ... the ruins formed a garrison for the protection of a gold-working race in remote antiquity. ... There is little room for doubt that the builders and workers of the Great Zimbabwe came from the Arabian peninsula. ... I have no hesitation in assigning this enterprise to Arabian origin, and to a pre-Mohammedan period.[28]

In his book later in the year he was slightly more ambiguous:

> the cumulative evidence is greatly in favour of the gold diggers being of Arabian origin, before the Sabaeo-Himyaritic period in all probability [i.e. before first century BC], who did work for and were brought closely into contact with both Egypt and Phoenicia.

While never admitting to Phoenician presence at the site, he played to the fascination with Phoenicia with comparisons to Phoenician buildings in the Mediterranean, and of biblical suggestions of the links between Phoenicians and the Sabaeans of Arabia.[29]

In the third edition of his book, Bent responded to feedback, noting 'it seems to me highly probable that in the temple of Zimbabwe we have a Sabaean Almaqah temple' – a context that would affirm the period from the second millennium until its conquest by the Himyarites in the first century BC. 'The builders were of a Semitic race and of Arabian origin.'[30]

The links of the medieval Arab trade with the central African gold fields were known, and the presence of pre-Islamic Arab traders on the East African coast was also known; so while the chronology was wrong, the suggestion of a link of these to the gold fields was not completely illogical, except that the archaeological finds gave no supporting chronology. In fact, we now see there was no interest in gold (or silver, tin or lead) in central and southern Africa until stimulated by the arrival of Islamic coastal traders.[31]

The alternative romance of the Phoenicians was hard to quash, despite the obvious reality that lacking a Suez Canal, Phoenician seamen had a Mediterranean focus. Herodotus had reported the Egyptian Pharaoh Necho hiring Phoenicians for an expedition from the Red Sea coast, and the Old Testament had Solomon using Phoenicians to create for him a fleet on the Red Sea. Both these suggest a situation of using them as mercenaries: no Phoenician activity on the East African coast has been found.

This notwithstanding, four years after Bent's work appeared, in 1896, Alexander Wilmot – also under Cecil Rhodes' sponsorship – published[32] a meandering and poorly structured survey of historical evidence on ancient Rhodesia, 'the Ophir of King Solomon', which endorsed with circumstantial material the Phoenician origins of Great Zimbabwe and the gold workings. Wilmot secured an introduction from the now world-famous novelist Rider Haggard. Here, some 11 years after his own inventive novel, Haggard was willing to support the origin of the sites he had been unable to visit himself, noting the gold mines had been 'worked by Phoenicians, or some race intimately connected with them', and supporting a Phoenician origin for the Zimbabwe ruins.[33]

Portuguese chroniclers had long been enthusiasts to identify the gold area in the African interior, known first through the reports of Arab traders, with the biblical Ophir, the source of wealth into the Kingdom of Solomon.[34] Ophir has indeed been located almost everywhere from Central Africa to Pakistan and even Australia!

In 1902 appeared a book of wild eccentricity by Irishman Augustus Henry Keane, who had left training for the priesthood to work in anthropology and linguistics and became Professor of Hindustani at University College London. Keane had strong views on the racial identity and racial hierarchy of humanity, which included an assessment of the Negro race as 'with no sense of dignity, therefore born slaves'.[35] In his retirement Keane developed a theory published as *The Gold of Ophir: whence brought and by whom?*[36] Here he pulled together diverse evidence supporting his views, while heavily criticising those who used the same (lack of) methodology to argue equally far-fetched ideas, such as the location of Ophir in the Indian subcontinent, or the linguistic identity Ophir = Afer = Africa. He took the relatively conservative view that biblical Ophir was not the source of gold but the port through which it was obtained, and located it in Arabia. However, he then positioned an active colony of Jews and Phoenicians on the Indian Ocean island of Madagascar, as a stopping-off point for the gold fields of Africa reached via Sofala! An emphasis of his approach would be reflected in numerous other wild theories in history and archaeology: the selection of individual similar words from different languages to suggest direct links, and of individual cultural styles in common.

The publication of Frazer's *Golden Bough* from 1890 had in fact shown many common elements shared across unconnected cultures.

To Keane the similarities of the isolated Zimbabwe sites to Sabaean and Phoenician buildings was clear; as was the link of Malagasy language to Sabaean and other ancient Semitic forms.[37] He conceded that the gold fields with which the medieval Arabs traded were operated by Africans, but thought they must be reworking ancient mines.

The main emphasis remained on the biblical era, and the gold that reached Solomon from Central Africa, by the use of slave labour working under the 'merchants of Tarshish' who built stone walls for defensive purposes. Bent had the relatively simple conclusion that pre-Islamic Arabs operated the mines for gold in areas with which the later Arabs traded. Keane muddied his arguments by involving Himyarites from Arabia, and Phoenicians, and Jews, and all using Madagascar as a base.

Such deliberate mixing and merging remained in much of the writing about mystic Rhodesia. For many writers pre-Muslim Arabs were not good enough, and it had to be Phoenicians. This continued right through to the work by Scottish racist Gayre in the 1970s.[38] A Pharaonic Egyptian source for Great Zimbabwe, advanced by Karl Peters in 1902, held less sway.[39]

While A.H. Keane was completing his *The Gold of Ophir* he had access to advance proofs of a book in press by Richard Hall and W.G. Neal, *The Ancient Ruins of Rhodesia*. Neal had been active in seeking gold through Rhodesia with the Rhodesia Ancient Ruins Limited, and provided information for the journalist Hall to write a popular book about his explorations, including stone ruins, burials and early mining sites in their scope. The book was divided into two halves: a fanciful description of the exotic origins of ancient Rhodesian culture preceded the actual description of numerous sites. The implication was that the description supported the interpretation but neither structure nor argument demonstrates that. The historical reconstruction and chronology was based on the work of other writers, while the subsequent site descriptions are pioneering records.

The book served to demonstrate the immense spread of the sites – some 125 are listed out of an estimated 500 – with stone-wall ruins across (Southern) Rhodesia, as well as the huge number of mining sites. Of these they listed evidence for ancient workings at almost 250, while stating that 'of the 114,814 registered gold claims now current (September 1900) in Rhodesia, considerably more than half have been pegged on the lines of ancient workings'. A chronology was assumed, which saw the finest architecture (that of Great Zimbabwe) earliest, with (still ancient) stages of architectural decline until the most recent where Africans attempted to copy the ancient style. The absence of burials from these ancient periods, they concede, is a mystery.[40]

Unlike Keane, Hall and Neal placed biblical Ophir in Rhodesia. In their model the settlement and gold working began under the Sabaeans and Himyarites of southern Arabia, who were succeeded by the Phoenicians from the Mediterranean. Gangs of slaves were used both for mining and construction.

Hall was then appointed curator of the Zimbabwe ruins by the British South Africa Company. He undertook fieldwork studies in 1902–4, some 11 years after Bent's, with excavations rough even by the standards of the time.[41] He presented an account of these in a popular book in 1905, with an introduction by Keane, adding a late preface to his volume in which he presented his conclusions after further recent work.[42] These were unnerving echoes of the complex fantasy created by Rider Haggard in *She* to which novel Hall pays tribute in his survey volume. In his sequence the site including a temple was originally created (using forced labour) by 'ancient builders' who were also responsible for ancient mine workings for gold. Dated some 3,000–4,000 years ago, these people had Semitic affiliations.[43] After their civilisation was ended by a plague the site became a ruin. Some centuries later, in medieval times (rather than the antiquity of Haggard), an organised Arab people exploited the gold mines of the area and intermarried with the local African population. The Arabs made Zimbabwe their headquarters, adding structural changes to the site. Distancing of the site from African achievements served well the European image of their role in the subcontinent.[44]

Such a claim was overturned by the scientific research in 1905 led by Egyptologist and prehistorian D. Randall-MacIver, and published in 1906, which placed this and other sites in a medieval dating and African cultural context. Such views were not widely accepted, Hall retaliating with his own book in 1909.[45] The black African contents of the site's creation was confirmed by further scientific investigation by Gertrude Caton-Thompson in 1929, who declared it 'medieval' in date and 'indigenous' in cultural content.[46] Anticipating dissent from the white community in the region, she expressed hope that the torch lit by MacIver and herself 'will not suffer extinction from the breezy cross-winds of the South African veldt'.[47]

Randall-MacIver thought the main period for Great Zimbabwe was the beginning of the sixteenth century or up to two centuries earlier, tied to the prominence of Arab Sofala.[48] With additional datable finds, Caton-Thompson suggested the origins of the site could be between the ninth and thirteenth centuries. Later work would distinguish between initial 'Iron Age' settlement in the tenth to eleventh century before a development that reached its climax in the fifteenth century, and then a sudden withdrawal from the site to other areas. She would note in her report to the British Association in 1929:

> It is inconceivable to me now I have studied the ruins how a theory of Semitic or civilised origin could ever have been foisted on an uncritical world. Every detail in the haphazard building, every detail in the plan, every detail in the contents apart from imports, appears to me to be typical African Bantu. It is also inconceivable to me how a theory of antiquity in the sense of Oriental archaeology could ever have been formulated by observant people.[49]

Many contemporary scientists, including Raymond Dart (see Chapter 3), rejected this work and adhered to the myth of the 'ancients'. Thereafter a gap arose between the archaeological interpretation of the sites, as the pinnacle of an Iron Age (black African) society trading with the east coast, and popular white opinion seeing a non-African origin for the site. The ideological weight of these debates became heavier during the conflict over white minority rule in Rhodesia. The 'mystery of Zimbabwe' remained high in white Rhodesia's image of itself, which put difficulties in the way of their government archaeologists who at times remained ambiguous in their writing about the site and other stone ruins.

Contemporary with Caton-Thompson's work the extreme South African nationalist politician Dr D.F. Malan used government funds to support German anthropologist Leo Frobenius. This energetic scholar, anthropologist, traveller in Africa and writer (1873–1938) had long advanced views of disappeared civilisations in the African past.[50] While Frobenius changed and developed these during his life, they included a lost civilisation, an 'African Atlantis' of white people in the African interior, which underlay many of the advanced African cultural developments.[51] However, his contribution to African studies had been profound.

With the support from Malan, Frobenius explored possible Indian roots to Zimbabwe origins.[52] Frobenius had developed a theory even wilder than his predecessors:

> the Zimbabwe colony was of the Sumerian–Babylonian civilisation, the centre of which was the Mesopotamian Valley … from Southern Arabia these people sailed to India and Africa. … Their object at Zimbabwe was purely to obtain mineral wealth … no fewer than 14 million kilograms of bronze were exported back to South Africa.

Caton-Thompson generously suggested that the reference to the alloy bronze might be a slip of expression for gold. After Malan's money passed hands Frobenius shifted his source of the Zimbabwe culture to southern India. However, his interests soon moved back to his wider work on African cultures.

Under such pressure there was a move away from presenting the scientific evidence. In a 1934 visitor guide by the curator of the site from 1910 to 1934, St Clere Arthur Wallace,[53] he notes the two datings, but that 'adherents to the ancient theory are in the majority' – this includes proponents of the 'Phoenicians, Carthaginians, Persians, Sabaeans, Grecians, Indians, Chinese, Parsees and others', and gives his own view that 'it is impossible to imagine [the Bantu] had anything to do with the actual building', though acknowledging that they may have been used as slaves in its construction. 'Nothing can be said with certainty. We do not know.'

In 1953 the Government Monuments Commission's guide to monuments referred to the earlier views but emphasised those of scientific archaeology. In 1972 this was presented unambiguously. But ambiguities had already begun to be introduced, and could be found in a 1976 handbook by a distinguished archaeologist working for the white government just before the independence of the state of Zimbabwe with open elections.[54] The antiquity and origins of Great Zimbabwe remained contested during the period of Rhodesia's unilateral declaration of independence under white rule, with interventions at the highest level of government to suppress the archaeological story.[55]

The European exploration for mining sites was guided by the numerous ancient mines in Southern Africa, reflecting many centuries of pre-European activity, though reduced in intensity before the arrival of colonial settlement. Despite the importance of the African gold trade to coastal Portuguese traders, the defenders of Zimbabwe's great antiquity were also involved in attesting a role for ancient civilisations in these mines.[56] Hall and Neal in 1902 were proponents of the Phoenician or Sabaean age for the mines, with a view that they had been abandoned since ancient times.[57] Modern miners' enthusiasm for reworking these sites destroyed much of the archaeological evidence.

All the writings on the exotic origins of Great Zimbabwe – or the wider range of ruins or ancient mines – appear focused on what they were *not*. They were not the work of African peoples. To argue this case was challenging. Excavations proved finds of African cultural origins, not exotic. Historical records of the Arabs and the Portuguese attest to the contemporary gold riches of the interior, the power of the Monomotapa chiefdoms and their occupation of stone-walled Zimbabwes. Indeed, if there had only been ancient gold and ancient cities, there would have been no Arab and Portuguese interest in the region. Bent's hypothesis of pre-modern Arab traders and settlers was the simplest alternative. But in the search for what was not African, the jumbling of Egyptians, Sabaeans, Himyarites, Phoenicians and Jews (Raymond Dart would even bring in the Chinese) weakened rather than strengthened the argument for exotic origins and laid the basis to support scientific research.

It is also ironic that the enthusiasm to use biblical references to Ophir and Tarshish came at a time – the final part of the nineteenth century – where biblical scholarship had clearly moved away from treating the Bible as history. The powerful need for the British South Africa Company to demonstrate a precedent in the exploitation of the Rhodesian gold fields brought about astonishing leaps of logic. The final analogy – that the gold fields of the ancient could only have been operated by using local African as slave labour – remained an interesting subtext.

A new thrust in the challenge to conventional archaeology of Southern Africa's prehistory – but probably not the last we shall see – came in 1981 when a South African publisher issued a volume by Cyril A. Hromnik arguing an origin for much of the continent's Iron Age developments in Indian gold-seekers.[58] Attention to the Indian Ocean dimension of Africa's history should be welcome; more attention had been paid to real and imaginary links to the Mediterranean and the Arabian worlds, and both trade goods in Africa and possible loan words attest to the importance of the continent in Indian Ocean trade. Hromnik's own background was in Indian Ocean history, with a thesis on sixteenth-century Portuguese trade.

But the book sought to undermine the whole of archaeology, and its diverse debates, with an extreme argument. Hromnik suggested that iron technology itself was introduced into Africa by Indians, and this was done for the purpose of assisting Indians to exploit the precious minerals of Africa. Without the initiative and motivation of settlers from the Indian subcontinent, Africans would have remained stone tool-using hunter-gatherers. The prehistory of the African Iron Age, as developed by archaeological research, was thus a myth. The selective evidence chosen by the author to back his case leant heavily on supposed similarities between words in Indian languages and in Bantu languages – an echo of Keane a century earlier.

A heavily critical article by a linguist and an archaeologist thus took seriously a book that might otherwise have been considered part of the outer fringe of science.[59] They dealt in some detail with the weakness of the linguistic argument, but recognised that the book lay in the realms of 'cult archaeology' despite its claims.

Given the nature of science, in which knowledge progresses by dispute and argument, it is inevitable that simplification and populist views will continue to attract a lay audience, as they have throughout the narratives of the deep African past.[60]

THE LOST CITY OF THE KALAHARI

A longstanding piece of mystic fantasy is the Lost City of the Kalahari. The idea developed from a mention by showman 'The Great Farini' in 1885–86, and was still featured by a popular novelist some 90 years later. Nevertheless it was taken seriously by the enthusiasts for an exotic non-African past, and this myth continued to have its adherents into at least the 1960s, inspiring 16 expeditions between 1932 and 1965.[61]

The Great Farini was the stage name of American William Leonard Hunt (1838–1929). His performances included crossing the Niagara Falls on a high wire and being a human cannonball, and he claimed to be the first white man to have crossed the Kalahari, on an 1885 expedition. As a minor part of this journey Farini mentioned encountering one, or possibly two, sites of ruined stone buildings. However, there were discrepancies between Farini's first reports of his journey and the details in his book-length account of his adventures; further discrepancies between the text and the map included in that book; and more distance between the described route and what he is likely to have been able to have accessed in a relatively short journey. The traveller's tale seems to have grown with the telling.[62]

The significance of the 'lost city' also grew in time. A newspaper account immediately following Farini's journey makes no mention of his discovering a 'Lost City'.[63] He presented a paper on his journey to the Berlin Geographical Society in November 1885, and in March the following year a paper in his name was read to the Royal Geographical Society in London and published in the RGS *Proceedings*.[64] This paper, addressed to a serious and sophisticated audience, was relatively matter-of-fact in its account of the journey and description of people and places. As a small part of his account Farini states:

> During one of our hunting excursions we made a discovery, a short description of which may be interesting. While hunting we came across an irregular pile of stones that seemed in places to assume the shape of a wall, and on closer examination we traced what had evidently once been a huge walled inclosure, elliptical in form and about the eighth of a mile in length. The masonry was of a cyclopean character; here and there the gigantic square blocks still stood on each other, and in one instance the middle stone being of a softer nature was weather-worn. A large stone, about six feet in length and the same in width, was balancing on this, and but for its great inertia would have been blown over by the wind. Near the base of the ruined walls were oval shaped rocks, hollowed out, some composed of one solid stone and others of several pieces joined together. These peculiar basin-shaped ovals were regularly distributed every few yards around the entire ellipse. In the middle was a kind of pavement of long narrow square blocks neatly fitted together, forming a cross, in the centre of which was what seemed to be a base for either a pedestal or monument. We unearthed a broken column, a part of which was in a fair state of preservation, the four flat sides being fluted. We searched diligently for inscriptions, but could find none, and hence could collect no definite evidence as to the age and nature of the structure. The approximate latitude and longitude of this remarkable relic of antiquity were about 23½ S. lat. and 21½ E. long., near the tropic of Capricorn.[65]

The discussion that followed the London paper did not even comment on the 'lost city' claim.

Farini's subsequent book-length description of the 1885 expedition included a mention of encountering ruined buildings of stone – not indeed a major emphasis of his accounts, but one that caught the popular imagination.[66] Dominant themes of the book included the unending slaughter of a great variety of game and the disparaging accounts of the racial types he met on the journey, together with description of some dramatic landscapes. Indeed, a major goal of the expedition had been a search for diamonds, to disguise which he had first travelled under another assumed name.

Farini's book expanded the description and interpretation of the ruins in terms inconsistent with his RGS lecture.[67] In fact his book mentions two sets of stone-walled ruins in ambiguous locations. The first looked like natural granites from a distance, but Farini 'felt certain they must have been brought here at some remote period by human hands ... they had lain exposed to the weather for a long, long time ...'.

The larger site was at an unconfirmed location at the foot of a mountain, where was

> a long line of stone which ... on examination, proved to be the ruins of quite an extensive structure. ... We traced the remains for nearly a mile, mostly a heap of huge stones ... and here and there with the cement perfect and plainly visible between the layers ... here must have been either a city of a place of worship, or the burial-ground of a great nation, perhaps thousands of years ago.[68]

While critics of Farini's writings took issue with many aspects of his traveller's tales, others – including A.H. Keane – took the comments about stone ruins more seriously. Expeditions in search of the Lost City began from at least 1932, when a venture sponsored by a motoring magazine was stimulated by reports that Bushmen had confirmed the presence of stone ruins. Searches for the Lost City continued – some leading to wild claims and wilder rumours, including one explorer who claimed not one but three lost cities. Many different locations were suggested for the Lost City, and a claim was made for 'ruins of the houses of 3000 to 5000 people of ancient Phoenicia, Arab, Ethiopian and Hottentot stock'.[69]

One of these expeditions, in 1956, included the writer and liberal activist Alan Paton, whose account of the journey, though stylish and wry, was not destined for publication; the manuscript appeared in print only 17 years after Paton's death.[70] It makes no suggestion that Paton saw this as more than an adventure (and escape from personal and political pressures); he had no motivation to support the Farini story. In fact he made no mention of the trip in his autobiography.

As late as 1964 two journalists claimed the discovery of a Phoenician settlement, a fort guarding an ancient mine, and newspaper reports suggested that this identification was supported by the eminent palaeoanthropologist Raymond Dart, and owed some inspiration to the vision of the Zulu mystic Credo Mutwa, whom we discuss below.[71]

A 1961 expedition felt confident it had found the site of Farini's discovery in the Aha Hills, and that on examination it was clearly of geological rather than human origins. But the location was disputed as being far from Farini's claimed route. More detailed studies suggested that neither the geography nor the timing in Farini's account of his journey was accurate, which of course makes more difficult the identification of the specific site that led to this claim. Nevertheless, in the absence of any archaeological site that corresponds to this claim, a natural geological formation seems to underlie the idea.[72]

In his bestselling novel *The Sunbird* (1972) Wilbur Smith exploited this story with great effect.

A hazy aerial photograph and a sinister curse – known only to the Africans – and Dr Benjamin Kazin stumbles on the archaeological discovery of a lifetime. ... For nearly two thousand years, a brilliant and unknown ancient civilisation has remained buried in southern Africa. Now at last the red cliffs of Botswana seem about to yield their secret. Under the lavish patronage of his old friend and mentor Lauren Sturvesant, head of one of the richest companies in the world, Ben and his green-eyed assistant Sally grope towards the mystery of the lost people. Magnificent cave paintings and the Bushmen's legendary City of the Moon are the unexpected clues to the first discoveries that point to the existence of an ancient city, violently destroyed centuries ago. But the magic of uncovering a lost culture is interrupted by dramas of a different kind: hunting scenes, romance, and the violence of African terrorists. And all are skilfully echoed in the splendour of the ancient world, as in a breathtaking sweep through time, the reader is transported back to the last days of the magnificent city itself. Combining adventure, suspense and a wealth of historical detail, *The Sunbird* is a brilliant imaginative feat.[73]

From the showman to the novel, the myth had come full circle and meanwhile had fuelled the wish for an exotic non-African civilisation out of reach of the accessible world of Southern Africa.[74]

CREDO MUTWA AND HIS FOLLOWERS

From Portuguese travellers to Rider Haggard, from the Great Farini to Wilbur Smith, the images of a mystic African past created for a European audience were those of other Europeans. They were therefore readily open to charges of inauthenticity by those who might otherwise have yearned for a greater exoticism (or a less racist) take on the real African past. To satisfy the needs of such an audience there emerged a black South African voice: Credo Vusa'mazulu Mutwa.

Mutwa (born in 1921) was an able creative writer whose published work was influential on white (especially English-speaking) South Africa and then on a wider world of readers who sought an authentic voice to confirm a mystic past and present of the African world increasingly beset by political change and conflict. After the democratisation of South Africa, Mutwa was taken up in cyberspace as a New Age seer.

The literary style employed by Mutwa (and his editors) neither reflected a specifically 'African English' nor the imposing echoes of biblical English used for quoted speech by some earlier writers. Mutwa presented a world of past history and current African belief that satisfied a yearning for a world of deep and powerful difference, a voice from within the society that was physically present to white South Africans yet little known or understood.

Mutwa cleverly laced his imaginative accounts of Africa's traditions with material gained from diverse ethnic sources, and references to words, names, events and images that might seem familiar to his readers, while his writing used words such as 'witchdoctor' and 'Bantu' familiar to whites. This gave them a sense of authenticity to the stories. Mutwa's own experience, according to his own accounts and claims, would have exposed him to a range of such information. An unpublished manuscript – an autobiography (with details at variance from those briefly sketched in *My People*), manifesto and account of further imaginative African legends and lore – has been published on a dedicated website, which reflects a range of New Age and eccentric views from around the world.[75]

At one extreme, Mutwa noted that he grew up as the attendant to his grandfather who was a 'witchdoctor', and much later in life he returned to his home to undertake training in these areas of traditional medicine and knowledge. However, his father was in fact a Roman Catholic (at one time a catechist) – hence the forename 'Credo' – and his early life involved mobility between his mother's family in Zululand, his father's family in southern Natal and his father who worked in different parts of the Transvaal. Mutwa seems to have been removed to the Transvaal by his father in his teens, and to have begun school there, before being returned to Zululand. Mutwa mentioned that he attended a Catholic mission school in Zululand.[76] He would thus have met people from diverse ethnic groups in his youth.

Despite his initiation as a 'witchdoctor', from his early thirties Mutwa was employed in a curio shop in Johannesburg where he dealt with and authenticated material culture, art and its background from a much wider range of southern Africa. He wrote from a base not in Zululand but from an urban township, Diepkloof. He moved to work in different parts of South Africa and by 2010 in his eighties he was living at Kuruman in the Northern Cape.[77]

Mutwa's first book, *Indaba My Children*, was issued in 1964 by Blue Crane Books of Johannesburg and republished in London by Kahn & Averill two years later; Grove Press were to reissue it in the USA with the subtitle 'African folktales' and it was reissued in Edinburgh in 1998.[78] *Africa Is My Witness* was the successor book issued by Blue Crane in 1966. A composite volume selected from both books was issued under the title *My People, My Africa* as an international edition by Anthony Blond in London in 1969 (and in New York by John Day Co.) and reissued in an international mass market paperback by Penguin in 1971 under the label *My People: the incredible* [sic!] *writings of Credo Vusa'mazulu Mutwa*, with a cover flash 'Writings of a Zulu Witch-Doctor'. Penguin chose to classify the book not as mythology or fiction but as 'Autobiography, Sociology, Anthropology'. In 1996 Struik in Cape Town published Mutwa's *Isilwane: the animal: tales and fables of Africa*, and a year later *African Proverbs* and his *African Signs of the Zodiac* and *African Symbols of Goodwill*.

In the mid-1980s United Publishers in South Africa issued *Let Not My Country Die*. Most recently in 1996 a small United States publisher issued *Song of the Stars: the lore of a Zulu Shaman* designed for a US New Age readership, with an introduction by a 'shamanic scholar'.[79] In 1997 Telkom, the South African telecommunications group, put out a small publication *Usiko: tales from Africa's treasure trove: vast secrets wrested from the womb of time.*

In 2007 Mutwa contributed a chapter to a book by his wife, Virginia Nkagesang Rathele, *Woman of Four Paths: the strange story of a black woman in South Africa*. The on-line text called 'biography' has not appeared in print.

Indaba My Children presented a narrative of an African past, echoing the form of myth and legend and told as if history. In grand and detailed accounts of people and places it echoes Homer and Virgil (both mentioned in the foreword to *My People, My Africa*). Using information from many sources, black and white, and filling in the gaps with a powerful imagination, the book served to create the image of a single southern African grand Bantu narrative. Distant places – Kilimanjaro, the Kalahari, the Amathole of the Eastern Cape – are woven into this narrative with different ethnic groups and individuals. *Africa Is My Witness* continued the story but had more of Mutwa's comments on recent history and current events, including what was read by some as a critical support for apartheid.

It was the international, shortened version of his work published as *My People, My Africa* that spread the Mutwa image. This book selected sections dealing with the supposed deep history of Bantu Africa, together with more recent history of the period of white settlement.

The narrative of Bantu history he created was an appealing fancy, which could be told without source, reference or evidence, being by implication derived from an oral history. Within this framework Mutwa echoed – but expanded on – the white myths, introducing African-sounding names to give authenticity to the text. Here again, in significant detail, was the invasion by the Phoenicians – the Ma-Iti – who sailed to the mouth of the Zambezi and invaded the African interior some 2,500 years ago and used Bushman and Bantu slave labour, especially for mining gold and even iron. Slaves were sacrificed to their goddess statue. An African description allows the reconstruction of their oared vessel, and Phoenician, Egyptian and Greek weapons are still hidden today by witchdoctors. An image of the Ma-Iti emperor is the so-called White Lady of Brandberg rock painting. Later we see the rise of the Munu-Mutaba kings who sold slaves to the Arabi, built their fortress of Zima-Mbje, which contains the hollow idol of the Ultimate Mother, with a bronze idol containing a stone with permanent radiating heat. Reflecting the image of tribal invasions to the south the Nguni, Mambo and Xhosa tribes argue over crossing the Zambezi at Kariba, until they finally do so (five million people in all). They reach the land of the fifth Munumutaba king, part Arab, part Hottentot, part Bantu, and his evil Queen Muxakaza. But they succeed in moving towards South Africa, where new tribal formations are made including the Zulu. Then the Portuguese arrive but the Arabi remain a threat, searching for and finding the treasure hoards of the Phoenicians.[80]

The detailed narrative of this account of early history merges into interpretations of aspects of white South African history – the murder of Piet Retief, the frontier wars of the eastern Cape, the Xhosa cattle killing and apartheid itself.

At one level all this can be classified as an entertaining book of myth and legend, appearing ten years after Tolkien's *Lord of the Rings* and weaving or adapting some elements of oral tradition of Europeans, Zulus and other ethnic groups into an imaginative creation. But more would be made of the book, which, as noted, was classified as anthropology by its publishers.

Mutwa cleverly teased his audience by stating the truth of what he writes: 'Much of what I shall reveal here will shock and anger many people – most of all my fellow Bantu, who resent having their doings and secrets exposed to foreigners.'[81] Mutwa had a welcome among those in white South Africa and beyond who sought an inner truth of African perceptions, understanding and history. South Africa's *Sunday Tribune* described it as 'an epic which may well rank as the most outstanding contribution yet made by an African'. The book was widely read, including by many English-speaking white South Africans; his writing was not translated into Afrikaans.[82] The writing, which filled a need for an African voice, was accepted as revealing previously hidden truths. But as an overseas reviewer noted:

> More frightening still is that those in South Africa with the necessary affluence to buy this book ... believe what they read there is the real, secret Africa. ... I spoke to several people who were shocked at the suggestion it might not be authentic.[83]

The critical responses to the early and landmark writings were dealt with relatively gently by some critics. Overall, within South Africa the work was not actively challenged, but rather ignored by serious local scholars, who had more serious issues to address. Some reviewers of the international publications were less forgiving. The *Times Literary Supplement* described *Indaba My Children* as 'an excellent and human book'.[84] Other reviews concentrated on the literary value rather than any claim to accuracy; 'a literary piece of considerable merit' was the review in *Africa Today*,[85] while a review in a UK academic journal suggested that the book 'is a linguistic triumph; but the reader must judge for himself where tribal tradition ends and speculative frolic begins'.[86]

One overseas critic did observe of *Indaba My Children* that

> the author is no old-fashioned tribesman as he appears in a photograph togged up in a ridiculous costume: he is an educated man of Africa using obscure and outmoded media to convey the frustrations of a people long subjected to a social system.[87]

Another took more harshly to *My People*: 'it is still an interesting document demonstrating the terrifying efficiency of the South African system of oppression in warping human minds'.[88]

Perhaps more realistically, Basil Davidson, reviewing *My People, My Africa* for the US *Saturday Review*, noted the book was out of place in a non-fiction list:

> The best one can hope of [the book's] publishers, who appear to have taken it as a serious work, is that they have been taken for a ride. ... The history he recounts, however, has nothing to do with the facts and probabilities now established...[89]

And most direct was the review in the first issue of a pioneering journal in the scholarly field, *African Historical Studies*:

> *Indaba, My Children* is utterly without redeeming historical value. It contains no authentic Bantu tradition ... it is a fraud. ... As a symptom of historical process this book is too tragic to joke about.[90]

In the 1970s and 1980s Mutwa became involved in a number of 'ethnic' displays and ventures, under the apartheid regime or its spin-off Bantustans. Accompanying the end of apartheid, which led to the democratic elections of 1994, it seems that Mutwa was more openly criticised as a fake, 'an old fraud, a charlatan'.[91] But while his star had descended in his own region, Mutwa's work would gain something of a cult status among the international adherents of New Age cults and beliefs, who looked to this supposed leader among South Africa's *sangoma* (medicine men) for mystical insights, and New Age adherents would arrive in Zululand in search of ancient truths. The US publication in 1996 *Song of the Stars* was essentially meeting the interests of this quite different audience from his earlier

South African work. Here Mutwa presents an account of his visionary shamanistic life and powers – a chapter on 'the common origin of mankind' echoes some of the wilder claims of before, with ancient Celtic and other links to Africa, but in a framework of idealistic philosophy rather than any serious engagement with historical process. Mutwa began to emphasise his experience of encounters with non-terrestrial aliens and his understanding of how aliens operated on our planet. A Mutwa interview has become of special appeal to those who believe in alien possession of reptile forms,[92] and the Credo Mutwa website appeals to those with very alternative views of the nature of the world. The importance of Mutwa took on a new role in adapting to supply spiritual need on a wide plane.[93] Africa has come to serve a new, contemporary, twenty-first-century form of mysticism.

There is a side story that provides a further link in the narratives of mystification of Africa. Mutwa's editor for his major book was Adrian Boshier, who was based at the Institute for the Study of Man in Africa established to support the work of Raymond Dart, which is discussed in Chapter 3. Mutwa paid particular tribute to the support and interest of 'a young man from distant England – Adrian Boshier, the anthropologist', but the role of Boshier in encouraging and aiding the work is unclear.[94] Boshier (1939–1978) was a controversial protégé of Raymond Dart and ally in Dart's eccentric views, and in Dart's pursuit with Peter Beaumont of the supposed early mining in Swaziland.[95] Boshier arrived with his parents in South Africa at the age of 16, and took to the African bush, uninhibited by the conventional barriers between white and black. He gained a reputation among the Africans with whom he travelled for his enthusiasm and ability as a snake catcher. According to his biographer, Lyall Watson – another Dart disciple – Boshier was instructed by a female diviner in her arts and in due course was initiated as a diviner in the Makgabeng area of the northern Transvaal (now Northern Province). Part of his appeal as a potential mystic in this community came from his liability to epileptic attacks, a medical problem that was to lead to his early death at the age of 39. Boshier was interested in the Late Stone Age rock paintings he found, which are conventionally attributed to communities related to the San (Bushmen), but Boshier showed specific paintings to Mutwa who attributed to them significance in African belief. It seems that Boshier and Mutwa may have fed each others' mythmaking, and Watson's writing helped cultivate this image. At one point Watson writes of links between north European ogam script and Arabic, and claimed that Mutwa possessed a slate that held Egyptian hieroglyphs, early Arabic lettering and European ogam script, a kind of African Rosetta Stone![96]

As Watson claims of Boshier, 'Ever since he had some under the academic umbrella of Raymond Dart, Adrian Boshier traveled with a sense of mission, dancing to the siren song of scientific discovery.' This began with presenting to Dart evidence of tool use that would support Dart's theory of the osteodontokeratic tool use by early *Australopithecus*. Dart arranged for funding for Boshier and then an official 'field officer' position in the Museum of Man and Science that fell under his influence. It was on Boshier's initiative that Dart began his work and claims for the earliest mining in the world at the haematite mines in Swaziland, part of a career of ambitious claims for the African past at odds with the scholarly consensus.

The creation of ideas of an exotic imagined African past within Africa is thus a tradition with its origins at the height of romantic Victorian imperialism, but one that has continued to echo to the present day. While there is much in African history and prehistory to amaze and excite, fiction can always go one stage further. The blurring between fact and fiction, fantasy and reality in Africa's past may continue to bring its dangers.

3
Looking both ways:
The enigma of Raymond Dart

The previous chapter looked at the cycle of ideas that brought exotic origins and distant invaders into the African past. The subsequent chapter will examine the work of some pioneer explorers of the fossil ancestry of humans in Africa. One of the most enigmatic characters in this story was a lifetime proponent of eccentric ideas in the first group while the founding father of work in the second: Raymond Dart, who lived from 1893 to 1988.[1]

Dart is remembered today for the discovery, description, naming (as *Australopithecus africanus*) and interpretation of the Taung skull from South Africa in 1925, as confirmation of Darwin's hypothesis of the African origins of mankind.

Dart's claims were described later that year in *Nature* by a leader in the field, Sir Arthur Keith, as 'preposterous', a view echoed by other researchers.[2] It would take until after other fossil discoveries in the later 1930s before the scientific community began to acknowledge the brilliance and accuracy of Dart's claim, and later before some major critics stepped back. But already by that date Dart had become a hero in South Africa, and the boldness and originality of his work built his reputation as one of the great figures in interpreting the human record. The conventional image in print is of a scientist ahead of his time, with a major breakthrough that took two decades for the world to recognise.

It is therefore ironic that in a very productive career of writing, together with numerous public presentations, the majority of themes and arguments that Dart pursued in archaeology and physical anthropology could indeed be described as 'preposterous' – clearly so in terms of today's knowledge, but many running directly against the methodology, knowledge and scientific understanding of his own time. These included the taming of fire, the osteodontokeratic, cannibalism and the killer ape, Boskop man, work on racial origins, on exotic invaders into Southern Africa from the ancient Near East, the Mediterranean and China, on phallic symbols and Stone Age miners. While Dart's description of *Australopithecus*

The young Raymond Dart and the Taung cranium, 1925. (Photo: Barlow Rand)

seems methodologically scientific, his analysis was one of many interpretations in his body of work made with less than strictly scientific methodology, but one that proved sustainable through the later scientific research of others.[3]

The German Leo Frobenius, 20 years Dart's senior, has been described as having 'spent his whole life in motion, between Germany and Africa, between the natural and the cultural sciences, between lunacy and scholarship' with 'a life-long proclivity to mix highly insightful ethnological analyses with wildly conjectural global histories'.[4] The 'lunacy' included Frobenius' own wild theories about disappeared civilisations in the African interior. Dart's and

Frobenius' paths crossed: they shared a mix of serious and fringe theories and both have reputations that have outlived them.

'MAN OF GRIT'

Raymond Dart was born in Brisbane, Australia – dramatically so, during the flooding of the town in 1893. He initially followed his family's strongly religious and fundamentalist views, and decided to become a medical missionary. At the University of Queensland, brought into contact with both zoology and geology, he moved away from his fundamentalist assumptions and changed his world view, seeing 'the discrepancies between Fundamentalism and the facts' and accepting an evolutionary model.[5]

Moving to Sydney University in 1914 to study for his medical degree, Dart was able to attend the 1914 meeting of the British Association for the Advancement of Science held in Sydney. Here he heard the (Australian-born) Grafton Elliot Smith (1871–1937), whose reputation as a distinguished anatomist is accompanied by his infamy (to archaeologists) as a leading proponent of hyperdiffusionism.[6]

Elliot Smith became a crucial influence on Dart's career, providing him with opportunities for employment but powerfully idiosyncratic outlooks on human prehistory. Dart attributed to Elliot Smith his leaning towards these interests, noting in 1929 that 'anthropology in recent years has received a great stimulus through the "Diffusionist theory" of Elliot Smith relative to cultures'.[7]

Dart was clearly an outstanding student. He took on a job of University Demonstrator in 1917 while still studying, then accepted a position as Elliot Smith's assistant at University College London, teaching anatomy but also beginning a programme of research in medicine that could have led his reputation in a quite different direction.

On Elliot Smith's recommendation, in January 1923 – aged only 29 – Dart moved to South Africa to take up the position of Professor of Anatomy in the Medical School of the University of the Witwatersrand in Johannesburg, which was to be his home for the next 65 years until his death in 1988 at the age of 95. He long remained active in writing, public presentations of his work and support of research that followed his own enthusiasms, with fieldwork often privately funded.

TAUNG AND *AUSTRALOPITHECUS*

Dart's career in Johannesburg fulfilled a valuable role in developing medical teaching – he was dean and head of the Medical School for 18 years. However, there was a major shift in his research interests.[8] As he was to explain:

> The abysmal lack of equipment and literature forced me to develop an interest in other subjects, particularly anthropology, for which Elliot Smith had fired my imagination.[9]

He added that

> here in Johannesburg, as with Elliot Smith in Cairo, bones had to be studied instead of brains. Physical anthropological issues screamed for initiation in this stupendous continent of Africa.[10]

Dart encouraged his students to collect fossils, and one of these brought in a fossilised baboon skull found at a lime works quarry in Taung(s) in the then northern Cape Province (today's North West Province). Dart showed this to geologist colleague R.B. Young, who arranged for further samples of bone-bearing breccia to be brought from Taung. It was one of those that contained the famous Taung child skull.

The breccia containing the skull was handed to Dart on 28 November 1924, and he began work on 1 December to free the fossil from the rock.[11] The South African teaching year had already finished for the summer, and fortunately this year Dart was not involved in external examining. The cleaning process took three weeks and was completed around 23 December, but clearly during the physical procedure Dart developed his unambiguous hypothesis that this was an early hominid, quite different from any found to date in Africa and evidence to support Darwin's hypothesis of the African origins of man. In another 17 days he completed his description, comparison, analysis, the naming of *Australopithecus africanus* and the bold statement that it represented 'an extinct race of apes intermediate between living anthropoids and man ... an extinct link between man and his simian ancestor'. The article was despatched together with its illustrations on 6 January 1925 (six weeks after the arrival of the find) to catch the boat to England; it reached the editor of *Nature* on 30 January and with the initial encouragement of Keith and others *Nature* published it on 7 February 1925.[12]

Indeed, Dart responded to local journalistic enquiries certain that the paper would be published in *Nature* by that date.

Such a process implies a rare confidence. The hypothesis was remarkable on two grounds. There was no reliable stratigraphic dating to provide a chronological framework for the find. Indeed, this has remained a problem; Dart quotes identifications of the limeworks deposit as 'probably Pleistocene', though he had thought it Pliocene.[13] The ancestral claim was primarily on morphological grounds and, since this was the skull of a child of about five years, the more difficult for comparative purposes. Further, the location, in the open dry lands of South Africa, contrasted starkly with the forest environment of Africa's great apes that had inspired Darwin's 1871 prophecy about the African origins of man.

In *Nature* a week after Dart's announcement, the four leading British scholars in the field commented on the claims: Keith, Elliot Smith, Smith Woodward and Duckworth.[14] In general they praised Dart's description of the material but put on hold their acceptance of his claims and classification while awaiting the full publication of the material. Keith doubted the creation of a new family, seeing *Australopithecus* as the same genus or sub-family as the chimpanzee and gorilla, and noted the need for geological evidence to settle its relationship. Elliot Smith too grouped the find with the African great apes and sought geological dating.

Doubts continued to be expressed about the claims made by Dart, and those who had supported their publication began to distance themselves from his conclusions. Most startlingly, Sir Arthur Keith, once he had studied casts of the finds in London, wrote in *Nature* in July 1925: 'An examination of the casts exhibited at Wembley will satisfy zoologists that [Dart's] claim is preposterous.'[15] He was referring specifically to Dart's claim for a new family and a position intermediate between living anthropoids and modern humans.

'Preposterous' is a strong word in science. At this time Keith was a leading proponent of the role of Piltdown Man, the British find that later proved to be a fake. And it was Keith who was to publish a detailed account of the *Australopithecus* skull, leaving Dart's own monograph unpublished.[16] Dart issued a shorter description of the teeth, but his further publications on the find were mainly about its significance, rather than more detailed scientific studies.

What confirmed Dart's claims was the discovery of further Australopithecines by Robert Broom and others in the southern Transvaal cave sites of South Africa from the mid-1930s onwards. These gave support to the hypothesis generated from Dart's single, juvenile, undated skull, and confirmed in the wider scientific world the high reputation that Dart had gained among his local South African supporters. In 1947 Sir Arthur Keith formally acknowledged Dart's claim.[17]

MAKAPANSGAT AND THE TAMING OF FIRE

Dart re-entered the area of detailed scientific work on *Australopithecus* with the finds at Makapansgat, in the northern Transvaal. Indeed, only five months after the Taung announcement, Dart noted the apparent presence of carbon in bone assemblages from the site and stated 'there seems little doubt from the evidence available that the bone-bed is the "kitchen-midden" result of human occupation at a remote epoch'.[18] But it was over two decades before he could test this bold statement. In a field project initially led by Phillip Tobias (who would become Dart's protégé), and continued under Dart's staff, Australopithecine fossils were discovered from 1947 onwards and described in great detail (and without challenge) by Dart in a series of technical articles. Ironically, he first ascribed them to a species different from both the Taung and the southern Transvaal sites, as *Australopithecus prometheus*. This pattern of a new species for a new find is typical of the fate that has befallen many hominin fossil finds at the hands of their discoverers.[19] Dart is also widely credited with suggesting the name *habilis* for *Homo habilis*.[20] In due course the Makapansgat finds would be considered by most scientists to belong to the same species as the Taung child, *A. africanus*.

Dart named his hominid finds as *A. prometheus* because he saw the use of fire as another skill of the early hominid community. Some of the vertebrate bones from the site were considered to contain free carbon, which he attributed to the deliberate use of fire by human predators:

> The special significance of the Makapansgat valley limeworks deposits in unravelling these early human mysteries lies in their being true hearths and thus providing information … concerning man's hunting skill, his probable weapons and his use of fire.[21]

Subsequent research and discussion has not supported Dart's claim for the human use of fire by *Australopithecus* at Makapansgat, or indeed for the presence of fire, and at least some of the blackening has been explained by manganese.[22] While there is still active debate about the dates for the first controlled use of fire, the claims for Makapansgat are not even considered.[23] In due course Dart seems to have backtracked on his certainty here.[24]

More strangely, Dart's confidence in the hominid source of fire at Makapansgat had persuaded him to identify a fossil baboon skull as *Australopithecus prometheus* two years before the actual *Australopithecus* was found, and to write a paper for this claim, which he withdrew before publication.[25]

It was, however, the Makapansgat site that led to one of Dart's most controversial claims, that of the Osteodontokeratic.

OSTEODONTOKERATIC CULTURE AND CANNIBALISM

The most famous of Dart's unaccepted claims was that the faunal assemblages that included the Makapansgat Australopithecines reflected a complex pattern of human selection (rather than accumulation by predators), deliberate fashioning, and use as systematic equipment of tools and weapons. Since he applied this to the fashioning of bone, teeth and horn he linked them by defining an 'osteodontokeratic' culture, which preceded the 'Stone Age', for no stone with signs of use were found with the Makapansgat breccia. This theme became the focus of Dart's lectures and enthusiasm, with numerous articles as well as a major monograph arguing the case.[26] In his personal memoirs he devotes far more space to this topic than to his landmark discovery and identification of *Australopithecus* at Taung.

What led to the osteodontokeratic hypothesis was the non-random occurrence of animal parts and the fractures on many of these. This persuaded Dart that the sample showed deliberate selection and preparation for tool use: saws or scrapers from teeth, use of long bones for clubs and so on. Individual bones he interpreted as tools of quite specialised function, including a dagger,[27] and even platters, bowls and drinking cups made from skulls.[28] Dart developed detailed descriptions of hunting strategies, including breaking open water turtles, clubbing animals and hamstringing them on the run. He saw the damage to baboon skulls as evidence of 'well aimed blows on the head with some sort of weapon', with the use of clubs to cause a double fracture. He went on to suggest that the Taung hominid had also slain the fossil baboons found there. He weakened his argument by hyperbolic language about the bloodthirsty regime reflected in these finds, and this led to hard lines being drawn between antagonists on discussions of human nature.

'Bludgeoning was characteristic of all South African man-apes.' The use of weapons in hunting, he suggested, was as much cause as effect of hominid bipedalism.[29]

Since there was damage to some *Australopithecus* skulls, similar to that seen on baboon skulls, Dart went further to argue that the victims of the hunters included fellow members of their species. Cannibalism in early humankind he defended as probable in the light of later anthropological and historical evidence on modern species.

The osteodontokeratic became a matter of faith for Dart's followers, who could see signs of human usage by looking at the materials, much as 'eolith' stone tools from the Pliocene had been supported in Europe and elsewhere. It was an interesting hypothesis and it had deeper impact, for it led to the popular image of human nature as the killer ape, popularised in writings such as Robert Ardrey's *African Genesis*.[30] The idea was always controversial and, while accepted by some prominent prehistorians, it was felt by many scholars to be unsupported by the evidence. Indeed, the vigour with which Dart repeated arguments for the osteodontokeratic reflected his awareness of the scepticism with which it was greeted by most scholars and scientists.

However, non-human explanations for the non-random accumulation – including hyena lairs and leopard predation – continue to be accepted as the most likely source of the selective process.[31] Later reconstructions suggest that the use of carnivore teeth on their prey created the impression of the 'well aimed blows to the head'. But Dart engaged in vigorous debate with his critics, and challenged from the start the carnivore explanation. The osteodontokeratic dominated the last years of his teaching career.

BOSKOP MAN

Dart's first article in the fields of palaeoanthropology and archaeology had been published in *Nature* in 1923, the year of his arrival in South Africa: this was a survey of the available evidence for a 'Boskop' race.[32]

Although now vanished from the narrative of hominin evolutionary history, Boskop Man, identified from discoveries made in the Transvaal in 1913 (and defined by Robert Broom in 1917 by the species name *Homo capensis*), flourished under Dart's tutelage for some time. The concept of 'Boskop Man' was applied to remains seen as pre-dating those of the Bushmen (San) and the 'Strandloper' community of coastal food collectors (assumed to be another extinct racial group), with a larger brain capacity than these more recent groups. Dart published a description of 'Boskop' finds from the southern Cape Province, identifying them as a race previously occupying all Southern Africa.[33] At this stage he was cautious about their affiliation, noting similarities with both Neanderthaloid and with more advanced Cro-Magnon specimens from Europe, and not committing to recognising a separate species *Homo capensis*.

Evidence of interbreeding or survival of 'Boskop' traits came to influence interpretation of other communities in both the fossil record and living communities, so that a skull might even be described as a Bush–Boskop–Bantu hybrid.[34]

At one level Boskop Man may be seen as no more than a classificatory framework that outlived its usefulness. The broader the range of available skeletal material to study, the weaker the case for this group, so that physical anthropologists came to side with the critics of the term:

> it is still a failing among not a few anthropologists … to plan vast migration routes of so-called prehistoric 'races' which are represented only by odd skulls … it is now obvious that what was justifiable speculation (because of paucity of data) in 1923, and was apparent as speculation in 1947, is inexcusable to maintain in 1958.[35]

Dart was locked to a paradigm of typological identity that created straitjackets into which it became increasingly difficult to fit the actual bodies.

RACIAL TYPES

The human biology, prehistory and history of Southern Africa were long dogged by a model of distinct biological races of humans, with the assumption that physical race, language and culture are inextricably linked, and with an extension that may connect behavioural characteristics to these groupings – Dart interlaced the 'childlike' physique of the Bushmen with their 'childlike' behaviour. In the 1920s such views were not unusual; in some South African historiography a linked classification survived into the 1970s and even 1980s, despite the artificiality of the model.

Such a typology stretched the evidence. Dart could not argue for pure physical races but rather for admixture: he described the Bantu tribes of the upper Zambezi and South-West Africa 'of an extremely mixed character with a dominating admixture of Bushman blood, and certainly strongly impregnated with Semitic and other Caucasian as well as Mongolian blood'.[36] In describing three 'Strandlopers' from Namibia (former South-West Africa) he makes comparison with Bush and Boskop types but adduces, as with the Southern Kalahari Bushmen, 'contamination not with the African Negro but rather with the brown and Mongolian stocks that are ethnically foreign to South and Central Africa'.[37]

Of course Dart was not the only scientist of his generation to identify distinct racial groups, and then find large samples forced them to a complex pattern of admixture to explain variance.

> I showed that the Bantu are constituted from a Bush and Negro matrix, but that before they fused, the Bush race had already been infiltrated with brown (Mediterranean) racial elements and the Negro with Nordic elements. Further, for the last thousand years or more, Asiatics of both Armenoid and Mongoloid character have been absorbed into the racial complexity which confronts us in the modern African population.[38]

An attempt to pull all this together exposed the limitations of the methodology. In his contribution on 'Racial origins' to Schapera's 1937 survey of African cultures of Southern Africa,[39] Dart conceded that neither European nor Bantu nor Bush is a pure race in South Africa, intermingling with Indians, Malays and other orientals. However, his narrative attempts to reconstruct a sequence of population movements that were increasingly complex and improbable: a Boskop race derived from previous admixtures, a Bush race arriving from the north and hybridising with the Boskop, the introduction of Mongoloid elements from Indian Ocean trading but more widely dispersed Semitic traits from northern ('Armenoid') origin. The Bush race had influence from ancient Egyptians, which showed why the Bush–Hottentot languages were so intimately related to the Hamitic group of languages. Facial features of the Negroid African populations of Southern Africa he calculated as 51.2 per cent Negroid, 25.0 per cent Bush, 22.3 per cent Caucasoid and 1.5 per cent Mongoloid. When this otherwise valuable book finally went out of print, Tobias wrote the introductory chapter to its successor and stated clearly 'a microtaxonomy of sub-Saharan peoples [is] most difficult if not impossible'.[40]

Within this model the sites of Mapungubwe and Bambandyanalo in the Limpopo Valley on South Africa's northern border, explored from 1932 onwards, were a particular challenge, associating African culture (linked to the Great Zimbabwe complex) with 'Bush–Boskop' human remains. Dart declined responsibility for analysing the skeletal material, but was involved in their interpretation, classifying the site as 'pre-Negro' and therefore further support for the non-African framework for the stone ruins of Southern Africa. Elsewhere he suggested an influence 'foreign to Africa and probably Mongolian' in one of the Bambandyanalo skulls.[41]

FOREIGN INFLUENCES ON AFRICAN CULTURE AND PEOPLE

Dart's adoption of Elliot Smith's cultural diffusionist views fitted well the views of European settler communities in Southern Africa that, as the indigenous peoples were uncivilised, non-African influences must be responsible for features that contradicted this.

Dart issued a manifesto of his hyperdiffusionist views in *Nature* in March 1925, only the month after announcing *Australopithecus africanus*. This paper is astonishing in its boldness and in its claims.[42] Here he lays out clearly his views of the Southern African links with, and influence from, the civilisations of the ancient Near East and elsewhere, weaving a selection of data chosen from within what, by then, was already established as a strong sequence of more scientific prehistoric information.[43]

One stimulus to Dart was claims for Babylonian or Phrygian hats in the rock paintings of the Later Stone Age in the Kei Valley in the Eastern Cape. Dart paraphrased this as 'the scene of the rape of a naked Bush girl by clothed foreigners wearing Babylonio-Phrygian headgear', seeing this also as the arrival of outside metallurgists into a Stone Age society.[44] Woven into the narrative of exotic links are isolated coin finds, place names, a photograph of a Zulu woman with ancient Egyptian headgear, and a panoply of unrelated and selected miscellanea that lie far from a calm scientific and testable methodology.

In several articles Dart saw sexual symbolism in the bored stone-digging stock weights of Southern Africa,[45] and phallic symbols elsewhere. He linked these to influences from ancient Egypt, Mesopotamia, Phoenicians or India.[46] 'The bearers of those [Mediterranean] cultures brought with them to South Africa not only their stone tools and aquatic ways of life but also their stories and myths.'[47]

Dart returned regularly to themes of exotic linkage. He could write:

> we are now in a position to state that the whole of the eastern portion of the African continent for some hundreds of miles inland ... was exploited by the *old colonists* ... from South-west Asia in remote ancient time ... these very ancient voyagers not only visited these territories and carried off their denizens, particularly their women, but also intermarried with them and settled down amongst them, bringing to them novel arts and customs.[48]

Other connections are seen: early Chinese voyagers' links with the East African coast from as least as early as the first millennium BC; different Chinese links with Southern Africa,[49] including Chinese hats as well as Phrygians are found in the rock paintings, and also ancient Egyptians, with the suggestion that the land of Punt in ancient Egyptian texts may have lain south of the Zambezi. Dart also referred to a mysterious undated 'galley' found near Cape Town, a find that has not been recorded in the literature.

The stone ruins and associated finds of the Limpopo basin loomed large in these discussions and in particular the African Iron Age site of Great Zimbabwe, discussed in Chapter 2, stimulated explanations of exotic origins.

Dart clashed in person with Zimbabwe's recent excavator Caton-Thompson at the 1929 meeting of the British Association for the Advancement of Science held in Johannesburg.

> He [Dart] spoke in an outburst of curiously unscientific indignation. ... After further remarks delivered in a tone of awe-inspiring violence ... he stormed out of the room. ... Miss Caton Thompson disposed of him allusively and effectively in a brief reply.[50]

Dart's memoirs concede to the conflict of ideas but indicate his preferred model:

> The distribution of ancient copper, tin and gold mines in Southern Africa, along with the comparison that could be made between bronze made in the Transvaal and the bronze statue of Pepi I of the 6th Dynasty [of Egypt] ... and the bronze gates of Shalmaneser in Assyria, demonstrated the ancient nature of the mining background to Rhodesia's ruins.

But he was also willing to emphasise Arab influence rather than more ancient sources, going beyond most proponents of that view in seeing the links as from the pre-Islamic Arab world.[51] He visited Great Zimbabwe for the first time in 1930, with a follow-up visit in 1935, by when he came to favour a Phoenician influence for the ruins.

A more extreme view – because it mixed his expertise in physical anthropology with his archaeological interests – was Dart's claim of wider Asiatic influence on both the cultures and populations of Southern Africa. An undated pendant from near Makapansgat was identified because its unusual form gave further evidence of 'foreign contacts of great antiquity'.[52] First argued in 1925, Dart repeated his views on foreign influence from the fifth millennium BC over a generation later.[53] Here he clearly identifies the influences on (Northern) Rhodesia from the maritime intercourse of Egyptians, Sumerians and Indians with a port of entry on the eastern coast of Africa. In 1929 he wrote of the need for anthropometric survey of Bantu peoples separated into their tribes. 'By such a survey properly carried out, my belief concerning Egyptian, Semitic, Arabic and Mongoloid infiltrations into the population … could be determined or rebutted.'[54] He identified Mongolian features among the San (Bushmen) – influences brought in by an Indian Ocean trading and sailing route. He first began to see Mongolian features in a Kalahari visit in 1936, to select Bushmen, whom he described as 'living fossils', for 'exhibition' in Johannesburg.

By the 1940s European physical anthropologists, who had witnessed the rise of racist ideologies in Europe, were moving away from the dangers of racial stereotyping. But relatively isolated in South Africa, Dart at this time remained tied to the older models. In a 1940 paper he sought to trace prehistoric and historic populations of Egypt in terms of the proportion of members of 'ideal' racial types based on skull shape.[55] Behind a simplified linkage of skull shape, skin colour, body hair and population movement lay the now very dated attribution of racial character.

Another even more juvenile. And less prolific, active and industrious, but far more light-hearted and happy type of mankind is the Negro type, … his blackness of skin is more akin to that of the Australian type, whose probably African but very ancient homeland is unknown. … The long-headed Bush (pygmy) stock of Africa and the short-headed Negrito (pygmy) stock of the south-eastern Asiatic islands [whose] characteristics reveal them as infants of the sapient human race. With their small (microcephalic) heads and their trustful, infant outlook goes their merry, dancing, care-free life. They are the children of men, the prototypes of fairies, gnomes and pixies.[56]

In a remarkable address in 1951, Dart accepted an argument that

if any people shows blood-group frequencies similar to a group of peoples not related to it ... the former traces back to the latter somewhere in its ancestry, or else the former has undergone crossing with the latter group or some similar people.[57]

He then used comparisons of the percentage of different blood groups in peoples throughout the world to create a detailed sequence of population movements – from northern Europe to South Africa, from the Nile Valley to Australia, from the Philippines to the Americas, within a chronology for four major migrations stretching between 7,000 BC to AD 100. These stages saw the successive 'negritization', then 'caucasianization' then 'indonesianization' of the Orient. Such a model would be dramatic as a set of general hypotheses; as a detailed narrative rewriting of prehistory it is quite remarkable. To Dart 'blood-groups provide our only clue to the hereditary pattern of races at the dawn of written history'.

Dart echoed this theme of improbable migrations in an article unambiguously named 'A Hottentot from Hong Kong' in which purely anatomical evidence is used to back the case for long-distance migration. But here he sees reverse movement of prehistoric populations dispersed from Africa eastwards as far as China, alongside Mongolian features reflecting intermingling with both Bush (San) and Bantu (Negro) populations of South Africa, reflecting their 'nautical contact with Mongoloid peoples'.[58] He continued to argue that

an unrecorded sea-traffic which was more Mongolian than Mediterranean ... once dominated the East African coast ... more remote in time than either King Solomon or Queen Hatshepsut. ...The ancient process of sea-traffic in the Indian Ocean ... carried Pygmy peoples eastwards and was thus responsible for the negritisation of the Orient.

He was a little more circumspect in noting the parallels between 'ships' of Sarawak and one from Okavango in Namibia.[59]

This and other selective evidence fed into Dart's early view that there was 'an endless procession of emissaries of every great navigating power' to South Africa in pre-European times, with the Indian Ocean routes bringing Asiatics to Southern Africa.[60] He clearly held to this view for much of his life – a line of argument diametrically contradictory to the line of development of scientific archaeology.

MINING BEFORE THE METAL AGES

Very early in Dart's South African work he was developing theories about mining that linked the subcontinent to the ancient civilisations of the old world. In June 1924, he wrote that the pre-European mining of Southern Africa could be attributed to 'an ancient people', with a hint that the source of nickel found in the bronzes of ancient Egypt and Mesopotamia might be sought in this region.[61] Five years later he advanced the argument more boldly, stating that the scale of the mining would 'preclude any belief that the products of the industry were consumed by a local population'.[62] This confirmed his views of Southern Africa as the probable source of nickel in the bronze of the ancient Near East, and the presence of the Bronze Age with 'the actual presence there at a remote age of skilled and intelligent craftsmen from a superior cultural area'. Noting distant biological influences into the Southern African indigenous populations, he concluded 'there can be little question that the South African Bronze Age synchronizes with the Bronze Ages of the nearest ancient cultures, namely, those of Egypt and Sumeria'.

Dart's enthusiasm for such debates on a wider range of topics in African prehistory was encouraged by the opportunity to join the eight-month Italian Scientific Expedition through Africa in 1930, during which he visited the ruins of Great Zimbabwe, which stimulated his support of the Elliot Smith diffusionist model. In Zambia he began one of his most persistent lines of argument, one that he continued until late in his life, that for ancient mining in the Stone Age. At Mumbwa Caves from excavation of cave deposits he and his colleagues claimed that Later Stone Age communities (with a picture of continuing Middle Stone Age artefact styles and indeed the persistence of hand-axe technology) had been miners of metal. Slag materials associated with Later Stone Age burials and artefacts were identified as showing 'traces of iron', and this led the group to a conviction that these hearths represented slag of furnaces used to smelt iron: 'the oldest-known iron foundry in the world'.[63] Recognising the conflict of this model with the associated Stone Age culture, Dart decided that indigenous labour must have been used by non-indigenous miners. On the absence of any iron finds from the Stone Age deposits, 'they might be explained by their having rusted away ... the more likely explanation is that the metal ... was too precious for any of it to be lost"[64]– a useful explanation for archaeologists wishing to prove any theory!

Within three years independent tests suggested the 'slag' was a cemented cave deposit, ironically the excavators' first hypothesis, and the iron finds were naturally occurring minerals.[65]

The ancient mining theme continued at the manganese mines in Chowa near Broken Hill (Kabwe), which he thought demonstrated contemporaneity with Mumbwa. Like many mines exploited in the twentieth century, this mine showed signs of pre-European use but with ambiguous cultural associations, and Dart concluded that 'the manganese mining community were predominantly Stone Age people' with the same mixed cultural material as at Mumbwa.[66] The mixture of material he explained by arguing that metal seekers and manganese gatherers of foreign origin, familiar with the uses of manganese, arrived among Stone Age people using 'very primitive' types of Early Stone Age implements. He considered this manganese mining pre-dated the Neolithic mines of western Europe.

For both sites Dart developed the view that substantial mining had been undertaken by Stone Age communities working for an external trade, and led by visitors from the Mediterranean:

the obvious channel for that cultural migration was the eastern coast-line, the sea and the water highways ... when the people came ... they arrived in a Moustierian community which had not yet been released from the trammels of Acheulian influences.[67]

For making metal with furnaces, 'either the metal-gatherers instructed the local inhabitants in that technique, or brought with them followers expert in that technique ... they founded their metallic enterprise amidst an old palaeolithic culture'.

He also argued that there had been a search for pyrolusite to be exported for glass making in the Near East. He allocated a chronology of 4000–2000 BC to this mining, and the primary link hinted at in the article was back to Ancient Egypt, though he was more cautious in putting this in print. The symbolism of haematite as a representation of blood explained the early haematite quarrying back to the Middle Stone Age.[68]

Given Dart's reputation in South Africa from his Australopithecine discoveries, his articles on both sites went straight into the distinguished pages of the *Transactions of the Royal Society of South Africa*.

Early mining returned later in Dart's life. In 1934 Dart first heard of finds of ochre on artefacts at Border Cave in Swaziland, and he pursued the idea of ancient ochre mining at a site he dated to the Middle Stone Age.[69] Excavations under Dart's mentorship waited until much later when his protégés Adrian Boshier and Peter Beaumont made controversial claims for archaeological work in Swaziland from the late 1960s, continuing the traditions of advancing ideas outside the conventional.[70] Dart and Beaumont announced these results from haematite workings at Ngwenya (Bomvu Ridge) as evidence for iron ore mining initially. They first dated this as nine millennia old and later dated the antiquity of mining to least 28,000 years old, and possible older.[71] They emphasised continuity with the mining claims for Chowa, reinforcing Dart's views of a foreign mining group:

> The claim made almost 35 years ago, that 'manganese was being deliberately mined in Zambia by a foreign people familiar with its potentialities in Late Stone Age time' ... have been fully justified.[72]

These claims have not generally been accepted by the archaeological community. However, the Swaziland research did make one claim that would last: that for the early first-millennium origins of the Iron Age in Southern Africa – where Castle Cavern produced fifth-century AD radiocarbon dates.[73]

EXPLAINING THE ENIGMA OF DART'S WORK

Raymond Dart generated multiple hypotheses and interpretations of Africa across the boundaries of archaeology, palaeoanthropology and biological anthropology, most of which were not sustainable, and many of which were dismissed or ignored by fellow scientists when they were made. The one that has stood the test of time – *Australopithecus africanus* – seems the exception, by good fortune as much as critical methodology.

Dart's ideas, their persistence and their popularity outside the scientific community can be attributed to the intersection of several factors, especially the nexus of Dart's personality and background with the society in which he worked for most of his life. South Africa was receptive to ideas that would not challenge the racial categories that reinforced perceptions of power and difference – from the past as well as the present. But it needed the individual whose personality, interests and influences could deliver this.

Dart was a physical anthropologist working after the Great War. In this period the discipline was grounded in a belief in racial typology, as a classificatory system and a practical approach to interpreting study materials: 'the underlying premises of inter-war physical anthropology took notions of innate racial difference for granted'.[74] This continued worldwide, alongside a widespread scientific enthusiasm for eugenics, until the rise of Nazism encouraged scientists to re-examine and abandon these approaches. Operating in the relative intellectual isolation of Johannesburg from 1923, Dart may have lagged behind some of the changes in approaches in physical anthropology, but he was not a pioneer in creating them.

What has been described as 'scientific racism' is not inevitably associated with practical racial discrimination. Dart, though never actively political, is credited with opening the Wits Medical School to non-white students, and with criticising discriminatory policies.[75] Early in his South African years he stated publicly there was no justification in biology for intolerance on racial grounds.

It happened that, for white South Africa, a racial typology model reinforced assumptions, political needs and economic structures in the interwar years. Then, following the National Party victory in 1948 and the gradual definition of the apartheid system, ideas of racial typology hardened in South Africa as they were being dissolved in science, but Dart was neither involved in nor responsible for those trends. Academics cannot take all the blame for the misuse of their ideas. In the apartheid era, Dart's followers could comfortably distance themselves from the most extreme racial paradigms and Dart could concentrate on different topics such as the osteodontokeratic.

Dart's enthusiasm for exotic origins and links in the past of the African continent, especially his challenge to the African origins of Great Zimbabwe, reinforced white prejudices and was echoed in Southern African white communities well into the 1970s. Isolated from European culture at the furthest end of a vast continent, historical links to ancient Mediterranean civilisations were immensely reassuring. But his early major claim for *Australopithecus* demonstrated the *African* origins of humankind. This was not just a challenge to those who saw Asian origins from the finds of *Homo erectus* (Pithecanthropus), but also the priority for Europe implied by the find of the fake Piltdown Man from England.

Further, Dart's actual studies of humans – from skeletal remains or living individuals – struggled to fit real evidence into the distinct racial typology, leading constantly to explanations of hybridity, as we have shown above. His own empirical research chipped away at the validity of distinct racial classifications, although he was loath to admit it.

The local acceptance in South Africa of Dart's views may also reflect the nature of 'colonial science'. The Australian Dart helped put South African science on the world map, and scientific achievement on the Southern African map.[76] White South Africa in the 1920s and 1930s was a fertile ground for someone willing to give the region a new role and status in world science, and the Taung find showed South Africa could house scientific research of world importance.

In 1925 Jan Smuts, prime minister until the previous year, specifically selected for praise the role of human palaeontology in South Africa.[77] Dart's discovery led to his immediate rise in status. Already a full professor at 29, he was made Dean of the Medical School within months of his discovery, and other honours followed and continued for the subsequent decades. In time Dart's status grew such that public criticism by others in the field was muted and indirect; in his later decades of work scientists were unwilling to say in print what they thought in private.

The disadvantage of such a pioneering role is of course isolation. The opportunities to test ideas among colleagues in the same disciplinary areas were few, though colleagues in other disciplines were encouraging.

We must look in part to Dart's personality to explain his approach to the fields of archaeology and physical anthropology. Having rebelled at university against his parents' fundamentalist religious beliefs, he continued to be a rebel (though some might suggest he endorsed a new fundamentalism). In his co-authored autobiography Dart wrote:

> I may be asked how it is possible in following the feckless hobby of an amateur detective to know where the trail will lead or what will prove the most valuable clue in the solution of human mysteries? Usually what helped me most was the general agreement of a lot of other people that I was on the wrong track! Knowing the fallibility of human opinion, especially popular opinions or

dogmas adopted without satisfactory reasons, it generally proved valuable to explore the reverse of the accepted view.[78]

An element here might be the brashness of the outsider to a world of science dominated by metropolitan Europe: the independent Australian character. Sir Arthur Keith would criticise Dart for 'his flightiness, his scorn for accepted opinion, the unorthodoxy of his outlook'.[79] More politely, Tobias describes 'his tendency to overstate the case' alongside 'his willingness to free his mind from the shackles of authority ... a man rich in idiosyncrasies, a born actor with overwhelming charisma'.[80] But what began as a radical approach to issues in prehistory would be seen as adherence to discredited ideas: instead of looking forward to new but untested ideas, looking backward to discredited ones.

Part of the explanation for Dart's approach is the baleful influence of Sir Grafton Elliot Smith, discussed in Chapter 6, the research scientist in anatomy who 'abandoned any pretence at scientific method ... his theory was formed and everything was squeezed into this theory'.[81] In an article after his retirement Dart acknowledged how when he first encountered Smith: 'he was now through his discoveries in Egypt revolutionizing our knowledge of how culture had spread throughout the world'.[82]

A major influence on maintaining that reputation through and beyond the last decades of Dart's life was Phillip Tobias, Dart's protégé and choice as his successor as professor of anatomy. Because of the widespread high personal and professional regard felt for Tobias, his championing and defence of Dart's reputation has had real impact. Tobias' work, as South Africa's leading physical anthropologist, actually contributed indirectly to undoing many of Dart's ideas, especially on racial classification but Tobias remained a strong public champion of his mentor and 'father-figure'.[83]

Finally, some of Dart's continuing influence must be attributed to his personal charm and charisma alongside the awe in which he was held, although many early students may have 'dismissed him as him "mad"...'.[84] As a source of encouragement, resources and institutional support Dart built and maintained a large circle of protégés and admirers, not always to the liking of the newer generation of professionals.

While Dart's publications included solid descriptive material in anatomy, physical anthropology and archaeology, his interpretative themes – most pursued doggedly throughout his life – represented a less than scientific approach. While one of these themes – the identification and position of *Australopithecus africanus* – has been accepted as a contribution to science, the others have been left behind. At the time that Dart advanced many of his wilder views, in the interwar decades and immediately after, prehistoric sciences were already established and growing in strength. Dart's views and lines of argument were leading in quite opposite directions, which he developed and adhered to for over five decades.

It is good to remember scholars for their lasting contribution to our knowledge, but we need to be aware that the process of creating that knowledge is not always clear, clean and methodologically sound.

Raymond Dart played a landmark role in the development of the scientific study of human origins in Africa, at the same time maintaining enthusiasm for the imagined past of the continent with passion and energy: a life that looked both ways, backwards to romantic invention and forward to new scientific approaches.

4
Egos and fossils

Among the most dramatic grand narratives associated with the African continent are those created by the discoverers of fossil hominins: the African ancestors of humankind. The changing models and images they created for human origins inspired world interest in Africa and continental pride in the African ancestry of all humanity.

Hunters for the fossil ancestors of humankind were the twentieth-century equivalent of nineteenth-century explorers. From the late eighteenth to the end of the nineteenth century world outside of the continent, awareness of 'Africa' was dominated by narratives of a succession of famous white explorers. As they faced hardship, disease, practical challenges and personal trials, books written by or about them on their return were bestsellers, often translated into multiple languages, and in the later period magazine and newspaper articles reported news (or the mysterious lack of news) of their adventures.

One theme for some of the great 'explorers' was of high moral motives: they suggested they were there to help bring civilisation to the heathen, expose and if possible suppress the Arab slave trade, and allow the entry of Christianity and productive commerce.

A second theme lay in competition between explorers; competition both as individuals and as representatives of competing non-African nations. In seeking to trace the Niger or the sources of the Nile, in reaching an area before a rival nation had established its claim, by informing potential traders, in representing their Protestant church against Catholic missionaries (or the reverse), they found in Africa a contested ground. Such contests would transform into institutional rivalry as nations declared protectorates or colonies in Africa, and churches established clear areas of missionary influence.

While expeditions included many individuals, the expedition leader was always the focus of attention, and the endeavour was always associated with its leader in the popular imagination.[1]

In the first half of the twentieth century much of Africa formed part of European empires and dominions. There continued to be

Sculpture of Louis Leakey making a stone tool, at the National Museum of Kenya. (Photo: Barry D. Kass@ImagesofAnthropology.com)

exploration, but this time as part of their paid duties by public servants working as surveyors, game wardens, district officers. For the most part their achievements ceased to be heralded as those of individuals. But a new kind of twentieth-century hero of African discovery emerged to take their place: the 'fossil man hunter'.

In African adventure figures such as Louis Leakey came to fill much the same role in popular imagination as Caillié, Barth, Speke, Livingstone and Stanley had done. And unlike the Victorian explorers who 'discovered' an area residents already knew was there, discoveries of early ancestors of humankind were genuine uncovering of the unknown.

There was thus scientific respectability to the cycle of great discoveries in the field that would come to be called palaeoanthropology, effectively a sub-branch of archaeology. After the discovery and identification of *Australopithecus* by Raymond Dart, discussed in the previous chapter, idiosyncratic figures such as Robert Broom, Louis Leakey, Richard Leakey and Donald Johanson became bywords for adventure combined with major scientific breakthrough. In turn these scientist-explorers could often fit the media image required of the lone adventurer in dangerous territory achieving the impossible with lasting impact.

The world of these discoveries was quite different from the operation of most science. The strongest backing for a piece of evidence in scientific research lies usually in its replicability. In the experimental sciences (say, chemistry) the basis for acceptance is that research methodology is made explicit, so that other scientists can repeat the experiment to prove – or attempt to disprove – the proposed results and their interpretation. In the observational sciences (say, astronomy or zoology) the described subject can be relocated and examined in the same or greater detail. 'Discovery' is the examination of evidence, the formulation of a nullifiable hypothesis, testing of the hypothesis against the evidence and conclusions that affirm the hypothesis and establish awareness of information, which can be further amplified, or modified, by further research. But as a leading palaeontologist noted, there is a tremendous bias towards the views of finders, rather than of interpretative and analytical scientists in the discipline of palaeoanthropology.[2]

Much of archaeological 'discovery' follows a similar pattern of calm development. Regions are studied, sites are located, sample excavations are made and resulting finds (artefactual, economic and contextual) are described and studied to contribute to scientific interpretation. While every spotting of a surface find, or thrust of the trowel or sieving of the excavated deposit may uncover some data, most 'discovery' is a modest contribution to incremental knowledge. And much of this interpretation is indeed *replicable*. The interpretative hypothesis may be that backed blades show use wear of scraping as well as cutting; or that offshore trade ceased with the arrival of a new ceramic tradition. It may be predictive: that elite tombs were located away from arable land, or that settlement in period x was seasonal between coast and uplands. Most information in archaeology is of this kind: augmenting knowledge in a way that can be tested by future work and be amplified, modified or eventually replaced.

This is distinct from the popular and media-driven image of archaeological discovery as the sudden dramatic uncovering of the unique and unexpected. This question leads the layperson to ask the archaeologist: 'what did you *find*?' They do not want an answer in terms of refinement of interpretations, enlargement of a sample, confirmation of a testable hypothesis. They want a material object – a royal tomb, a gilt statue, a hoard of coins or an inscription that undermines assumed knowledge. And of course, from time to time, such an event does happen, such an object or site is identified and announced and archaeology enters the media to confirm the illusion that the discipline at its best is focused on an unending search for the unique and physical, not for the systematic expansion of knowledge and understanding that fill all the annual issues of over 400 journals and vastly more monographs. The image of a Heinrich Schliemann, or a Howard Carter, if not Indiana Jones, has come to haunt the archaeological community.

Most research is group-based. The increasing tendency is for the scientific papers that reports the results of research to appear over the names of all those involved in the research; not just the leader of the team, or the writers of the article. Indeed, some of those listed as authors may have contributed no words to the paper, may not even have seen it, but receive their authorship acknowledgement because of a fieldwork or laboratory contribution to data.[3]

That contrasts with both the image and the tradition of the pioneer fossil hunter associated with a major discovery. That is one strand that has often appeared to fulfil and match the fantasies of popular 'discovery' – the hunt for fossil hominins, the ancestors of humankind and their closest relatives.[4] And in the history of the sub-discipline of palaeoanthropology and the work of associated prehistorians, it is hard to avoid the conclusion that many of the participants – encouraged by the media and the demands of raising financial support – have played up to this image of the explorer/ discoverer/pioneer.

The classic 'moment' in palaeoanthropology has become the announcement in the pages of a scientific journal such as the weekly *Nature* or *Science* of a new discovery, together with its naming – and the immediate reporting of this announcement in the international print and electronic media. This commonly followed a commitment to silence and secrecy following the actual unearthing of the relevant find. Such an approach supports an image that the most important prehistoric research is a classic uncovery of the unexpected and unique. The science is clear and clean: the announcement comes first in a highly reputable journal, following peer review – but ironically, the detailed publication of the find and its context may take years, sometimes many years, to appear, and more seriously, some complete formal descriptions have never been published.

Perhaps the strongest contrast between this area of research and other fields of archaeological enquiry lies in the frequency with which claims have been made for uniqueness. This is seen in the crucial question of taxonomy: classification. For much of the long history of research on fossil hominin sites and their associated finds, the emphasis has often been on dissimilarity, not similarity, on difference rather than links, on the individuality of new data rather than their contribution to enlarge the pool of information available for study.

The subjective element spreads from 'lumpers' to 'splitters': those who prefer fewer taxa to those who prefer more. This operates both as classification by species and classification by genus. Both 'splitters' (those who favour multiple species and genera) and 'lumpers' (those who prefer a classificatory and phylogenetic scheme with fewer taxons) vary in the criteria they consider essential to their classificatory scheme. It can be argued that the overall tendency from the earliest finds of fossil hominins was effectively to 'patent' the find by naming it formally as a new species or even a new genus.[5] The fundamental of a patent is that future users respect the claims of the patentee, but in fact subsequent finds now seen as from the same species would be 'patented' under another name, occasionally even when reported by the same scientist.

Since the late nineteenth century over 60 species and around 30 hominin genera from Africa or Eurasia have been named by their discoverers or those assigned by the discovery team to present their finds in the scientific literature. Most of these were subsequently recognised as similar to other finds and merged with those species names, while new finds followed the same pattern of claimed novelty. Thus today there are still about 7 genera and 26 hominin species recognised, many of them recent announcements.[6]

The pressure to identify a find as a new species comes from a mixture of personal ego, national pride (the nationality of the discoverer or the discovery location, which may differ), the enthusiasm of scientific research, the isolation of individual researchers, or the pressure for funding support, which recognises that unique finds are more likely to attract sponsorship in a competitive market. Africa has seen scientists name a large number of species, and then seen them merged by subsequent analysis into existing taxons.

The hominin genera of Africa with the longest acceptance are *Homo* and *Australopithecus*. The genus *Paranthropus* named by Robert Broom in 1938 was merged into *Australopithecus*, but many scientists now consider it as a separate genus again. Meanwhile genera have been named for earlier hominins – *Sahelanthropus*, *Orrorin*, *Ardipithecus*, *Kenyanthropus*. But finds separated as separate genera have been merged into *Homo* or *Australopithecus*: *Africanthropus*, *Telanthropus*, *Atlanthropus*, *Tchadanthropus*, *Zinjanthropus*, *Paraustralopithecus*.[7] The classic French–English rivalry over African territory has been projected back a few million years before the nineteenth-century scramble for Africa.

Robert Broom reclassified his 1938 find of *Australopithecus transvaalensis* ('Mrs Ples') as a new genus *Plesianthropus*, though it was later merged into *Australopithecus africanus*.

Within *Australopithecus* individual finds have been allocated by enthusiastic scientists to their own species, only to have them moved by consensus into existing taxons. Louis Leakey's *boisei* has survived on its own, but Dart's find from Makapansgat in the Transvaal, named *Australopithecus prometheus*, was regrouped with his Taung find as *africanus*. Despite the corralling of the earlier finds into a reduced number of species, there has been a blossoming of new australopith species with *Australopithecus* (or *Paranthropus*) *aethiopicus*, *A. afarensis*, *A. anamensis*, *A. bahrelghazali* and *A. garhi*, augmented in 2010 by *A. sediba*.

Our own *Homo* genus has also seen a number of temporary taxonomic visitors in African palaeoanthropology, especially finds initially described as separate species but subsequently considered to be *Homo sapiens*: these include *H. capensis* ('Boskop Man'), *Homo rhodesiensis* ('Broken Hill Man'), *H. australoideus africanus*,

H. drennani, H. kanemensis, H. helmei, H. florisbadensis, African-thropus njarasensis, and *H. leakeyi.*

While some of these names reflect articles reclassifying existing finds, others mark the enthusiasm of pioneer workers in Africa for their discoveries and their significance.

SOME PIONEERS

Fossil hominid hunters had established reputations in Asia and Europe; figures such as Eugene Dubois (1858–1940) and G.H.R von Koenigsvald (1902–1982) in Indonesia and Davidson Black (1884–1934) in China had set an image for the European in difficult and distant lands making a personal scientific breakthrough that would change the perception of human origins.

The career of Raymond Dart was described in the last chapter. Dart put palaeoanthropology into the popular imagination from his announcement of *Australopithecus africanus*, and, as we have shown, he played up the image of the scientist/discoverer with numerous further claims of less sustainable value. His identification of *Australopithecus africanus* has held up while his support for *Homo capensis* and *Australopithecus prometheus* as separate species did not.

Robert Broom (1866–1951) was 'a character' and a pioneer in African fossil hominid exploration.[8] Trained like Dart as a medical doctor, he moved from his native Scotland to South Africa, initially as a doctor then to teach zoology and geology at the college (and future university) in Stellenbosch from 1903 to around 1909, while being affiliated to the South African Museum. He then returned to medical practice, alongside continuing his research interests. In 1918 he published a report on the 1913 find identified as Boskop man (*Homo capensis*). He became a supporter of Dart's 1925 claims for early hominid finds, and in turn Dart with support from former (and future) prime minister Jan Smuts helped Broom secure a position at the Transvaal Museum from 1934 at the age of 68.

That provided a base where he could undertake his own field research, and it was Broom who uncovered the australopithecine remains at the Transvaal cave sites of Sterkfontein (from 1936), Kromdraai (from 1937) and Swartkrans (from 1948). At the first site the find of the australopithecine *Plesianthropus* ('Mrs Ples') marked the entry of Broom into the study of early humans.

Already in his seventies, Broom's demeanour as the very formal elderly Scottish doctor was as renowned as the remarkable discoveries he made and the claims for their antiquity. These were made with his own physical efforts to explore sites and both to excavate and prepare the fossilised materials.

Broom continued working and writing to the end of his life at 84; his assistant, John T. Robinson, continued his work on the Transvaal cave sites and they have remained subjects of active field research.

THE PHENOMENON OF LOUIS LEAKEY

Most people who could name a figure associated with major African finds of fossil hominids would first think of Louis Leakey (1903–1972). Leakey is associated in the popular imagination especially with Olduvai Gorge in Tanzania, site of numerous finds of which the most famous announcements were 'Nutcracker Man' – *Zinjanthropus* (now called *Australopithecus*) *boisei*; and *Homo habilis* ('handy man'), together with some of the earliest stone tools known.

Leakey and Olduvai became publicly known worldwide through the *National Geographic* magazine (whose associated Society was proud of funding his later activities); from widespread lectures, television programmes, and popular books. 'Doctor Leakey' thus became the definitive image of the pioneer explorer scientist, and Olduvai the image of the classic discovery site of archaeological and palaeoanthropological science. Added to this was the romanticism of Leakey's birth and upbringing in Kenya, his confidence with African people, his association with adventurous female students of African wildlife, and his rugged image. Just as the lasting image of Elvis Presley has been that of his later years rather than the years that brought him fame, so the lasting image of Louis Leakey is of an older man in dusty khaki boiler suit standing in the African savannah, speaking to a group of admirers, or testing some stone tools, or holding a fossil hominin cranium.

The lifetime work and commitment of Leakey can be credited with major extensions of our knowledge of African prehistory and the fossil ancestry of humankind. His achievements were both direct, in a lifetime of fieldwork, writing and interpretation; and indirect, in his support and sponsorship of others. His work is a reflection of his personality and drive, rarely self-critical, passionate and zealous, with a proprietorial approach to areas of time and space where he focused his research. Occasionally his passions led him down false paths; at times, like others in palaeontology, he held firmly to beliefs longer than scientific process would allow.

Nevertheless his is not a simple story.[9] The work that led to his major discovery of *Zinjanthropus* was underfunded, had limited institutional support or public recognition. But this find led to a totally transformed period of funding and public support, for a period during which ironically Louis Leakey withdrew from much active African fieldwork and diverted his interests into other directions.

His own research, especially in relation to fossil hominin finds, is an exemplar of the yearning by pioneer fossil hunters to put their imprint on knowledge through unique finds, unique naming of these finds, and a defensive and personalised approach to these names and their implied taxonomy.

Leakey was part of the phenomenon noted above, where new species or genus names were given to finds that more sombre appraisal attributed to existing taxons. His research led to major discoveries of *Homo erectus* and to the type fossil for *H. habilis* at Olduvai, the first member of the *Homo* genus and master of toolmaking. The earlier finds that Leakey called *Zinjanthropus boisei* continue to be thought a distinct species, but not a distinct genus.

Leakey's work in 1932 on Kenya's Lake Victoria produced a number of fossil finds. His naming of *Homo kanamensis* in 1935 initially met acceptance in the scientific world,[10] and as Leakey considered it to come from very early deposits, the new species was proclaimed as an early African human ancestor. However, it proved impossible to confirm the accurate context or geological age, an embarrassment that cast a pall over Leakey's early career. In due course most but not all palaeoanthropologists would reclassify this material as *Homo sapiens*.

As with Raymond Dart, Louis Leakey's enthusiasm for the uniqueness of his fossil hominin material proved accurate at some but not all times. His fervour, dedication and astonishing energy in physically demanding contexts was matched by what could also be described as rushed, zealous, 'pig-headed' attitudes, with a strong tendency to overstate his case; his wife-to-be Mary was warned 'genius is akin to madness'. Leakey's conviction that *Zinjanthropus* was not an australopithecine remained firm, and preceded his opportunity to make comparisons with the South African australopithecine material.[11] He remained insistent it was a new genus. Whether it needed the attribute of a new genus or not, *Zinjanthropus* served to change the financial basis of the Leakeys' research endeavours.

There was long debate too over the crucially important find made by Mary Leakey at Olduvai: one of the finds that would in due course be named *Homo habilis*. The definitive naming and report was the work of the distinguished South African anatomist Phillip Tobias, but in the years of his careful research Louis Leakey initially felt the find was non-*Homo*, then became confident that it was an early member of the *Homo* genus, before further evidence persuaded Tobias to place the new species in the *Homo* range.[12]

There was less controversy over some of the earlier fossils found. The naming of the fossil ape *Kenyapithecus wickeri* found at Fort Ternan in Kenya in 1961 and *Kenyapithecus africanus* at Rusinga Island have survived, as have the subspecies of Proconsul, all of the Miocene age. His main rival in the study of this period, the American Elwyn Simons, characterised Leakey's views as 'The fossils that I find are the important ones; they're all on the direct line to mankind. But the fossils you find are extinct side branches.'[13]

Leakey's career can be contrasted with that of Raymond Dart, who was born ten years earlier but survived Leakey by sixteen years. Both were energetic, passionate and dogmatic. But Dart came to shun the professional criticism and surround himself with protégés who did not criticise his work (even if, as with Phillip Tobias, in practice they undermined it). Leakey was equally individualistic but recognised the need to work with specialists of other disciplines, and in particular came to rely on the solid commitment and methodology of Mary Leakey, so that his reputation has survived in a quite different way.

Another complexity to the Leakey story is one that contradicts many popular images of the successful scientist, operating with widespread fame and international support. Leakey's major research and discoveries were in fact almost entirely undertaken in circumstances of severe financial restraints and physical hardship, over a long period extending from 1924 to the discovery of *Zinjanthropus* in 1959. This last find, and the belief that it was associated with the earliest stone tool-making, served as the catalyst to attract (from the USA in particular) the level of funding and support that had been missing from the decades of work. But, ironically, from this stage on Leakey ceased to be the major active player at Olduvai and his wife Mary Leakey directed the work there from 1960 to 1983. Fame and resources only came Louis Leakey's way when the major work had been done, and at a time when his own health set some limits to his own field activity. Equally significantly, the reputation attached to him individually led to fund-raising attached very much to the individual, the image of the explorer-scientist, and allowed him to fund quite different projects, including primate research and misguided studies into ancient America, while Mary continued the hard slog of systematic field research and analysis at Olduvai, Laetoli and related sites.

Thus when the pioneering work was being done Leakey was much less well known and operating in hardship. Once he was being supported by foundations and a base of passionate fans he was neither working in the field not focused on the same priorities, and it was the much more self-effacing Mary who survived the very different challenges arising from the changed circumstances to continue the solid field research.

The main period of Louis Leakey's pioneering work, from 1924 to 1959, was one of substantial energy, often in tough physical circumstances operating on very limited resources, and learning his skills as he went along.[14] The spread of his studies was immense, perhaps too broad – his monograph reports extended from vertebrate fossils of the Miocene era (23 to 5 million years ago) to the Later Stone Age sequence of East African hunter-gatherers to the anthropology of the Kikuyu among whom he grew up.

The discomforts to achieve such results, alongside the hard work of the excavations or field survey themselves, included tough treks, campsites in poor location, attacks by mosquitoes, the danger of snakes and wildlife, very restricted range or even quantity of food, poor or limited – sometimes extremely limited – water, alongside the challenge of maintaining vehicles and other equipment in remote areas.[15] At a long-term project like Olduvai there could be some improvement, by building modest local living quarters, but there was never the comfort of well-fitted field research premises in the main period of Louis' research.

While some of this was inevitable in rugged terrain without the facilities of urban life, the shortage of cash exacerbated it.[16] As with many archaeologists of the era, there was no separation between life and work, no divide between funding for the Leakeys' personal life and that for their research, so that effectively they personally funded much of their own research for many years, and set operational budgets accordingly. Leakey's early work at Olduvai, Kanjera and Kanam cost much of his limited resources and those of his first wife Frida. When, in 1932, they returned from Kenya to Cambridge University, where Leakey was then working, the family including a baby were in poor accommodation. Using Frida's dowry they were able to buy a house. but the tensions between Louis' priorities and those of a family man were substantial. The marriage ended after he had met Mary (Nicol) in 1933; she shared his willingness to face hardship for the sake of research, and maintained the same priorities fifty years later after Louis had become a media figure.[17]

The divorce prejudiced the British academic system against Louis. After his period registered as a postgraduate student at Cambridge he had held a research fellowship, but he no longer had a salaried position after 1935, when he was already 32 with the financial responsibility for himself and Mary and, in theory, for the two children of his former marriage. A salaried position in his field would long stay denied to him. Recognition for his contributions was real, but did not pay the family bills. It was a major breakthrough when in 1941 the Kenya Government appointed him an *honorary* (i.e. unpaid) curator at the Coryndon (later National) Museum in Nairobi, bringing the valued benefit of housing, which the Leakeys could use as their home base when not in the field. Finally, at the end of 1945 at the age of 42, he accepted a salaried position at the museum and for the first time had some modest personal financing. He was able to use the position – and the salary – to balance his fieldwork and research priorities with the needs of the museum, a pattern he continued for another sixteen years, past the age many colonial civil servants would have retired.[18]

Leakey was not the easiest of employers. An enthusiastic young British archaeologist, Merrick Posnansky, was brought by Leakey in 1956 to work as curator of prehistoric sites in national parks, and would late recount Leakey's opposition to promoting and proselytising prehistory to a wider local audience, alongside a paternalistic attitude to Kenyans, especially urban Kenyans, which set him at odds with the rising urban nationalist movement.[19]

Following the *Zinjanthropus* find the National Geographic Society paid Louis a (modest) salary from 1961 and continued to renew this arrangement. This allowed him to stand down from his formal museum duties, while staying in an honorary position and on the museum's board; ironically, his successor was unseated and replaced by Louis' son Richard seven years later.

For individual projects Leakey had been able to get some support from outside East Africa. The US-based Wenner-Gren Foundation's Viking Fund helped a rock art project with £2,000 in 1951, businessman Charles Boise contributed £1,000 to the Miocene research in 1948 and the Kenyan Government responded in kind with £1,500, after which both parties continued with further grants for this work. Boise offered to support the work at Olduvai Gorge for seven years from 1951 – work that led to the fossil find named in his honour *boisei* and which allowed a new generation of funding, although it was spread so broadly that projects such as Mary Leakey's work at Olduvai remained at times short of cash.[20]

Tough conditions often exacerbated by inadequate funding did not help Leakey's periodically poor health; indeed, in 1942, a baby daughter died from dysentery.[21] During Leakey's very early research work in 1924 he had the first of a number of attacks of malaria, was passing blood and vomiting; thereafter he commonly had epileptic fits with loss of consciousness, increased by tiredness in the field; in 1948 he was hospitalised with gall bladder problems but still undertook major field seasons; he experienced kidney stones, glandular fever, and the debilitating effects of the waterborne disease bilharzia. By the time after the *Zinjanthropus* discovery that the funding world discovered and began to support Louis Leakey, arthritis too had begun to affect him.

The major funding from 1960 thus came at a time when most research workers would be cutting back on practical fieldwork and bringing that cycle of their life to an end, and in many ways that is what Louis did. His energies went into delivering what his supporters expected: lecture tours, social events, meetings, media interviews. Fatigued during his 1967 tour in the United States, he collapsed or had a further epileptic fit; the following year he had a hip replacement but still undertook fundraising work; early in 1970 he had a minor then major heart attack that led him to take serious rest; in early 1971 an attack by a bee swarm stimulated a stroke. At the end of that year, at a conference in Ethiopia he was passionate, mentally alert and reasonably mobile, but less than a year later he died in London, aged 69.

The watershed was the 1959 find of *Zinjanthropus boisei*, which at the time the Leakeys saw as the culmination of the work Louis had begun in 1931 at Olduvai – a site not in Kenya where he held an appointment but in neighbouring Tanzania. The timetable of the transition was short, in the research lifetimes of the Leakeys. On 17 July Mary made the find – a surface find, not the result of excavation. The apparent association with stone tools suggested this was a hominin toolmaker.[22] The find was announced over Louis' sole name in an issue of *Nature* dated only a month later.[23]

Leakey flew with his find to colleagues in South Africa and to a congress in Congo, then on to London and finally (sponsored by the Wenner-Gren Foundation) to the USA. This last journey changed the lives of all in the Leakey story. Here he found a vast public audience and an immediate sponsorship from the publishers of *National Geographic* magazine. For a while they were his major sponsor, though in the mid-1960s the Wenner-Gren Foundation funded work at the research centre Louis had set up near the Museum in Nairobi.

The *National Geographic* support was tied to particular projects despite its salary support for Leakey. But given the personality cult that was being established in the USA around Louis Leakey it became possible for him to establish a level of independence through which he could pursue other interests. This was achieved by a very American style of operation appropriately named The L.S.B. Leakey Foundation for Research Related to Man's Origins. The prime basis of this was wealthy Californians.[24] While its committee had academic members, it was the personality that attracted the financial support and by definition it was unlikely to be critical of the uses to which Leakey wished to put the funding. Resources therefore went only partially into African archaeology and palaeoanthropology, where Mary Leakey continued with her solid work. Louis Leakey funded a number of untried researchers to undertake primate research in Africa and South-east Asia, an initiative that produced some remarkable results, though initially met with criticism from the scientific establishment. More troublingly, Leakey pursued a vision of early humanity in North America and the work he supported and encouraged at the Calico site, appropriately enough in California, was a low point in Leakey's later work.[25] He persisted in his confidence that human settlement in the Americas was earlier than the present evidence supported; that the site of Calico was the test site and that stone finds there were human artefacts and a circle of stone a human hearth. Opposition to these claims was widespread; often muted, though Mary Leakey was more open in her scepticism.

Mary remained focused physically and intellectually at Olduvai, well beyond Louis' death in 1972. In the later years of work there she concentrated on writing up the finds and their interpretation. Finally, in 1983, after 20 years there, she moved back from Olduvai to Nairobi, continuing her Olduvai studies towards their definitive publication, a process that saw the final large volume of the Olduvai Gorge monographs appear in 1994, two years before her death.[26]

Mary and Louis' son Richard, in seeking to establish his own reputation in palaeoanthropological research, found himself increasingly in conflict with his father. This became most marked when he was unable to secure funding from the Leakey Foundation.[27] Richard's own field research was to lead to major results. In the Omo Valley of southern Ethiopia and at Lake Turkana (Rudolph) in Kenya he organised expeditions that contributed significant new finds to the fossil record, especially from Koobi Fora in Kenya. From 1989 his career moved, initially into a role as director of wildlife conservation and later in opposition politics in Kenya.

ENTER DONALD JOHANSON

While Louis Leakey was establishing a reputation as the leading researcher on fossil hominids in East Africa, he had no-one to challenge this. When American Donald Johanson sought to establish such a reputation in the 1970s, he could only do so by toppling the dominant role of the Leakeys: by then Richard and his mother Mary.[28]

Johanson began his youthful field research in East Africa in friendly cooperation with Richard Leakey but rivalries emerged, personal and professional. Neither had the personality to bow to the other's expertise or ambition: after initial collaboration and later collegial rivalry relations came to the point where Richard would refer to Johanson as 'a scoundrel', and sought to avoid his company.[29] Mary's attitude would be one of hurt and sadness rather than open hostility. Johanson's ambition and personality was a driving force to make major achievements in palaeoanthropology, but he did so in a way that would cause concern in the wider discipline.

Johanson was able to operate independently of the Leakey world in his major expeditions at Hadar in the Afar depression of Ethiopia. The 1974 discovery of a cranium nicknamed 'Lucy' was the most prominent find, being classified as a new Australopithecine, *A. afarensis*, dated 3.2 million years ago. This led to conflicting views between Johanson and Richard Leakey over the pattern of human evolution.

Other conflicts between Johanson and the Leakeys began to emerge, which came to represent ownership claims on the past and also on sites. Johanson identified a find from Mary Leakey's work at Laetoli as the type site for the species he named from his own Afar site *Australopithecus afarensis*, but then took over the description of Mary's site and work in the 1978 scientific meeting that announced this species.

Scientific rivalry took a much more unpleasant turn in 1985. A convention in archaeological work is that scientists do not intrude on the sites of other scientists. Olduvai Gorge was not only associated with Mary and Louis Leakey but the subject of her continuing research and description. However, the site did not 'belong' to Mary nor was it in her now home country of Kenya. Within two years of Mary's return to Nairobi to write up the long research Johanson obtained a permit from the Tanzanian government to take over 'the Leakeys' site' and began fieldwork of his own there in 1985. This inevitably caused distress to Mary Leakey and a negative reaction from many of her admirers; it perhaps reflected a cultural divide between different generations of researchers and between the US – now dominant in financing African fieldwork – and others.[30] Johanson ignored these reactions and proceeded to exercise his legal permit to work at Olduvai.

Arguably in response to the turmoil caused by large egos and lives building empires, hominin research in Africa has become less focused in recent years on individuals. Articles appear under multiple authorship. Research projects funded from outside Africa are carefully controlled by local governments and operate in close collaboration with local institutions. African students are supported for overseas study and on-site training and build up longer-term relationships with their non-African colleagues. But underlying the field is still the hope for the unique find, the excitement of the breakthrough discovery, and the temptation to make a claim that will put a unique find into the textbooks with a revision of taxonomy and the hominin evolutionary story. It remains an area where passion and drive of individuals' impact on the scientific scene, and where unexpected finds – such as the dwarf hominid from Flores in Indonesia found in 2003 – can upset assumptions and stimulate passionate arguments between those active in the subject.

5
Stirring the gene pool: Human ancestors from Africa to the wider world

If much of the twentieth century witnessed debate about the earliest African ancestors of humankind, the most recent decades have seen the grand narratives of the emergence in Africa of fully modern humans, defined by physical type, or genetics, or behaviour; and of the stages by which humans and their ancestors left the African continent.

As discussed in the last chapter, the continent of Africa has been the prime location for studies of human evolution. Here the line of primates that led eventually to humankind, all grouped as 'hominins', split from the line of the African great apes. Here developed the australopithecines, and from Africa their early *Homo* descendants left to occupy many parts of Asia and subsequently Europe in stages of migration described as 'Out of Africa 1'. Most (though not all) scientists look to Africa for the origin of truly modern humans around 200,000 years ago, who left the continent around 60,000 years ago ('Out of Africa 2') to populate Asia, Australia, then Europe and later the Americas.

The contribution of Africa to these major themes of human prehistory has, inevitably, attracted many grand theories and sweeping claims. The evidence of fossil remains, still few in number, has not always easily tied in with the more plentiful archaeological evidence. While some scholars have adapted and changed their views as new finds were made, others have been more dogmatic and defensive. And some models, which might fit the geological, anatomical or archaeological evidence, have been pursued despite conflicting with the geographical realities of the continent, requiring improbable movements across water or arid land barriers.

As evidence had been uncovered, analysed and reanalysed, the core questions and debates have changed significantly. There have been major debates from Darwin onwards about the origins of the line that led to humans: where the first hominins emerged (Africa,

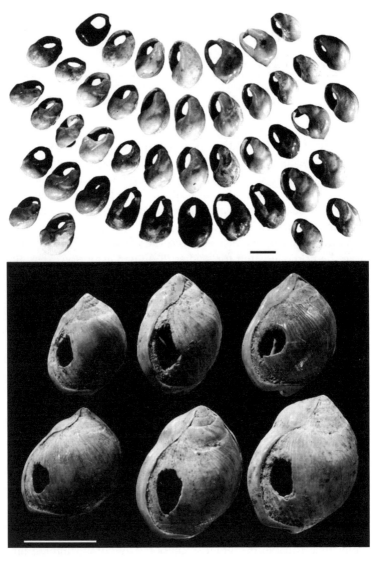

Modern human symbolic behaviour: perforated *Nassarius kraussianus* shell beads from the Middle Stone Age of Blombos Cave. (From C. Henshilwood et al., *Science* [2004], 34, reprinted with permission from AAAS)

Asia or Europe); how and when they spread through Africa and within Eurasia.

There has been substantial change in the questions asked about the origins and spread of anatomically and behaviourally modern humans. Europe saw modern humans first arrive in the continent a little over 40,000 years ago equipped with new technologies and new cultural attributes including social complexity and symbolic, non-functional behaviour as represented in art and ritual. A Eurocentric view of Africa took the assumption of a similar single emergence of modern humans until it became clear that our anatomically modern species emerged in Africa much earlier, with dates being pushed back and now considered as around 200,000 years ago. This was well before the emergence of the cultural and symbolic forms that mark modern human behaviour, and arguments have developed on what characterises the modern human mind and when this is manifested in the archaeological record. Finally, there is the question of dating and interpreting the necessity and the cultural ability for these modern humans to leave Africa and spread into and beyond Asia, a migration dated only around 60,000 years ago. The emergence of modern human behaviour is later than the development of modern human form.[1]

Treatments of these issues have reflected not just new evidence but ideological approaches, changing interests, changing methodologies as well as, at times, special pleading.

THE AFRICAN ANCESTRY OF THE HUMAN LINE

Raymond Dart's announcement of the Taung australopithecine fossil in 1925 as humankind's earliest African ancestor provided strong support for Darwin's suggestion that the origins of humanity should be sought in Africa. Until Dart's discovery, the fossils found in Java and China had led a consensus of an Asian ancestry of humankind, and the 1912 finds at Piltdown in England, not exposed as a forgery until 1953, further complicated the debate.

Australopithecines lived in the savannah regions of eastern and southern Africa, and the first of our genus, *Homo habilis*, stemmed from the australopithecine line but also lived alongside the last australopithecines from ca. 2.3 million years ago. The subsequent hominin, called *Homo ergaster* or *Homo erectus*,[2] emerged in Africa about 1.8 million years ago. *H. erectus* is also found in South-east and East Asia by 1.8 million years ago, very close to the date it is first seen in Africa, and reached Europe by 1.4 million years ago.

A primary question is how, when and why *H. erectus* expanded its range from Africa into Eurasia. This may have been in several stages. Early *H. erectus* with a core chopper technology left sub-Saharan Africa around 1.8 million years ago and is found in North Africa, Georgia and into East Asia. An additional spread of new cultural forms – the hand-axe technology of the Acheulian, which originated in Africa – may have moved into south-west Asia and beyond around 1.4 million years ago. Finally, there is a more widespread movement into Asia around 800,000 years ago associated with fully formed Acheulian technology. It is more difficult to define the age of the final *H. erectus*, especially in Asia, where there is little agreement over the dating and classification of later finds.

Some broad sweep theories have suggested maritime departures to reflect these movements out of the African continent, noting three possible crossings. None of the evidence, however, requires a maritime crossing to explain the movement of *Homo erectus* between Africa and Eurasia. The stretch between Tunisia and Sicily is of some 145km, but the earliest Sicilian occupation shows links from the north, not the south.[3] The Strait of Gibraltar between Point Marroqui in Spain and Point Cires in Morocco is today 15km across; at the lowest sea levels of the Pleistocene it would have been 5km across but with fast-flowing channels.

That the Strait of Gibraltar was a real barrier to movement by the ancestors of modern humans is emphasised by the prehistory of the Neanderthals. Neanderthal settlement spread through central and southern Europe from at least 200,000 years ago, and in the face of pressure from modern humans may have lasted longest in the southern Iberian peninsula, up to at least ca. 28,000 years ago, yet even under these pressures did not have the cultural ability – watercraft – to cross the Strait of Gibraltar into North Africa. Nor is there evidence that the contemporary moderns in North Africa crossed at this time into southern Spain.[4]

For the period of *H. erectus* there is likewise no evidence of humans crossing between Africa and southern Arabia, where the shortest distance is the 32km of the Bab el-Mandab across the Red Sea between Yemen and Djibouti. On a small-scale map there appears to be adjacency but such a distance (double that of the Strait of Gibraltar) requires both watercraft and propulsion. Even at times of reduced sea level there was no land bridge contemporary with hominin occupation of Africa. Nothing in the Arabian archaeological record would require the use of a water crossing here for pre-modern hominins.

The sole land bridge from Africa to Eurasia is Sinai; more specifically, it is across areas of Sinai that lie between marshes and lakes. In a climate like that of today some 70km of the western Sinai boundary is passable by land. Historically the main transit route was along the northern fringe of Sinai, leading from Egypt's Eastern Desert, but there is also a parallel interior northern route, still avoiding the arid interior of Sinai. In wetter periods of the Pleistocene the areas that could be crossed by foot would be narrower. In drier periods the incentive to enter Sinai would be less. The grand sweep of migrations and movements fitting the anatomists' models is therefore limited to a small area of transit zones and a small number of likely periods. Damper, warmer periods would allow both settlement and transit of the Eastern Desert–Sinai region while the onset of subsequent cold, dry glacial periods would depopulate the area. This is relevant to the Bab el-Mandab: the lowest sea levels and shortest land crossing were at the most arid and inhospitable times.

The initial movements out of Africa thus fit a geographic framework best seen as natural movements of a population occupying the Eastern Desert in periods of warmer, wetter climate and moving into a Sinai with similar ecology through limited transition zones. The influence of climate similarly limited early hominin migrations and settlement in Europe.[5]

The movement from eastern Africa through to Sinai was through today's Eastern Desert, not along the Nile Valley, since the Nile did not flow during much of the period when *H. erectus* left Africa – the period from 1.8 million years ago to 800,000 years ago. Even in the wetter climatic phases the Nile Valley would have been less attractive for settlement than the adjacent desert zones, and the distribution of archaeological material seems to endorse this view.[6]

This gives a timetable before 800,000 years for movements across Sinai. From 800,000 to 170,000 years ago there was probably no other faunal movement between the two continents.[7] The period of warm wet interglacials dated from around 130,000 to 71,000 years ago, and another interglacial from 59,000 to 24,000 years ago are a frame for later migrations.

There have been recent arguments that challenge the idea that *H. erectus* developed in Africa and spread into Asia, suggesting the reverse may be possible.[8] Such an approach needs further discussion, but is more likely to be resolved by new finds together with the redating of existing finds, rather than discussions based on current evidence.

The strongest argument against *Homo erectus* being the first hominin outside Africa lies in the anatomical comparisons of *Homo floresiensis* (known only as early as 74,000 years ago) with the hominins that pre-date *H. erectus*.[9] Access to the Indonesian island of Flores by the ancestors of the Flores 'Hobbit', whether *H. erectus* or not, was most probably accidental, with the result of a tsunami being the most likely explanation. At periods of low sea levels, there was still a minimum of 80 kilometres of open sea to cross in migrating from mainland South-east Asia, across the Wallace line between Bali and Lombok, to the land that includes Flores. The conscious movement by watercraft would be outside the cultural abilities of *H. erectus*. But there is evidence for accidental voyaging. People have survived tsunamis and been transported by clinging to natural vegetation rafts. In 2004 an Indonesian woman and an Indonesian man were rescued five and eight days respectively after being washed out to sea by a major tsunami.[10]

THE EUROCENTRIC MODEL OF MODERN HUMANS

Today a major question is why there was such a long gap between the emergence of anatomically modern humans by around 200,000 years ago and their much later spread around 60,000 years ago from the African continent; and the related question of the emergence of the modern human mind. This gap emerged through recent research and revised chronologies. In traditional surveys of African prehistory it was not a major issue, with assumptions that were made often based on European models.

All prehistory classifies primarily by material culture, and the stone tool assemblages have given their name to the classificatory schemes. In Europe and in south-west Asia the weight of evidence supports the replacement of Neanderthal populations using a Middle Palaeolithic (Mousterian) flake tool industry by modern *Homo sapiens sapiens* with a more complex and adaptable Upper Palaeolithic blade tool industry. These modern humans arrived as a 'package' of modern physical type, new technologies and advanced behaviour, around 40,000 years ago. The Upper Palaeolithic peoples soon exhibited a wider range of advanced behaviours, including cave painting and mobiliary art. The spread of modern humans through Arabia, Asia and the first hominin settlement into Sahul (New Guinea and Australia) similarly represents a 'package' combining physical and cultural innovation.

This was a readily comprehensible model, which was applied confidently to North Africa, but one that proved not to apply to the rest of the African continent.[11] One of the leading figures in African prehistory from the mid-twentieth century was Desmond Clark. In his 1959 survey of southern Africa,[12] the Middle Stone Age, with a distinctive stone tool technology and the use of fall traps and pit traps for game hunting, was correlated with the Upper Pleistocene, and the Later Stone Age (microlithic industry) cultures with the subsequent Holocene (now dated to the last 12,000 years). Under such a model, modern humans and their culture had a late arrival in the southern part of the continent.

In a survey of East Africa's prehistory published soon afterwards, again the Middle Stone Age was attributed a late emergence, after 40,000 years ago, with Later Stone Age emerging in the Holocene.[13]

By 1970, in Desmond Clark's new popular survey of African prehistory, a simpler picture seemed likely in Africa.[14] *Homo erectus* used an Acheulian technology, an African Early Stone Age comparable to Europe's pre-Neanderthal Lower Palaeolithic, and the end of the Acheulian was still being dated to 60,000–50,000 years ago. Early (i.e. archaic) *Homo sapiens* emerged and spread into equatorial regions and deserts of north-eastern Africa. Intellectual and technological advances went hand in hand with this and stone tools developed in forms classified as Middle Stone Age. It then seemed possible that fully modern humans emerged outside Africa[15] and are found in Africa 'before twenty thousand B.C.' and associated with blade technologies in northern Africa, with less developed Middle Stone Age industries south of the Sahara continuing to or even beyond 10,000 years ago. However, Clark noted that some Middle Stone Age sites, still thought to be associated with pre-modern *H. sapiens*, had evidence of possible art and ritual through accumulation of minerals from which paint could be made.

Clark anticipated later debates by arguing that truly modern humans were distinguished by possession of speech, and that the development and spread of modern humans allowed behaviours enabled by speech and language. It was, however, the Later Stone Age cultures of Africa from ca. 10,000 years ago that mark this, a later arrival of language that most would accept.

The thought persisted that the Middle Stone Age only started late.[16] But more detailed work, especially in Southern Africa, slowly extended its timescale back. There remained uncertainty on how earlier Middle Stone Age fossil hominin finds should be classified –

as archaic or truly modern. Until the 1980s it was possible to see the emergence of modern humans as no earlier in Africa than elsewhere.

By a major 1985 summary of current knowledge, the antiquity of anatomically modern humans had been extended back to 100,000 years.[17] The Middle Stone Age industry of coastal Southern Africa described as Howieson's Poort, technologically less sophisticated than the blade industries of the European Upper Palaeolithic, was seen as extending back almost as far. It was no longer possible to apply to sub-Saharan Africa the Eurocentric model of a single migration of modern humans, with advanced culture and modern cognition arriving in a single movement to replace earlier populations. The African origin of modern humans seemed most likely but the chronology and spread remained to be examined.

MULTIREGIONALISM AND GEOGRAPHIC BARRIERS IN THE EVOLUTION OF ANATOMICALLY MODERN HUMANS

Although the single African origin of modern *Homo sapiens sapiens* came to be the dominant model, from 1984 an alternate hypothesis – 'multiregionalism' – argued that modern humans evolved not in one location to replace earlier populations elsewhere, but throughout the region of pre-modern humans by gene flow within these large populations.[18] A single *Homo* species evolved in a similar direction across the vast region of Africa and Eurasia as a single breeding population: as new traits emerged locally they spread by breeding to other regions, to become the modern human species.

The model was pioneered by US physical anthropologist Milford Wolpoff who has defended his views vigorously in numerous publications. The model has a neatness in fitting some of the variability in hominin skeletal remains, especially in East Asia, and was supported by Australian Alan Thorne as the best model to explain the robustness of some early Australian fossils. The multiregional hypothesis would allow for greater archaism at any point of time at the peripheries of the breeding population of the evolving species.

Among the arguments against this approach is the requirement to have regular gene flow between Africa and Eurasia in the period during which modern humans emerged. When the hypotheses was first advanced, the early African dates for *Homo sapiens sapiens* were not yet available, and the priority of Africa in the development of modern humans was not yet established. The question of dating the emergence of modern humans was a more open question. Now that modern humans are dated back to around 200,000 years ago in Africa, ecological and geographical barriers to the model have become higher.

The multiregional hypothesis has a theoretical elegance but is undermined by geographical realities. Genetic exchange between Africa and Eurasia would require significant and frequent population movement across Sinai, between the Levant and the Nile Valley or the deserts of North Africa. These arid zones are marked by an absence of other faunal movements in the relevant period, 800,000 to 170,000 years ago, in which significant gene exchange (migration or breeding) would be required.[19] The multiregional hypothesis would require gene flow across wide areas, to allow a widespread population of pre-modern humans to develop into a single species of modern humankind. A small migration across land or water can lay the basis for a large new population, but the evolution of a whole population spanning Africa and Eurasia requires substantial movements within the whole area. For the whole pre-modern population to evolve into modern humans across this region would mean frequent criss-crossing of Sinai. But the new dates for early modern humans in Africa place this requirement in the period of aridity when there would be least reason for hominin occupation of the arid zone or such regular population movements. What may therefore suit the patchy evidence of scattered skeletal material does not therefore readily fit the physical environments in which it would have to take place.

An intermediate view has emerged between the extreme claims of the multiregional hypothesis and the model of a single new modern population replacing all previous hominins. This would see some interbreeding with earlier hominin groups, including the descendants of *Homo erectus* in East Asia, allowing hybrid communities, especially in areas of Asia, and this fits some of the biological evidence. But to reach this stage in understanding battle lines were drawn between two strongly argued camps: the multi-regionalists and the 'Out of Africa' proponents.[20]

PHYSICALLY MODERN HUMANS

Known dates for the first known anatomically modern humans in Africa have gradually been increased with a date up to 200,000 years ago being now considered likely.

'Modern humans' (*Homo sapiens sapiens*) are distinguished in skeletal remains from Neanderthals (*Homo [sapiens] neanderthal-*

ensis), but also from archaic forms of *Homo sapiens* variously (and confusingly) referred to as *Homo sapiens sp.*, *Homo antecessor*, *Homo helmei* and *Homo heidelbergensis*.[21] The conventional argument is that the Neanderthal species or subspecies from ancestral archaic *Homo sapiens* (DNA suggest a divergence between 600,000 and 350,000 years ago) and were the hominin species in Europe and south-west Asia until late Pleistocene, when they were gradually replaced by the arrival of modern *H. sapiens sapiens* who had evolved elsewhere.[22]

To the majority of scientists modern *H. sapiens* originated in savannah Africa. The cranial and post-cranial bones of 'Omo 1' found in 1967 by Richard Leakey and team at Kibish in Ethiopia, considered as *anatomically* modern human in form, have subsequently been dated at close to 195,000 years ago.[23] A more archaic-looking cranium, 'Omo 2', is also attributed to this date.

Cranial material found in 1997 at Herto in Ethiopia's Afar depression is of modern human form, dated to the late Middle Pleistocene at around 160,000–154,000 years ago.[24] The Upper Herto level, which included the modern human remains – attributed at discovery to a new subspecies *Homo sapiens idaltu* – had stone artefacts, which the excavators classified as typical of final or transitional Acheulian: these were some bifaces together with Levallois flake tools typically associated with the African Middle Stone Age. The community lived at the edge of a freshwater lake and butchered hippopotamus and other large mammals. The excavators suggested that deliberate burial was present, involving defleshing and partially cutting up the body.

These anatomical finds from dated archaeological contexts tie in with interpretations from geneticists' studies of mitochondrial DNA, which initially suggested a common ancestor to contemporary humans around 200,000 years ago.[25] These have generated hypotheses to date the divergence of all modern humans genetically, with 'mitochondrial Eve', the last common ancestor of modern humans, dated around 170,000 +/– 50,000 years ago.[26] The East African genetic origin of modern humans is emphasised by studies of subsequent genetic diversity.[27] After ca. 75,000 years ago many more remains exist of anatomically modern humans, though the specific dating of many lies within only broad frameworks.[28]

With present finds and their dating, the emergence of modern humans in Africa well pre-dates their presence in Eurasia. This could be considered the result of scattered and selective field research if it did not tie in so well with the dating provided by genetic studies, a field not available to earlier researchers, and increasingly the basis on which human evolutionary prehistory is being written.

MODERN HUMAN BEHAVIOUR

The Middle Stone Age cultures of Africa, with which early modern humans are associated, do not in themselves necessarily mark a major breakthrough in cognitive abilities or symbolic behaviour. The search for markers of such change has become an area of competition between field researchers, alongside debates about what it means to be fully human.

If there was a change in human behaviour without a change in human anatomy, what were the stimuli? 'A neurological change that launched the first modern human ability to manipulate culture as an adaptive mechanism' is one formulation.[29] The arrival of functional speech has been suggested as the particular innovation that marks the transition to modernity.

There is a strong argument that social advance required social interaction with the ability to describe abstract ideas, suggest forward plans, and organise a group of individuals around a forward project. Such an approach would certainly be required for waterborne migration, but it would also be required for competitive strategic hunting and trapping. The key to such strategies could lie in the development of language. The potential of the human skull for expressive speech is a precursor but not a necessary cause for language. The verbal expressions needed to respond to basic needs, indicate basic emotions and convey these in the context of hunter-gatherer economy are fewer and simpler than in a society that needs to achieve consensus for a forward plan. Studies combining psychology and archaeology argue the significant emergence of advanced language can be dated much later than the emergence of modern human anatomy.[30]

Certainly language would be a prerequisite for most of what is seen as modern human behaviour and for the skills required for their spread. Aspects of behavioural development would include more advanced *planning* for tool use (the cores that produced blades in the European Upper Palaeolithic or the multiple tools of the Later Stone Age). They include the taming and use of fire, and travel including water crossings. But they especially include non-material developments: personal adornment, art and design, ritual including burial, as well as communally constructed open camp sites. The ability to envisage a potential outcome is a mental one; the ability to convey this to others requires language, and language at a developed level. There is a clear adaptive advantage in the possession and development of language. Put at its strongest,

> The nature of language as a symbolic communications system 'created' the human mind, capable of logistics and planning apt for all environments, of reifying concepts, of distinguishing 'us' from 'them', of the invention of the supernatural, of investigating its own workings and the past.[31]

Armed with advanced mental abilities and language, major steps could be taken in human social development. Yet the archaeological evidence in Africa is of different stages of behavioural innovation, with different views on what is a marker for modernism.

In economic development, the Middle Stone Age of coastal southern Africa shows settlement from ca. 127,000 to 57,000 years ago[32] exploiting coastal resources but not fishing. Meanwhile river fishing is seen in the Middle Stone Age elsewhere in Africa. On the southern African coast there seems to have been a reduction in population after 57,000 years ago, before the Later Stone Age emerged ca. 24,000 years ago, with fishing as a core part of the economy.

Neanderthals are known to have buried their dead but with limited ritual; the pattern may just be that of disposal to keep the dead out of living areas.[33] Cultural artefacts associated with these burials may be inclusions by chance rather than deliberate grave goods. Did Neanderthals have language skills? There is no evidence that they did either from their cranial physiology, or from their range of demonstrated societal skills, although some artefacts associated with Neanderthals including decorative uses and scoring marks have been described as non-functional.[34]

In the earliest period when Neanderthals occupied Europe and south-west Asia, anatomically modern humans occupied Africa, but they were only marginally more advanced than the Neanderthals in stone tool technology and overall cultural achievements: they were 'cognitively human but not cognitively modern'.[35] Possible attributes of fully modern human behaviour are diversity of artefact types, shaping or bone and other organic materials into formal artefacts, art, spatial organisation of camp sites, distance transportation of raw materials, ceremony or ritual (art or burial), higher density, cold climate survival and fishing.[36]

The collaborative effort required to make complex traps, snares and projectiles and trap large mammals also requires both organisational skills and language; such finds are seen only in the latter part of the Middle Stone Age of Africa and in the Upper Palaeolithic to the north.

The control of fire has many implications: it encourages social interaction, it allows a broader range of settlement, it impacts on food preparation and can be used in hunting. While the *use* of fire has great antiquity, it has been suggested that the *control* of fire is part of the ensemble of modern human social behaviours, and may be represented only in modern human communities.[37]

The emergence of advanced culture is pinpointed by archaeological finds that represent a growing competition by scholars for iconic signs of mental agility. Decorative beads are such an icon: found at Enkapune ya Muto cave in Ethiopia around 40,000 years ago, at Mumba in Tanzania about 45,000–40,000 years ago, and at Border Cave in Swaziland about 38,000 years ago.

From Blombos Cave in coastal South Africa finds associated with technological advances in the later Middle Stone Age stone tools at about 40,000 years ago are seen as major modern steps.[38] Here were bone tools shaped for piercing, gouging or drilling, incisions on a bone, which the excavators considered possibly decorative, and an economy including fishing as well as shellfish collecting.

Further work from the same site of Blombos, pushed back to ca. 75,000 years ago evidence of Middle Stone Age bone tools, engraved bone and engraved ochre, together with a far more dramatic find: snail shells clearly drilled for use as a necklace, a use confirmed by wear marks. And later finds suggested that engraved ochre was used even earlier, possibly as early as 100,000 years ago.[39]

Comparable evidence from other sites is still limited: engraved ostrich eggshell at Diepkloof ca. 55,000 years ago, engraved bone at other Middle Stone Age sites. The southern African coast remains the centre of the competition to find early examples of modern human behaviour. The use of fire to harden silcrete in toolmaking has been identified at the site of Pinnacle Point around 72,000 years ago and possibly much earlier. This site of Pinnacle Point presents evidence for early use of marine shellfish food resources, probably as early as ca. 164,000 years ago.[40]

There is archaeological support to an interesting hypothesis: that it was the use of shellfish that increased human cognition and ability. In this model population pressures moved hunter-gatherers from the arid interior to the coast, gave stimuli to use the new coastal resources, and these shellfish enabled the development of new cognitive abilities: an emphasis on 'encephalisation'.[41] Biologically encephalisation is the increase of brain size to body mass, whereas it was the increased *use* of the brain that seems to coincide with increased shellfish use.[42] Specifically the long-chain polyunsaturated fatty acids essential for brain development occur in shellfish (both marine and freshwater) at higher levels than terrestrial food sources. The new evidence from coastal sites seems to extend back the period in which some shellfish were exploited, and the period in which some elements of symbolic behaviour can be identified: no single sudden breakthrough of a linguistic and behaviour revolution can be located. Nor perhaps will it be: if the arid periods of the later Pleistocene in Africa coincided with the lower sea levels of the glacial maxima, then the first evidence for intensive coastal exploitation may lie under water.

Perhaps the most definitive proof of advanced behaviour, the advanced mind and social organisation that required forward planning, social organisation and the use of language, is water crossings. While many consider the probability of a water crossing from Africa to Arabia across the Red Sea, there is even stronger support for deliberate water crossings into Australia, when as part of the Sahul land mass it was separated from South-east Asia by water stretches. Humans, who reached Australia by 50,000–40,000 years ago, could only have done so by a series of island-hopping journeys in reasonable water craft carrying a large enough breeding population to establish a mainland community.[43] And the recent claims for human settlement on Crete before 130,000 years ago add complexity to this discussion.[44]

But what has changed in recent years is the confidence that the emergence of modern human cognition, symbolic thinking and language coincided with the spread of modern humans from Africa: while 'Out of Africa 2' may be dated to around 60,000 years ago, the emergence of the modern mind is being pushed back in a narrative that is continually being changed, both by new discoveries and by new arguments on what it means to be truly human.

OUT OF AFRICA

There is limited archaeological and palaeoanthropological evidence to date the migration of anatomically modern humans from Africa. Interpretations of the geological and climatic timeframe help to narrow possibilities and suggest a framework in which migrations were likely or possible. It is from genetic studies that the most detailed images of the human spread have emerged, and these have pushed the search for archaeological record into second place.

Recent debate has focused on the timescale for the departure of modern humans from Africa, the route and the context, with a date around 60,000 years ago cited as a probable timing. Genetic evidence suggests this may have followed a lengthy period in which modern humans lived in separated groups in southern and eastern Africa, and in relatively small numbers: at the lowest point perhaps only in the thousands before seeing significant population growth.[45]

There was one 'false start' in the spread of modern humans. Skeletal finds generally seen as anatomically modern were found at the Israeli sites of Skhul and Qafzeh, with a dating of 120,000–90,000 years ago, but with the probability that this brief expansion from Africa was later repelled and replaced by the Neanderthals who occupied the region.[46] This migration may have been in a warm, wet phase but seems *not* to have been down the Nile Valley. Instead this migration may have been across water systems extending through today's deserts to the Mediterranean in the period 130,000–117,000 years ago.[47] These water systems then dried up, preventing further population movements, and through a climatic window of dispersion into the Levant.[48]

The ability of modern humans to plan water crossings and construct watercraft is demonstrated by the presence of humans in Australia by ca. 45,000 years ago.[49] The movement of a breeding population sufficient to settle a new continent required planning and organisation as well as the technological skill to build rafts or boats capable of 'island hopping' and at times crossing strong currents.[50] No other primates crossed the barrier between South-east Asia and Sahul (the continent that linked New Guinea and Australia during periods of low sea level).

Comparisons of archaeological finds of the Middle Palaeolithic and Middle Stone Age in the Horn of Africa, the Nile Valley and eastern Sahara, the Levant and the Arabian Peninsula do not show clear cultural continuities between any of these areas, at a level sufficient to draw a clear migratory link.[51] Indeed, the similarities are greater between Arabia and the Levant to the north.

Genetic analysis suggests a departure of modern humans from Africa within the period 70,000–55,000 years ago, when sea levels were lower and climate more arid.[52] If we accept a push–pull model then the pressures arising from increased aridification would create the incentives to cross the growing Bab el-Mandab strait. The weight of evidence leads most to accept a single dispersal event from Africa.[53] Both genetics and logic suggest such a migration would involve only a small number of colonists. Alternatively, if migration in periods when warm, wet climate encouraged and supported broader areas of human settlement, even those were probably interglacial periods when sea levels were at their highest. Such a model best suits migration across Sinai with its band of ecological continuity between Africa and south-west Asia. Or did the major migration(s) occur at a time when the advance of cold, dry climate forced people to migrate through hostile space – in the case of the Bab el-Mandab, a water boundary leading to a no more promising zone on the Arabian side? We cannot be certain that the exact timing of climatic changes in one region of Africa applied throughout, let alone beyond, the continent. It is possible that abrupt deterioration in climate – Heinrich events – prompted movement, and if such movement did not reach more hospitable territory the movement would continue; within one generation a substantial movement could be undertaken leaving no archaeological trace.[54]

The apparent growth in Middle Stone Age populations of savannah Africa around 80,000 years ago was not sufficient to create population pressure that led to migration.[55] Archaeological evidence has been interpreted to suggest the later Middle Stone Age of Southern Africa had a period of minimal population between two short-lived cultural groups: Stillbay at around 71,000 years ago and Howiesons Poort from ca. 65,000 to 60,000 years ago, close to the date that sees the first modern human migration out of Africa.[56] But the genetic evidence does show expansions within Africa in this period of 80,000 to 60,000 years ago, and the migration by around 60,000 years ago of the relatively small group of individuals ancestral to modern Eurasian populations. More detailed studies of African populations, based on mitochondrial DNA of the female line, have suggested quite distinct lines of population development in modern humans within Africa from as far back as 200,000 years ago.[57] Only one of these populations led to the expansion out of Africa.

The issue, then, is whether a migration was through Sinai by land, or by boat across the Bab el-Mandab and following the coastline from there. The genetic evidence and the most convenient climatological framework would fit a model of coastal migration: following coastlines, exploiting the resources of the coast and river mouths as well as their hinterland, and following round southern Asian coasts rapidly enough to reach Australia before, perhaps well before,

45,000 years ago.[58] Such a model is often assumed to require a water crossing at the southern Red Sea to reach southern Arabia. But rapid coastal movement might also pass through the north-eastern arid zones of Africa, into Sinai and from there into Arabia. In the paucity of archaeological material nothing actually requires a water crossing to take modern humans at 60,000 years ago from the Horn of Africa to Arabia; a land route through Sinai could be the route even at this stage. Arabia had been occupied earlier by Acheulian communities whose origins were ultimately through Sinai.[59] The argument against a Red Sea crossing is that it was not repeated, even when higher sea levels in glacial periods made it a shorter route. Those same glacial periods reduced the eastern Sahara and Sinai to uninhabited arid stretches. A movement of a small founding population for modern humans in Eurasia – perhaps including only 600 women – has been considered likely, but such a population movement is still an easier movement through Sinai than across the Red Sea.

There is only limited archaeological material either from north-east Africa or from Arabia and south-west Asia from the periods of the main migrations of modern humans. There is not enough to say whether migration was across the southern Red Sea from the Horn of Africa into southern Arabia (the Bab el-Mandab route), or through Sinai into either the Levant or Arabia. A migration suggested by genetics can be used to examine the small collections of artefacts, but the artefacts on their own do not demonstrate migratory routes.[60]

A comprehensive recent survey of the evidence from Arabia for early human climates and settlement failed to confirm any evidence or necessity for a crossing of the Red Sea by the first modern humans.[61] Arabia was on the route by which humans spread along the coast from Africa into Asia, but the current record could allow the movement of modern humans from Africa into Arabia and beyond across the land link of Sinai. In periods of wetter climate they entered the interior; in arid periods settlement was in three 'refugia' areas, one on the Red Sea. The absence of cultural connections with Africa in the later Middle Stone Age suggests little movement from Africa into Arabia in the Upper Pleistocene; cultural connections seem closer to the Levant than to East Africa.[62] The main movement between the continents would be no later than 74,000 years ago. There was high rainfall in the period 130,000–120,000 years ago, then a further peak in wet conditions at 82,000–74,000 years ago, before the onset of arid conditions.[63] The genetic evidence from today's population also shows 'no traces of autochthonous M lineage in Arabia that could support the exit of modern humans from Africa across the Bab al Mandab strait'.[64]

Further exploration of the Middle Stone Age and Middle Palaeolithic of north-east Africa, Arabia and south-west Asia may in due course give large enough samples for a typological relationship. But meanwhile it is the genetic research that is making most of the running. And much of this sets links and timing between East Africa and southern Asia without refined chronology of the arid zones of western Asia. The rapidity of the spread is emphasised, with a timetable that reached India by ca. 65,000 years ago and would reach Malaysia and possibly the Andaman Islands by 55,000 years ago.[65]

As a recent summary notes, genetics 'continues to indicate an out-of-Africa dispersal at around 70,000–55,000, which is 5000–20,000 years before any clear archaeological record, suggesting the need for archaeological research efforts focusing on this time window'.[66] Genetics has taken over from archaeology, and from the study of human skeletal remains, the role of tracing the stories of human origins in Africa, and their spread from Africa to populate the world.

We can thus see that the essential accounts and interpretations have changed, both for the emergence of modern humans and for the role of the African continent as a backdrop to those changes. Until Dart's announcement of *Australopithecus africanus* in 1925 it was possible to place early hominin evolution in Asia rather than Africa. For two generations more it became possible that modern humans had evolved outside Africa and had migrated with new advanced cultural and mental abilities into much of Africa as they did into Europe. It was possible to advance a 'multiregional' view that modern humans evolved from earlier populations across a broad area of the world, though this view acquired only a minority of adherents. Then gradually, with genetic studies powerfully supplementing the more limited archaeological and palaeoanthropological evidence, the longer timescale of modern humans in Africa could be contrasted with their shorter timescale (but rapid migration) in Asia and Australia. Between these more empirical studies came the question of when modern cognition and the modern mind can be said to have emerged, and the link of this to the emergence of language. It is in this more philosophical area that future debates may be strongest, as new studies, finds and interpretations continue to fill out the story of human origins in Africa.

6
Ancient Egypt and African sources of civilisation

The role of ancient Egyptian civilisation in world history (including that of Africa) has inspired many writers but has also led to exaggerated and imaginative claims with widespread impact.

Ancient Egypt has been a constant source of fascination to everyone from the readers of Herodotus' *Histories* in the fifth century BC to the twenty-first-century visitors who crowd every museum exhibition of mummies. But there are wide differences in the context and location in which ancient Egypt is seen. To some it is clearly part of Africa, while some think of it primarily as part of the Mediterranean world, alongside the civilisations of Greece, Rome and the Levant. To others it is the western extent of a 'Near East' that extends as far as Iran, or at the centre of a 'Middle East' that includes the Maghreb.

Egypt has also been given different positions in world history. A sequence of writers with otherwise incompatible views has been drawn to the argument that diverse cultural traits could be traced back to the pharaonic civilisation of the ancient Nile Valley. Unified in the emphasis on the influence of Egypt, how they applied these views led them in quite different directions.

Many invented ideas about ancient Egypt have stayed in the amateur world of the 'lunatic fringe', followed by those with a fascination for the mystic, or the need to fill television time. The riddle of the sphinx, or the mystery of the pyramids, or the predictive value of the 'pyramid inch', made for ongoing entertainment, outside the framework of serious ideas. But several scholars have developed arguments about ancient Egypt that have been considered much more serious contributions or challenges to the consensus. In the early twentieth century Sir Grafton Elliot Smith developed ideas of Egypt's role that would later be described as hyperdiffusion, but especially looked north and east. West African writer Cheikh Anta Diop from the 1950s set a new role for Egypt as an African society, arguing both its influence on Africa and its (African) influence on classical and subsequent European culture. Such views were taken

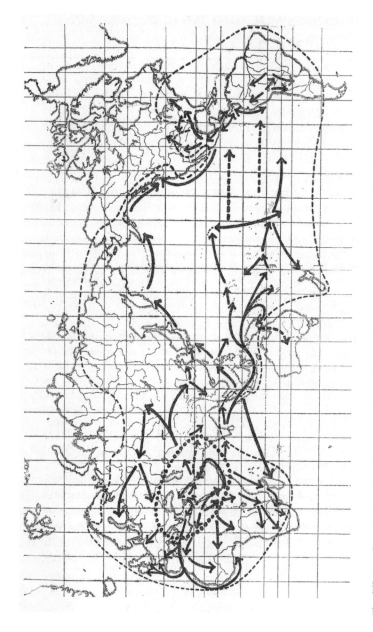

The diffusion of world culture from Egypt, according to Elliot Smith. (From *Human History* [1934 ed.], 489)

up again with the rise of black consciousness and negritude. Then in the last twenty years the work of Martin Bernal, broader than suggested by his title *Black Athena* has challenged ideas about the relationship of early civilisations in Africa, Asia and Europe.

THE HAMITIC HYPOTHESIS

An early model that encompassed Egypt and other North African societies was the 'Hamitic hypothesis', which reflected the interface of biblical heritage with the nineteenth-century European interest in race that accompanied imperial expansion. In the Book of Genesis Noah's sons and their descendants spread to populate the earth: those of Japheth spread north, the Semitic races descended from Shem and the Hamitic races included the Canaanites, Egyptians, Libyans and Cushites (in Sudan and Ethiopia) from their brother Ham. In medieval Europe this led to all non-Arab Africans being seen as 'sons of Ham'. Because Ham was cursed by his father for seeing him naked, the 'curse of Ham' came to be seen as explanation if not justification for the enslavement of black Africans.

A subtler use of the Hamitic concept emerged in the nineteenth century, with the view that an expansion of people who spoke Hamitic languages, and were racially distinct from black Africans, was responsible for cultural advances in many parts of Africa. The conflation of language, physical characteristics and culture was a common theme in nineteenth-century science alongside the yearning to classify human races with the same precision than Linnaean biology had applied to the plant and animal kingdoms. Such views continued until the rise of Nazism showed the dangers of a simplistic approach to race, and most scholars retreated from the racial model.

However, it was in 1930 that the most definitive statement of the Hamitic hypothesis appeared, from the pen of anthropologist (and Sudan specialist) C.G. Seligman in his *Races of Africa*. He defined as a group linked by language and physical type 'the Hamites who are "Europeans", i.e. belong to the same great branch of mankind as the whites'.[1] His argument was essentially that the pre-Islamic societies of Africa owed their cultural development to a series of Hamitic migrations by non-negroid peoples, probably from north-east Africa, which had introduced into passive negroid societies social change and technological innovations. The level of Hamitic influence in groups such as the Maasai or the Tutsi would continue to be debated.

Apart from relatively late Semitic influence ... the civilizations of
Africa are the civilizations of the Hamites, its history the record of
these peoples and of their interaction with the two other African
stocks, the Negro and the Bushman, whether this influence was
exerted by highly civilized Egyptians or by such wider pastoralists
as are represented at the present day by the Beja and Somali. ...
The incoming Hamites were pastoral 'Europeans'– arriving wave
after wave – better armed as well as quicker witted than the dark
agricultural Negroes.[2]

Eastern Hamites included the ancient Egyptians, Nubians, Somalis
and most Ethiopians, while Northern Hamites included Berbers,
Tuareg, Fulbe and the indigenous people of the Canary Islands.

Although Seligman's book continued to be published in new
editions through until the mid-1960s its model of linked cultural,
linguistic and physical identities was by then long dismissed.[3]
However, as an important study of the Rwanda massacre of 1994
has shown,[4] the distinction between supposedly 'Hamitic' Tutsi
and Bantu Hutu emphasised by the Belgian colonial authorities
underlay the eventual massacre of Tutsi. The Hamitic hypothesis
had extended from an antiquarian archaism to contribute to a
political tragedy.

GRAFTON ELLIOT SMITH AND HYPERDIFFUSION

The early twentieth century's leading advocate for a world-changing
role by the ancient Egyptians was the Australian anatomist Sir
Grafton Elliot Smith. Even more than his protégé Raymond Dart,
he used a distinguished reputation in anatomy to advance views
well outside his field, in archaeology.

Smith was born in 1871 in the New South Wales country town
of Grafton, where his father was a school principal.[5] He studied
medicine at the University of Sydney and had clinical experience
before turning to research in anatomy. Although his research was
initially on the brain of Australia's monotremes, his distinction
was based on his work on the human brain and its evolution. This
significant research contribution to human anatomy was recognised
both by a knighthood and by the Fellowship of the Royal Society.[6]
He died in 1937.

Smith also worked in descriptive areas of physical anthropology
in the later part of his career, both in the description and the interpretation of fossil hominids. He was one of the initial group who

studied the Piltdown fossil, found in 1912 and only exposed as a forgery in 1953.

Smith's main interest in antiquity, and the development of his eccentric ideas, began when he secured a post as professor of anatomy in 1900 in the Government School of Medicine in Cairo, a post he held until 1909. This was a period of major international archaeological research in the Nile Valley, and inevitably Smith was asked to examine finds of mummies, in whose brains he took a particular interest. This stimulated a broader interest in archaeology and led him to develop ideas that took him well away from the mainstream of archaeology and indeed Egyptology.[7] Alongside his researches in his own field of human anatomy he began to write and speak widely in public on his theories, despite their dismissal by the specialists in the field.

In essence, Smith took the view that an invention – in material culture, economic or social development – could happen only once and that the spread of such an innovation must be from a single location. To him ancient Egypt was the source of most ancient innovations. From modest expression of these views he moved to a passionate advocacy – 'preaching his gospel'[8] – of the views that would later be described as 'hyperdiffusion'. Most archaeologists and historians would recognise changes in material culture or society reflecting a mixture of spread of ideas and items – diffusion – and local innovation. To Smith only diffusion could apply.

His theories began gently enough, in his 1911 book *Ancient Egyptians and the Origin of civilization*,[9] reinforced in its second 1923 edition. Much of this book presents an interpretation of the biological history of ancient Egypt which, even though it may not match current knowledge, is not outside the paradigms of physical anthropology of the time. The emphasis of the work is on northern links – Smith dismissed a black negroid element in ancient Egypt.[10] He makes the main links with south-west Asia, emphasising an incursion around 3,000 BC, of a 'Brown race' of Alpine or Armenoid people. Much of his discussion, not atypical for the period, was on the influence of Egypt on the culture of Sumer and Elam at the dawn of civilisation. Almost as an afterthought, at the end of his book, he extended the argument that Egypt through its influence on south-west Asia had originated the cultural changes of Europe in the Neolithic and metal ages, notably spreading the art of monumental stone building from Egypt's pyramid age to Europe's megalithic monuments. But he saw the stone monuments of the north Mediterranean and Western Europe as 'crude copies of the more finished and earlier monuments of the Pyramid Age'.[11]

He wrote that 'Ideas and culture do not spread among uncivilized people except by settlement amongst them of those who practice the new arts and hold the new beliefs. But these settlers need not be great in numbers.'[12] Even these perspectives, while chronologically unsound, are not illogical. But finally Smith jumped into the claims that would dominate his work: that metalwork and other cultural elements spread in all directions from Egypt. Some of this was by land; but he also claimed Egypt was a greater maritime nation than is usually accepted and that Egyptian-style ships are seen from Scandinavia to eastern Africa and beyond.[13] Trade, in particular the search for precious metals, was the driving force, and in a breathtaking summary Smith first advanced his views that Egyptian seaborne influences extended into the Pacific and across to the Americas.[14]

Mummification, which had drawn Smith into interest in antiquity, he took as a prime example of a once-only invention. Because mummification is found as far afield as New Guinea and the Americas, this would represent an extreme test case for loyalty to his ideas.[15] It therefore caused significant dissent that he was chosen to write the section on anthropology in the twelfth (1922) edition of the *Encyclopaedia Britannica*, an opportunity he took to proselytise his views as if they were established.

Smith's ideas found no sympathy from Egyptology. Flinders Petrie, long a colleague of Smith's at University College London, soon recognised the dangers of Smith's approach – he diarised his reaction to a Smith lecture as 'much disgusted', scribbling 'no .. no ... nonsense ... no evidence whatsoever' in his copy of Smith's book on Egypt.[16] But Smith did find support from those in other disciplines[17] – W.J. Perry in Manchester, the writer Warren R. Dawson, and people from anthropology and other disciplines seduced by his approach including W.H.R. Rivers in Cambridge (whose literary executor Smith became) and anthropology colleagues in London. Rivers in due course 'went the whole way with me in recognizing the initiative of Egypt in the creation of civilization ... [and] played a very material part in securing any hearing at all for my heresies'.[18]

Between *Ancient Egyptians* in 1911 and his death in 1936 about a third of Smith's output of over 300 books and papers lay in his theories of archaeology and human history. His work developed an expansion of the reasons for human expansion: the search for elixirs, the 'givers of life'. The claims grew with each book.[19] The substantial tome entitled *Human History* (1929) is ambitious in its detail, effectively a selective prehistory and history of the world in the application of Smith's racial and diffusionist models. Gone are any reservations about the model and its application.

Mankind split into different races from a central Asiatic origin. The negro race in Africa subsequently expanded into India during glacial periods of the Pleistocene.[20] The racial descriptions fall into the categorisation that still remained; negroes exhibit physically primitive traits, and 'affinities with the apes are commoner than they are in most other peoples'.[21] But all humans were once of black skin colour. In early times negroes from Africa reached Melanesia after following the Asian littoral. But the book pays no further attention to Africa's Egyptian links. Smith's main interests are in the spread of cultures and developments into Europe, Asia and beyond, initiatives created by the 'Mediterranean Race'. He paid particular attention to the spread of megalithic monuments and to the question of primacy for the origin of civilisation between Egypt and south-west Asia. These were indeed live topics at the time; Smith's fellow Australian, the great archaeologist Vere Gordon Childe published his *Most Ancient East* in 1928.[22] But in the 'asides' the argument again went well beyond the evidence: mummification spreading from Egypt to Europe, to India and Indochina, New Guinea, Australia and on through Polynesia to the Americas. Smith hints at grander claims: a Greek origin of Buddhism, for example.[23]

One notable observation on Smith's work is how little attention it paid to Egypt's role in the continent where it sits. Influences to Europe, the Middle East, Asia, even the Pacific and the Americas are outlined but Africa is barely mentioned. It was left to his follower Raymond Dart to explore these dimensions of the diffusionist model, as discussed in Chapter 3.

The maps that appear in Smith's final book on the theme, *The Diffusion of Culture*, could equally be used as demonstration of the fallacy of the argument. One shows the once-only invention of the boomerang making its way from ancient Egypt through India to be taken up with enthusiasm in Australia, before being passed from there to the Americas. We have Roman-style armour in Hawaii, Greek art styles travelling via Indonesia to the Americas, and numerous other cultural elements in the Americas owing their spread to Oceanic voyagers. 'The conclusion that Egypt invented seagoing ships and that vessels of these distinct types encircled the world is now an established fact.'[24]

At a conference to commemorate Smith's work in 1974, scholars generally praised his professional anatomical work. Those in historical fields distanced themselves from his views in human history with varying degrees of politeness.[25] But loyal disciple Raymond Dart defended his mentor, turning on its head the chronology that disproved the influence of pyramid builders on European megalithic cultures, and it was clear than hyperdiffusionism was not completely dead.[26]

CHEIKH ANTA DIOP AND THE CIVILISING ROLE OF AFRICA

The work of Senegalese writer and scholar Cheikh Anta Diop (1923–1986) stimulated influential new views on the position of Egypt in the history of both Africa and of European civilisations. Diop argued the case that ancient Egypt was a 'negro' society and that it was black Africa that brought civilisation to Europe; he made emphatic distinctions between African and white European cultures.[27] He also argued that ancient Egypt was both an influence on, and an example of, black Africa cultural norms. Like Smith and Dart, Diop worked across disciplinary areas. Born in colonial French West Africa, he was trained in Paris as a physicist and went on to direct Senegal's radiocarbon dating laboratory (as well as engage in Senegalese political life). While a student in France he developed broad historical interests and began his writing on the African basis of ancient Egyptian civilisation.[28] He presented this initially as a thesis, then developed his arguments as a book in 1955, *Nations nègres et culture*. His thesis was issued in book form in 1959 as *L'Unité culturelle de l'Afrique noire*, and another study was passed as a doctoral thesis and published in 1960 as *Étude comparée des systèmes politiques et sociaux de l'Europe et de l'Afrique*. A second major volume appeared in 1967, *Antériorité des civilisations nègres*. These books and several articles were published by the influential journal and book publisher *Présence Africaine*, founded in 1947 by the (also Senegalese) cultural and political activist Alioune Diop.

These were important and constructive arguments in the context of a French tradition which, like the British, had long underplayed the identity of Africa's past,[29] reflecting Victor Hugo's declaration in 1879 that Africa had no history. France had its share of eccentric theories, from colonial official Maurice Delafosse's claim for Judaeo-Syrian origins of a fourth-to-eighth-century kingdom in ancient Ghana, to Abbé Henri Breuil's espousal of the 'White Lady' of Brandberg in today's Namibia as evidence for early penetration from the Mediterranean.

Diop's innovative ideas were taken up in French progressive culture, and the core elements of both were introduced to an English-reading audience with a US volume in 1974, which combined selected chapters from his two main French books.[30] After a long period when they had been ignored they were then dismissed in the non-Francophone scholarly world. But they came to engage with the emerging identity politics of the black diaspora, especially in the United States.

In France and francophone Africa, however, Diop maintained a reputation as a leading influence, in a culture where the beauty of ideas is sometimes valued higher than their factual accuracy. Marking 40 years since Diop's first book, in 1995 there appeared a tribute volume by one of his main disciples, Théophile Obenga,[31] and a year later a more distanced critique of his work by François-Xavier Fauvelle. In an introduction Elikia M'Bokolo notes 'to each his own Cheikh Anta Diop'.[32] Fauvelle sought to explain Diop in the context of the cultural significance rather than the content of ideas – the importance of Diop's ideas lay in *his* truth rather than *the* truth. 'Truth and ideology are not opposites. They are simply not performing in the same register.' In his study he downplays the archaism in which people were either negro or Aryan, in which the Egyptians had just 'changed colour'.[33]

In his native Senegal, Diop was honoured by the renaming of the University of Dakar in 1987 as the Université Cheikh Anta Diop. Delivering a keynote speech there in July 2007 on France's perspectives on francophone Africa, French President Nicolas Sarkozy avoided any reference to Diop's name or work.[34]

Several themes are interwoven in Diop's argument: the black African racial identity of the ancient Egyptians; the African nature of elements of Egyptian civilisation; the influence of ancient Egypt on many areas of Africa; and the influence of (black African) Egypt on Greek and other societies.

From today's perspective the fundamental flaw in Diop's work is that he worked within a racial model that Europeans had developed: 'only three well-defined races exist: the white, the black and the yellow. The so-called intermediate races probably result solely from crossbreeding.'[35] Educated in Paris in the late 1940s his ideas evolved in a period that used such assumptions: by the 1950s views of distinct racial identities were on the retreat in physical anthropology and by the 1960s the idea that 'there are no races, only clines' was widely accepted among scientists.[36] By the time of Diop's second French volume in 1967 he was arguing within a model no longer supported by scholars; and by the time of his English translation in 1974 the discrete racial model was thoroughly discredited in science, but not in popular discourse. Confronted with the question of whether ancient Egyptians were white or black, Egyptologists would in subsequent decades argue that this was a false question: the Egyptians were Egyptians, with a range of physical character-istics that reflected their location, development and spread along the length of the Nile.[37] But Diop's work was addressing more popular prejudices and stereotypes, and formed an essential part of the *négritude* movement that contributed self-esteem to many in Africa, especially former French colonial Africa; he wrote of 'racial self-retrieval'. And eventually he responded to criticisms of a racial model with a softening of his 'black race' narrative.

Not surprisingly, if human history had to place an ancient people into one of three distinct racial groups, then the European classifica-tion of Egypt as white had to be challenged. The only alternative was to place ancient Egypt as black. Diop's rebuttal of white assumptions was therefore a necessary rejoinder – an essential correction to the attempts to group all of ancient Egypt into a white, or Hamitic, or Mediterranean, or other distinct non-African box.

But in arguing the case that ancient Egyptians were negroid, his evidence was highly selective and his claims over-ambitious. Diop reported a grab-bag of links and features to pull Egypt into its African context: linguistic coincidences, an eclectic choice of social, political and cultural similarities. Artistic representations were used for his racial allocation: in ancient Egyptian artistic representations 'it is impossible to find ... a single representation of the white race or the Semitic race. It is impossible to find anyone there except Negroes of the same species as all indigenous Africans.'[38] Diop was able to trace selective quotes from many early writers referring to the African links of Egypt. The same selectivity applied to place names: the dangerous task of linking apparently similar sounds to give a common origin, a logic that allowed Diop to note a possible origin of 'Paris' either from the Egyptian goddess Isis or in a West African Wolof word. Diop unwittingly revealed the inadequacy of the 'similar names' approach when he observed without irony or comment how similar is the word for men in the languages of both Eskimo and the Wolof from West Africa![39]

Diop extended his arguments and interests to the cultural linkages of 'black Africa' with 'black' Egypt. He mapped commonalities between cultures of sub-Saharan Africa and ancient Egypt. He suggested that ancient Egypt was physically and culturally part of a larger 'Africa' than others had allowed, and distinguished the harsh values of a patriarchal European culture with the more enlightened values of an Africa that was broadly matriarchal – until its Islamisation.[40] Having constructed a range of African 'norms' in Egypt, he then saw these as reflecting the positive elements endowed on Greece and beyond. He would develop his concepts of homogeneous norms of African culture in new books.[41]

In his first writings he assigned negroid physical identity not just to ancient Egypt but to the Elamite civilisation of south-west Iran and to the Phoenicians of the Levant.[42] He could therefore complement the influence of (black) Egyptian culture on the origins of Greek civilisation with an influence from (black) Phoenician culture, themes that would be taken up by Martin Bernal. He did not develop further a few other suggestions such as pre-Columbian America's links with Africa.[43]

Western Egyptologists were late to engage with Diop's challenges, and began to recognise the value of reassessing Egypt's African links.[44] However, the increased field research in many areas and periods of African archaeology has failed to show significant outreach from the ancient Nile Valley into areas of Africa beyond Nubia to the south and the Libyan deserts to the west. Few now would see an advantage, other than in political reversal of western trends, in calling ancient Egyptians 'black' except as a reminder that they were not 'white'. As Brace notes, 'The old-fashioned chimerical concept of "race" is hopelessly inadequate to deal with the human biological reality of Egypt, ancient or modern,' emphasising the negative impact of applying current crude racial labels to ancient societies.[45]

The wider influence of Diop's ideas came with the first English language translation of his work, *The African Origin of Civilization: myth or reality*, published in 1974 and derived from two of the French volumes. In a foreword Diop stated that his goal was 'restore the historical consciousness of the African people'.[46] This edition had particular influence on African American perspectives of black and African history. Translations of other work of Diop's appeared in the United States: *Precolonial Black Africa* (1987), *The Cultural Unity of Black Africa* (1989) and finally the book *Civilization or Barbarism* (1991), but these were mainly publications of record.

There had been a small but important pioneering tradition of Afrocentric history in black American writing from the nineteenth century, which had fought to rescue the image of Africa's past.[47]

However, none had the detailed presentation and interpretation of historical data that Diop's work offered. The work of Cheikh Anta Diop on race, alongside that of Basil Davidson on historical pinnacles within Africa (discussed in Chapter 7), served a strengthened black American identity in the middle decades of the twentieth century. Whether or not Egyptians were racially 'negro', it was timely to remind those in the black diaspora that from the African continent came mathematics and monumental architecture, astronomy and medicine, and writing. It presented a neat contrast to suggest that ancient Egyptians were black, and that the first whites in Egypt came there as slaves, after capture in war.[48] The selectivity of cultural elements makes a parallel with Elliot Smith though with a very different agenda.

Modern Afrocentrism, especially as pursued in the United States, has solidified into a widely held set of beliefs. These views relating to ancient Egypt have been summarised as being: that the ancient Egyptians were black, had greater achievements and greater influence on Greece and Rome than had previously been believed; their civilisation originated south of the Pharaonic territory and extended contacts that maintained its links to other African cultures; and professional Egyptologists have conspired to hide these truths.[49]

But, as Howe observes, 'there is an irony in Diop and his followers adopting naïve diffusionism as an antiracist creed'.[50] One African scholar has suggested that 'champions of Afrocentricity are often among the most Westernised themselves'.[51]

MARTIN BERNAL AND BLACK ATHENA

A weakness of the Egyptocentric views of Elliot Smith was that he advanced regional hypotheses that for the time he was writing were not impossible, but then with minimum evidence he extended his argument to a worldwide pattern. Diop also used limited evidence from other areas in the context of his sweeping arguments on Egypt's influence.

By contrast the British scholar Martin Bernal has advanced a convincing argument – that of the sidelining of ancient Egypt's influence on ancient Greek culture – but then weakened this argument with an eclectic and antiquarian range of detailed evidence that has not stood up to wider scrutiny nor presented a model that met wider acceptance.

Bernal (born 1937) was initially a specialist in Chinese language and history who studied and taught at Cambridge University before moving to Cornell in the USA. He was the son of a distinguished Marxist physicist and grandson of an equally distinguished establishment Egyptologist, Sir Alan Gardiner. He would later claim that he initially wanted to study the history of Central and Southern Africa, and turned to Chinese history because at his university, Cambridge, African history was not taught at the time.[52]

His interests shifted from the languages of the Far East to the languages of the Near East. In three substantial volumes published in 1987, 1991 and 2006 Bernal advanced his bold reinterpretations of ancient history under the title *Black Athena*.[53]

Well before he had presented the detailed argument in the third volume Bernal had become the centre of discussion and controversy with many articles and books of dissent, these in turn being answered by the author.[54] In a sense, the more Bernal wrote, the weaker his arguments seemed to scholarship but the more appealing to his admirers. The writing was complicated by his predicting and summarising in each volume what future volumes would argue and prove.

There is no doubt about the astonishing spread of Bernal's investigations and the depth of his research into archaeology and linguistics of Europe, Asia and Africa. The sequence and structure of his arguments is the reverse of the conventional. The 1987 volume predicting his proofs generated immediate debate and his archaeological second volume appeared before the major ripostes (in 1996) and his reply to these (in 2001). When he finally presented his detailed linguistic evidence in 2006, the debate was almost over, in the sense that most scholars had already taken sides and had firm views of his approach. Indeed, the impact of the third volume was minimal compared to earlier work, with few published reviews and few sales compared to the earlier volumes.[55] And this final volume of detailed proof differed from that he had originally planned.[56]

The core argument is that much of ancient Greek culture and society derived from the east Mediterranean: from the Levant and Egypt. To Bernal this had once been accepted in western scholarship ('the ancient model') until an emphasis on the European links and Indo-European, Aryan ethnicity of Greece replaced this approach from the nineteenth century. Thus Bernal was restoring an earlier understanding with a 'revised ancient model'.

Part of the cause of the change of emphasis from east Mediterranean to Europe had origins, Bernal argued, in racial prejudice. In particular a withdrawal from the emphasis on Near

Eastern links reflected an anti-Semitism, as the Phoenicians were a Semitic-language group.

A complex ambiguity was created by the title of the three-volume set, *Black Athena*. Bernal at different times stated he was not interested in race, and his critique of the Aryan model was reflecting anti-Semitism. But in presenting his new model, his emphasis on Egypt (not a culture with a Semitic language) led to emphasis on its Africanity. In the introductory volume Bernal noted his discovery, late in his research, of the Black American emphasis on ancient Egypt as an African civilisation or even as a black civilisation.[57] His title seems to pay homage to this tradition, even though Bernal was unwilling to say that Egyptians were racially negroid. He did mention black characteristics of certain pharaohs, but the thrust is more on undoing the racial simplifications of earlier writers than making a major manifesto about the racial identity of the Egyptians whose influence on Greek and European civilisation was so profound. The title is almost a yearning, by the author or his publishers, to be relevant to the identity issues of African Americans and others in the black diaspora, though it would later be observed that 'Bernal cannot be called an Afrocentrist'.[58]

The great strength of Bernal's approach is to emphasise the cultural borrowings of Greece from Egypt and the Levant – Bernal gives the period 2100–1100 BC as the key – and correspondingly 'the political purpose of *Black Athena* is, of course, to lessen European cultural arrogance'.[59] This approach had been played down in the European historiographical emphases dating from ca. 1790 to 1830, though he does concede that certain areas of scholarship had subsequently recognised the eastern influences on art and of course especially the origins of the Greek alphabet in the Phoenician script.

Egyptologists long supported a model of Egyptian influence on Greece, and classical scholars were reminded by Bernal of the Near Eastern links of early Greece and the tradition in European scholarship that had acknowledged this. Where Bernal failed to gain support was in the scope and nature of Egyptian influence. His work appeared to most as selective or biased in the way in which archaeological evidence was used and applied, and not least in the selective approach to language and place-name parallels.

Ancient Egyptians did not write vowels in hieroglyphic, hieratic or demotic scripts – indeed, not until the Coptic script, which was derived from Greek letters, did vowels appear in written Egyptian language. This increases the apparent similarity of the consonants in an Egyptian word to those in a (vocalised) Greek word, and allows for the subjective selection of apparent similarities on which hypotheses of real historical links can be built. Early in his arguments, well before presenting detailed argument, Bernal claimed that up to a quarter of Greek words could be traced to Semitic origins and another third from ancient Egyptian, a view unlikely to gain expert acceptance.[60] Comparisons of place names have long been a dangerous quicksand for writers trying to make historical links – among those Bernal advanced is originating Athenai (Athens) in an Egyptian *Ht Neit* (house of the goddess Neit).[61] Such selective comparison of place names, ironically, reflects a late-nineteenth-century tradition of antiquarianism that had disappeared from much scholarly discourse.

Archaeologically Bernal supported the hypothesis that the Hyksos – the probably Canaanite outsiders who ruled Lower Egypt in the seventeenth and sixteenth centuries BC – conquered Crete and possibly established colonies in mainland Greece. He also lent support to the suggestion that the expulsion of the Hyksos from Egypt may be reflected in the biblical account of the Jewish exodus from Egypt.[62]

For the present study, the interest of Bernal's thesis lies in the African identity and links, for if Europe owed its cultural origins in large part to Egypt, and ancient Egypt was a racially black and culturally African society, this provides support for the arguments advanced by Diop, and with less complexity by many African American writers that Europe's culture derives from Africa's culture.

In practice Bernal's ideas, especially at the superficial level suggested by his trilogy's *Black Athena* title, generated simplistic acceptance. His major critic, Mary Lefkowitz, seems in part to have stimulated to rebuttals by her black students complaining she had failed to teach that Socrates was black! Initially this level of racial identity is not what he claimed, but in due course Bernal came to acknowledge that much of his support came from the diaspora community of African descent, and this led him to group himself with writers of extreme views, such as George James, author of *Stolen Legacy.*[63]

Earlier Bernal saw the Egyptian culture as a combination of the peoples of the Upper Nile Valley (Upper Egypt and Nubia, within the African continent) and the cultural stimuli not of Africa but of south-west Asia – a conventional view in much archaeological interpretation.[64] The African links come later. 'Egyptian civilization was fundamentally African ... many of the more powerful dynasties which were based in Upper Egypt ... were made up of pharaohs whom one can usefully call black.' Specific southern pharaohs are considered black.[65] The title of the three volumes came to refer to his arguments and the debate as a whole, and to bias an approach that initially had included Semitic impacts on Greece as much as those from elsewhere. Bernal's critics ranged from those who dissented from his interpretations of archaeological sequence, linguistic and place-name borrowings, to those who saw his contribution as a dangerous addition to the negative ideologies of racial identity, a fiction that contributed 'symbolic myths of ethnic supremacy'.[66] It is perhaps the emphasis on race, on blackness, that is the least convincing of Bernal's arguments and least important to his core argument within the academy, but the one that has had greatest resonance outside the academy.[67]

Late in his writing, in his third volume, Bernal engaged with the African past more directly by discussing the origins of the major language groups. Working within a genetic model of linguistics, he played down (though did not ignore) the influence of loan words in comparison of languages, and this brought him back to some recent archaeological debates.

He accepted the classification of a large Afroasiatic language family, distinct from the Indo-Hittite family (an enlargement of the classic Indo-European group). He linked the spread of both of these to the spread of agriculture. But he accepted the argument of those linguists who identified a common language ancestral to both of these – Nostratic – with an earlier origin, which he located in the specialised hunter-gatherer communities associated with microlithic stone industries.[68]

The Afroasiatic family is one of four continental language groups that the great historical linguist Joseph Greenberg had identified, alongside Nilo-Saharan, Niger-Congo and Khoisan, which is associated with the pre-Iron Age communities of southern Africa, the San (Bushmen) and Khoi (Hottentots). Bernal suggested links between Afroasiatic and Khoisan languages, and placed its origins in the Rift Valley area of East Africa.[69] After this daring suggestion, though, Bernal returned to his main theme of the Egyptian and Semitic substratum of Greek language and Greek civilisation, with an emphasis on consonantal similarities in terms and place names. Few authorities would find this strong supporting evidence for

Bernal's major thrust of the influence of the east Mediterranean on Greek culture.

Thus in different ways 'Ancient Egypt' has been used as a tool for different arguments and disputes relating to core concepts in language, culture and physical race from at least the early nineteenth century. It is likely that there will be many more uses and abuses of Ancient Egypt as a pawn in future debates.

7
Old states good, new states bad

For more than one generation in and beyond the English-reading world, the most influential and widely read author on the African past was Basil Davidson.[1] His books combined a fine, even brilliant, writing style (he had been a professional journalist) with careful perusal and good understanding of background scholarship. If a reader in Britain or the USA or Anglophone Africa had read just one book on the history of the African continent in the 1960s, the 1970s or even later, the chances were strong that it had been written by Basil Davidson. In the 1980s an influential eight-part television series on Africa's history *Africa: a voyage of discovery* written and presented by Davidson reached a new audience including many in African countries.

In filling a gap, Davidson initially placed emphasis on those great achievements of the African past that reflected powerful states, and created a 'canon' of historical black pride during the period that saw both the triumph of independence movements in Africa, and the growing self-confidence and identity politics of the African diaspora. Davidson moved beyond, but did not renounce, his historical emphasis on the state. Thus through the period that colonial territories were transformed into newly independent states, the strongest images of the continent's past were of powerful past states.

This created an image of Africa corresponding to what Orlando Patterson summarised as 'princes, pyramids and pageantry'; what Ali Mazrui has labelled 'romantic gloriana … admiration of kings, emperors and eminent scholars of the past … predicated on a respect for hierarchy and stratification' in contrast to an image of 'romantic primitivism' with an emphasis on egalitarianism.[2]

But the trajectory of Davidson's own writing is a model for the broader passage of progressive western thought, from ideals and optimism through more selective engagement, to a critical assessment of the power elites of the new African independent states and finally to a profound dismay at much in the post-colonial experience. In 1959, early in the sequence of independence for African colonies,

Covers of Basil Davidson's classic works, 1970 editions.

Davidson would 'rediscover' in print the glory of past African states. Thirty-three years later, under the title The *Black Man's Burden: Africa and the curse of the nation-state*, he would sadly distance himself from the present African states whose pattern had left so many progressive western intellectuals and African citizens alike despondent.[3] Davidson's first writings on Africa were political and so were his later writings; his commitment to 'African history' was a political act.

In 1981 two African critics wrote that in the 1960s

> Africa was interested in cult heroes, and these it got. In so doing, it seems, Africanist historians divested themselves of their professionalism. ... African postcolonial historiography has instead distorted the past so as to glorify the precolonial era, and by implication the postcolonial era.[4]

At one level, we can contrast the positive approach to the African past by Davidson and his followers with the critical approach to the realities of the present. But the relationship is more complex. Woes of Africa's present came to be blamed on the nature of the state and those who controlled it, yet the historical glories selected initially for the canon of African history were specifically the centralised and powerful state formations. The supposed glories of the past came to inspire those creating new states of the present; while many outside the state apparatus continued to admire the old states while expressing horror at their modern successors.

CREATING A CANON OF AFRICAN HISTORY

The mystification of the African past discussed elsewhere in this book had been one form of attack on the integrity of its history. A far greater attack was its deliberate omission from the narratives of world history. 'African history' as an academic discipline or field for serious writing and study emerged very late in Europe and North America, and even later in other parts of the non-African world.

The European framework that fostered the study of African history was that of decolonisation and the post-colonial responsibilities and links. During the colonial administration of Africa there was interest in the anthropology of native peoples, often seen in a timeless 'ethnographic present'. As the colonial administrations increased and solidified, interest grew among Europeans in the history of their own administration.[5]

With the post-war trend to decolonisation began a move to greater interest in the past of the African peoples within the former colonies. African history as such began to be taught in Europe from the 1950s.[6] The *Journal of African History* began in 1960, under the editorship of John Fage and Roland Oliver, whose *Short History of Africa* was published in 1962. The more interdisciplinary *Cahiers d'études Africaines* began the same year, and in the US *The [International Journal of] African Historical Studies* began in 1968.

African Studies in the US had grown massively in the period to 1970. At that date some 1,800 individuals, mainly academics, identified as Africanists, with political science, history and anthropology the dominant disciplines. This compared with an estimate of 20 Africanists in 1950 and 200 in 1960![7] Senior teachers and researchers, especially in history, were still being drawn from overseas.

But part of the stimulus, a new era in African Studies outside Africa, came with the rise of Black Studies in the USA. This reflected the identity politics of Americans of African descent and the new confidence that followed the civil rights movement of the 1960s. The intellectual, political and cultural movements from the time marked a shift away from and emphasis on inclusion and non-discrimination to a community pride among black Americans, and support for tertiary-level courses in Black Studies, which included an emphasis on the African past. Teaching of African Studies relied on individual Americans who had been drawn to the continent, often as a result of Peace Corps assignments.[8] However, the broader field of Black Studies, with its emphasis on the black diaspora and the United States in particular, was largely taught by those with African American ancestry.

Black Studies appeared as a focused result of the political movements that followed the civil rights campaigns of the 1960s. An early initiative lay in a course at San Francisco State College in 1966;[9] thereafter 'Black studies history is remarkable because its establishment in 1968 was a sudden event.'[10] A walkout of many black academics from the 1969 meeting of the US African Studies Association meeting was one reflection of the times. Overall, it was student demand, on the back of the social movements, that led to the creation of Black Studies courses. The influential *Journal of Black Studies* began in 1970 with an editorial:

> Seldom in the history of academic disciplines has an area of study been born with so much pain and anguish as Black Studies, also called Afro-American studies.[11]

Though by the mid-1980s some students in more elite institutions preferred the rigour of African Studies to the Afro-American field.[12]

Writing initially for a British audience, the most popular writer on the African past became Basil Davidson. His work proved timely as it was already established when the US saw growth in Black Studies, and his accessible writing style together with his particular approach to the African past fitted the identity needs of the new black students, more than the measured professional history of Fage, Oliver and their protégés.

A LIFE OF COMMITMENT

Born in 1914 – and dying in England at the age of 95 in July 2010 – Davidson's path is illuminating, as a case study of the 'Old Left'. Leaving school at 16, he moved to work as a journalist for national papers both before and after the Second World War. During the war use of both his knowledge and a cover as a journalist took him to various secret assignments, the most significant of which was undercover work with anti-fascist partisans in Yugoslavia in 1943–4 and in Italy in 1945. On leaving the army, this future radical held the rank of Lieutenant-Colonel and several war medals.[13] His experience with guerrilla forces in wartime Europe would heavily influence his later engagement with guerrilla armies in African independence struggles.[14]

In the post-war years Davidson was involved in the Union for Democratic Control (UDC) – a left-wing and by now anti-colonialist foreign policy pressure group. He was for a while its secretary and wrote pamphlets and reports for the UDC on world, European and African affairs.[15]

He continued to be employed as a newspaper journalist until 1961: for *The Times* in Paris from 1945 and as leader writer, then the *Daily Herald* and the *Daily Mirror.* But he balanced journalistic writing with books and pamphlets on world affairs, where he could advance progressive views tied to a passion for peace and social change. His interests were diverse, but in due course came to move away from European affairs and to focus on Africa.[16]

Davidson recorded his first chance encounter with Africa and its past.[17] A wartime transfer in 1941 from England to Cairo was routed via Banjul and Lagos ('a perfectly horrible place to be') to a refuelling spot in northern Nigeria where an impressed soldier pointed out to him in the distance the tall walls of a centuries-old African town nearby – the city of Kano – which stimulated his curiosity.

Davidson's work with the UDC led to a conference on Africa and then an invitation from radical labour leader Solly Sachs to visit South Africa. He undertook his one and only visit there in 1951. This led to his 1952 book *Report on Southern Africa*,[18] received by some critics as the work of a fellow-traveller of communism because of its support for the rights of the majority. A more sympathetic review[19] noted the quality of his reporting and writing but regretted his lack of contact with local Africans and his preference for industrialisation, Europeanisation and improvement from above.

In 1952 he visited West Africa and co-edited a book published the next year on the politics of West Africa, which was to see the first independence of a British African colony in Ghana.[20] The volume included some historical overviews but received a critical response in reviews. In 1953 Davidson was to visit Southern and Northern Rhodesia as well as Swaziland, which required the authorities to let him travel via South Africa despite the National Party government declaring him a prohibited immigrant the year before.[21]

A further contribution to contemporary politics came in 1955 with *The African Awakening*.[22] This recorded an account of the author's 1954 journey through (Belgian) Congo and (Portuguese) Angola, backed up by statistical information, to argue the evils of two of Africa's most savage colonial situations, and to celebrate the nascent African nationalism. He would maintain his interest in the politics of these regions in later writing, specialising in the liberation movements of Portuguese African colonies.[23]

Davidson's disturbing and critical writing about colonialism and his celebration of independence movements in Africa led to his being banned from several territories, a fortuitous event as (after taking the opportunity to visit archaeological sites in Sudan) he moved to writing on Africa's past. This was a theme that did not require visits to politically sensitive or strife-torn regions.

Old Africa Rediscovered was issued by British publisher Victor Gollancz in 1959, and reissued in the USA the following year under the unambiguous title *The Lost Cities of Africa*. Lost ... rediscovered ... this was indeed the recovery not just of finds by archaeologists but of knowledge that had been omitted from the corpus of western historiography. But it was a selective and celebratory volume – necessarily so to attract an audience. It was at least in part the success of the book that allowed Davidson to survive from his own writing and cease employment as a newspaper journalist in 1961.

This was followed by another major book. In 1961 *Black Mother* was issued in the UK, also by Victor Gollancz. Its subtitle was *Years of trial*; the US edition the same year was subtitled *The years of the African slave trade*. For publication in the US the main title, a phrase innocent in Britain but offensive black argot in the US, eventually had to be replaced and the book was reissued in 1980 as *The African Slave Trade: precolonial history 1450–1850*.

Further contributions followed with subtly changing focus. *The African Past* in 1964 was an edited and handy collection of documents. *Africa: history of a continent* in 1966 was a narrative retelling of African history, reissued in subsequent editions as *Africa in History: themes and outline*. As an excellent writer Davidson was brought in by educational publishers to work with academics on educational textbooks: a survey of West African history in 1965, of East and Central Africa in 1967; *The Africans: an entry into cultural history* in 1969 (in the US called *The African Genius*) and in 1978 *Discovering Africa's Past*. In 1984 *The Story of Africa* was published to accompany the eight-part television series he hosted, and in 1994 a collection of essays from different contexts was brought together as *The Search for Africa*.[24]

LATER WRITING AND APPROACHES

Davidson's first writing on Africa was as contributions to contemporary political issues, before he claimed his place as the great populariser of Africa's deep past. He returned to write on themes of the present, and included books on modern African history that linked in with new titles on contemporary politics.

One major theme of his writing was support for the remaining movements for independence. As France and Britain disengaged from their African colonies, Portugal remained in Africa. Davidson – who had travelled in Portuguese Angola in 1954 – returned to write powerfully and with passionate support about the political, and by now military, African movements against Portuguese rule.

This journalism and writing on contemporary African politics involved him in energetic and sometimes dangerous travels, which had started with his trip to Angola and the Belgian Congo in 1954. In 1962–3 he met with leaders of the Angolan liberation movement in Zaire, and of the Mozambican liberation movement in Tanzania. He visited areas of Guinea-Bissau outside Portuguese control in 1967 and then went into Mozambique the following year. In 1970 there was a major trip in Angola, and in 1972 in Guinea-Bissau and to Cape Verde on the eve of independence.[25]

He maintained active political lobbying in support of the liberation movements of Portuguese Africa alongside his influential writing on the topic. New books appeared including *Which Way Africa? The search for a new society* on African politics (1964, revised 1967), and volumes on Guinea-Bissau (1969), Angola (1972), Ghana (1973), Southern Africa (1976), Eritrea (1980) and Guinea-Bissau with Cape Verde (1981), and a survey *The People's Cause: a history of guerrillas in Africa* (1981).[26]

Davidson wrote more broadly about African modern history and political change, in a model that both led and reflected a broad consensus of western progressive hopes, thoughts and analyses. With the advantage of hindsight these can be seen as shifting optimisms. When all of Africa was colonised, hopes of many progressive westerners lay in decolonisation, which spread from 1956 to 1968. With initial disappointment in the nature of the post-colonial state in former British and French colonies, passion and optimism moved to those with radical rhetoric fighting guerrilla wars against entrenched Portuguese colonialism. Disappointments in the troubled birth of these nations were replaced by hopes for a democratic Zimbabwe (which had an all races vote in 1980), then South Africa (in 1994).

In a sympathetic but also thoughtful and critical review of Davidson's work to mark his 80th birthday in 1994, the year of South Africa's first democratic elections, Stephen Howe noted the gap between positive forward expectations and backwards assessments in Davidson's writing.[27] The same special journal issue dedicated to Davidson reflects the mixed feelings by progressive thinkers of disappointment at Africa's recent trajectory, with one last gasp of hope at South Africa's imminent transition, a transition that would soon lead the left to the same distanced disappointment.

In the years from 1994 to 2003, it was estimated that 9,210,000 people died as the result of conflicts in Africa, and the subsequent years have seen dramatic further conflicts.[28] Oxfam estimated that conflicts in Africa *since* the end of the Cold War have cost the continent over $150 billion. By 2005 51 per cent of the population of Africa were still living on less than US$1.25 a day,[29] with the World Bank estimating in 2009 that half of the population of sub-Saharan Africa were living in extreme poverty, a proportion that had not changed since 1981. There were an estimated 22 million HIV-positive people in sub-Saharan Africa, with 1.5 million deaths annually from AIDS-related causes. With such trends alongside continuing civil conflict, hopes and expectations for social and economic development declined in the views of many analysts.

Perhaps most distressing to the progressive writers and activists of the period were the reports, frequent in conversation but rarely reported in print, when people from rural communities told researchers that they had been better off, both economically and in other ways, under colonial administrators than under the new urban elites who controlled the state.

Although Davidson did lean towards optimism and hopes for substantial political and social improvement in newly independent African nations, his books were not simple paeans of praise for the new leaders, nor dismissals of failure and disappointment in the start of post-colonial states. He acknowledged that colonial masters of English and French territories could be replaced by self-seeking elites. He witnessed the overthrow of Portuguese rule following the democratisation of Portugal itself, then the challenge in the former territories of civil wars or coups. This was not the new Africa he had expected.

Many of these dilemmas he sought to address in his 1992 book on the failures of the African nation state.[30] Here he distanced the failures of the modern state from the achievements of the pre-colonial state, arguing it was the continuation of a European state model that could be blamed for the present ills. But he avoided a possible corollary of this – that tribalism and tribal identity would be a more stable form of government if pre-colonial models were to be revisited.

Two major shifts have been suggested for in Davidson's work: first a shift from a belief in the possibilities of capitalist development towards the necessity of a socialist model; then more significantly from his hopes for emerging nationalist movements to his 'sharp rejection of the nation-state model itself'.[31] Davidson – but by no means he alone – had tied his flag to the mast of successive liberation movements only to be distressed when they failed to meet the expectations placed upon them.

OLD STATE GOOD, NEW STATE BAD

The period of Basil Davidson's life and work spans a path from radical optimism to radical pessimism by observers of Africa, underlying the hopes followed by disappointment at the post-independence development of African states. The state apparatus of post-independent Africa, with few exceptions, would be seen as the result of concentrating power into self-seeking centralised elites (whether defined by ethnic affiliation, family self-interest or the self-preservation of military cliques). While modern nation states in Africa have seen powerful criticism, the selective emphasis of Davidson's most influential work was on the powerful centralised states of the past, with his early work appearing to glorify these.

At the height of the black history movement, the distinguished Caribbean scholar Orlando Patterson reviewed the models and paradigms of current thinking: those that saw the (US-dominated) black history movement as one that celebrated survival, those that saw it as dominated by themes of catastrophe, and those that stretched further back into the black past with what he called 'contributionism' – an emphasis on Africa's contribution to world history, forged by selectivity. Patterson characterised this as based on 'princes, pyramids and pageantry' – but that is a fair description of the emphasis of Davidson's earlier historical surveys.[32]

To say Davidson's historical surveys glorified the achievements of early states is not to say it could readily have been otherwise. For a writer and publisher to gain an audience in a new and unfamiliar topic dramatic selectivity is necessary. Whereas a later audience studying the whole gamut of African history in a university course might take a wider approach, the aim of Davidson's first books and their publishers was to attract a general audience who might thus become interested, surprised, entertained by the pasts that were being 'rediscovered'. Davidson took the time and publishers took the risk to create books introducing the history of a continent previously said to have no pre-colonial history, and this proved a successful venture for both parties.

The first, 1959, edition of *Old Africa Rediscovered* (published on both sides of the Atlantic)[33] was issued the year *before* the independence of 17 British, French and Belgian colonies, including Nigeria, Congo, Chad and Senegal. Its coverage was early history, before the colonial impact. But it did allow a link to the present in a final section of glowing optimism 'History begins anew'. Davidson celebrated the imminent decolonisation and a different future: 'the beginning of African emancipation, the joining of the people of Africa to the common family and equality of man'. Here much of the main hope lies in the erosion of the nation state model:

> An independent federation of the lands of French West Africa would eclipse the size of all the medieval empires of the Old Sudan. African peoples followed their own road in the past: there is nothing to say they will not follow it, constructively, creatively, again.[34]

By the time the 1970 edition was issued by Longman, Davidson's reputation in African history was already high and, more significantly, African history had seen the growth and consolidation of the 1960s alongside much new archaeological and historical research, and a boom in African Studies in the USA on the back of the rise of Black Studies and cultural awareness. This new edition would reach to a student as well as a general audience. He did not rewrite or revise, but he did omit his positive forecasts in his penultimate paragraph about West Africa, which had seen the Biafran secession and war in the intervening years, with the loss of up to a million lives.

His introduction notes a few of the advances in knowledge in the intervening period: the Hamitic hypothesis had finally died; radiocarbon dating had significantly filled out the African sequence and further areas had been opened up to archaeological exploration. More significantly Davidson wrote:

If there has been a change of emphasis during the 1960s, it has been mainly towards righting the balance of appreciation of the so-called 'stateless societies'.[35]

But it was the centralised states of powerful kingdoms that dominated the book. After an initial background chapter on pre-state societies, three-quarters of the text dealt with the major states and urban settlements visible through their architecture and art: Meroe and Kush, the succession of military states of West Africa, the East African entrepôts, Axum in Ethiopia, Great Zimbabwe and the other stone-built settlements of south-central Africa, while other chapters addressed trade between Africa and the wider world. The image of the African past was one of centralised power, wealthy trade routes dominated by powerful potentates and symbolic architecture that could only emerge through the centralised state. Here were African rulers and elites demonstrating their equality with power and rulers elsewhere. The title of the US edition *The Lost Cities of Africa* was realistic.

On the basis of his reputation from this book, TimeLife Books commissioned from Davidson a text to accompany a highly illustrated book, *African Kingdoms*, in their series *Great Ages of Man*.[36] It was here that a subtle warning appeared on the glorification of Africa's powerful states, in a preface by the then doyen of Anglophone African history Roland Oliver.

Some readers may feel that in evaluating the African past Davidson tends to be romantic and eulogistic. They may be assured that this is a matter of interpretation, not invention; Davidson commands his sources. If he assesses them too admiringly for some tastes, he also rights an old imbalance.[37]

THE SLAVE TRADE, COLONIALISM AND MODERN HISTORY

Old Africa Rediscovered excluded the colonial era and ended with the arrival of Portuguese on Africa's shores. The impact of that contact was explored in the successor volume first issued in 1961, *Black Mother*. While intended to explore the relations and impact of the period of Africa–Europe contact over four centuries, it became primarily a study of the Atlantic slave trade. The villains are clearly the maritime trading nations, the traders and their clients. But the book does not disguise the underlying evil without which the maritime trade was impossible: the enthusiasm of communities of the western coast of Africa to sell human beings to the European traders. It was not the Portuguese or Dutch or French or English who took men and women prisoner in Africa; they provided the financial stimulus for local chiefs and their subjects to sell on captives and prisoners, then to capture vast numbers to fill the burgeoning demand.

Davidson could observe that 'the kings and emperors of medieval Africa never developed the same autocracy and tyranny as their contemporaries in Europe' and that the slaves of the period were closer in status to feudal vassals, but contact with the 'modern' world of Europe rapidly changed that.[38] The slave trade itself helped a breakdown of social structure, in Davidson's view, yet what in *moral* terms might be a breakdown, in practice created a strong new coastal economy based in the new commodity, live humans, whose exchange value exceeded that of precious metals and other commodities.

Was this entirely the replacement of a medieval 'Merrie Africa' and its values by a harsh modernist commerce? The book casts most African slavery before the Atlantic trade in a conciliatory light, but the record of human sacrifice at the death of a ruler raises questions about this. The practice is found as far back as Kerma in second millennium BC Nubia, and again in sixth-century Nubia. Davidson notes it was 'inseparable from the traditional ritual and religious requirements' of a number of early African societies, but suggests it may have involved acceptance by retainers until an inflation in sacrifice stimulated by the Atlantic trade.[39] In Ashanti society, however, an observer saw the sacrifices as prisoners of war or criminals spared only for such sacrifice.[40] Whatever the patterns – and given the varied societies of Africa there were numerous different patterns – the attitudes of African societies to human rights and dignity was far from that of the feminised, egalitarian, pacific natural culture argued by Cheikh Anta Diop (see Chapter 6) as the antithesis of masculine, militaristic, white Europe.

Published in 1961, in the early years of many independent African states, *Black Mother* could look back on the horrific impact of European contact with Africa as a cycle that encompassed both the Atlantic slave trade and the succeeding colonial era that was only just ending. It could thus end in an upbeat forecast, where supporters of 'the renaissance of Africa are welcomed by the lifting voices of a new life in Africa itself: inexhaustible, ever-quickened, keen with hope'.[41]

A longer sweep of African history was included in Davidson's 1966 book, *Africa: history of a continent*,[42] which was reissued in subsequent editions with the same structure as late as 2003 under the title *Africa in History*. Its successive editions appeared therefore alongside the dramatic period of African political and historical development. This was a powerfully written book for the general reader, which built on the same story but extended Africa's history to modern times. It thus engaged with the more accessible knowledge of its readership, who could be assumed to have awareness both of imperial endeavours and then the moves to decolonisation. This was a compromise between the emerging field of history within Africa, and of Africa as part of the wider imperial narrative.

The emphasis of much of the pre-colonial history was the same, with chapters entitled 'Ancient Glories' and 'Tropical Achievements', but the historical coverage does extend more broadly than the glories of ancient African states. It touches on themes of development and change – the Tallensi of Ghana come in for treatment as a successful non-state society, and the smaller societies of Africa showed the balance of individual rights with social obligations that marked a natural African democracy.[43] The rulers of African states have varying treatments, which sounds more positive set in the past than applied to the present. Thus '... the traditional role of an African king as an essential regulator in the distribution of realised wealth. The king accumulated but he also distributed.'[44] Without the benefit of foreseeing the future bloody clashes, the book could suggest groups such as the Hutu 'think it wise to make themselves the tribute-paying vassals of men for whom warfare and government were a professional duty and not a guarantee of privilege'.[45]

Two-thirds of the book is dedicated to Africa before the impact of European trade and colonisation. The remainder deals with the impact of contacts with the external world: trade, including the slave trade, imperial conquest and colonisation. Thus a contrast appears between the positive (the glories of the past), and the negative (the imposition of European influence and power). Despite the narrative of powerful warring states, Davidson suggests:

> Much of Africa was not in turmoil before the colonial invasions. There were vast regions of this massive continent where the old ways held firm, and where little occurred to disturb the quiet unfolding of traditional precedent and custom ...[46]

This binary opposition would be a massively influential one. To the general reader using such a book as their image of the continent, Africa before the Europeans was one of achievement and glory: at times a kind of 'Merrie Africa' with noble kings, great art and architecture and heroic history. The ancient Malian state was 'a golden age of prosperity and peace'.[47] In contrast the arrival of the Europeans brought disaster, slavery, loss of power. Depending on which edition was being read, the movements bringing liberation from colonialism provided the opportunity to reassert that ancient glory.

Such is not to say that Davidson as the populariser of African history slid over complex issues or sought to mislead his reader. But selectivity in historical works of synthesis is inevitable and fits the needs of specific readers and the publishers who need to reach them. Any reader would feel a contrast between the positive accounts of the African states of the past and the negative view of the colonial states that followed them. The colonised peoples were the basis for future hope. That hope fluctuated through the different versions of the book, as the final part of the book was revised at different stages of the post-colonial experience.

In 1966, Davidson completed his first edition with a section on 'Reconstruction' in the final chapter 'Towards Liberation'.[48] By then the Congo crisis, Biafra and other false starts to independence had scarred the continent. Davidson would refer to states

> beset with troubles ... setback and disillusion ... rulers who appeared content to relapse into positions of personal privilege and to repress ... every effective criticism or popular movement aimed at regeneration. But even in these countries ... the hopes and pressures of liberation continued to exercise an influence towards expansive change ... all this ... could only promise well.

Rural reconstruction was slow or absent. It soon became clear that political and economic solutions accepted on the day of independence could be regarded as no more than provisional. But hope lay in those 'more thoughtful people' who were arguing for pan-Africanism, for non-capitalist and socialist development. Davidson was ultimately optimistic about 'new and outward-thrusting thoughts and policies that promised to be capable, at last, of clothing the aspirations of unity and progress in the armour of a new reality'.

In the 1972 edition, this text was retained but augmented. The difficulties facing Africa were 'more difficult than, ten years earlier, they had seemed to be'.[49] Instead of moving toward greater transnational units some pressures were in the other direction. Economic development had been disappointing, not least under the influence of rich overseas nations. 'Africans have many immediate reasons for pessimism.' But ultimately 'the need to use these years constructively was seen as the central challenge of the 1970s'.

Sadly and symbolically, when the text of the book was released two years later in a 1974 revised edition under the new title *Africa in History: themes and outlines*, the title of the final section had changed from 'Reconstruction' to 'Efforts at reconstruction'.[50] This maintained but expanded the same message on the recent past and the potential future, putting more emphasis on the economic pressures on Africa from outside. 'But it would be wrong, in the context of this book, to end on a depressing note.' New ideas and concepts were emerging, though where is not stated, and 'this ferment heralds the action that will clothe aspirations of unity and progress in the armoury of constructive change'.[51]

By the 1991 edition, the author had to look back at the recent years and observe that 'the continent in the 1980s had plunged more deeply into acute impoverishment and political confusion'.[52] The wars, dictatorships, military coups and economic decline showed up the African states that relied on brute force as 'intellectually hollow structures, without the least moral substance ... they belonged to the detritus and debris of Africa's modern history'. Any future hope for Africa lay in the emergence of democratic structures of self-government at the base of society, or of federal unities than bypassed the limitations of post-colonial states. For this reason, argued Davidson, Africa's mood was 'not without its mood of stubborn optimism'.[53] And this optimism in 1991 was heralded, in Davidson's introduction to the new edition, by the release of Nelson Mandela in South Africa. 'Relief from persecution in South Africa ... might act as a liberating force for the whole continent.'[54]

In the 2001 reissue and subsequent reprints no changes were made; the book continued to end with the view of a resilient optimism.[55]

Thus while the final chapter was amended, extended, modified and changed in mood, the bulk of this influential book retained the same focus: the past achievements of Africa, and especially of powerful African states, before the negative impact of encounter with the European world. If the reader could no longer be convinced that the post-colonial state was delivering for the good of its people, the pre-colonial state was generally spared from such criticism.

Davidson's later writing did not revise or abandon his enthusiasm for the deep African past. But his political commitment led him to focus on writing about Africa's present with a more critical voice. His 1978 book *Africa in Modern History*[56] was effectively the long-delayed sequel to *Old Africa Rediscovered* and *Black Mother*. In the meantime with rapid changes in Africa the near future had become the recent past. Echoing comments at the end of other books, the author saw capitalism as a limiting factor and nationalism as a major inhibitor to human progress in independent Africa; transnational unity could bring greater hope. He explored these issues in greater depth when the trajectory of most post-independent states had been set; in his important and troubled study of 1992 unambiguously entitled *The Black Man's Burden: Africa and the curse of the nation state*, where he – like many other writers – considered some of the issues arising from the first decades of post-colonial Africa.

Perhaps in response to some critics of his state-focused enthusiasm, Davidson's essay written in 1990 for a publisher in military-ruled Nigeria qualified the image of all-powerful rulers. In the kingship-producing culture in Africa the rulers 'were the accepted and convenient apex of the pyramid of social cohesion', and if they became tyrants 'the checks and balances of custom and ritual would pull them down'.[57] This is certainly what many of Africa's citizens, including the new post-colonial intellectuals, wanted to hear as hope for their own future.

In his 1994 collection of essays Davidson reprinted a 1987 lecture that spoke of 'I remain most unrepentantly an optimist, an observer convinced of the grandeur of Africa's self-transformation'. But in a piece written for this volume he would look back at the period of his optimistic writing and conclude:

> Thirty years or so earlier there had seemed, for Africans, to be time and opportunity for everything while the beckoning threshold of anticolonial independence opened out, as it appeared, upon endless possibilities of progress. By the outset of the 1990s, in one of history's reversals, these possibilities could appear all too completely to have vanished from the scene.

Africa's structures of government and administration 'had lost or thrown away the legitimacy that comes from people's recognition and acceptance'.[58]

The grand narrative of African history popularised by Basil Davidson is probably the most influential of those discussed in this volume, and was inspired by a commitment and hope for the African future. We cannot ignore the irony that emphasis on the glories of the African past focused on the achievements of societies with a powerful centralised state apparatus, while much of the pessimism about Africa's future lies in critiques of the nature of the new elites who came to power in the modern state.

8
The present of the past

Earlier chapters of this book have described some of the grand narratives of African pasts that reflected particular social, political or individual contexts. In addition to historical narratives, broad philosophical and ideological approaches to Africa past and present continue to have wide influences both positive and negative.

Historians of Africa within and outside the continent have long debated the models and ideologies that dominate their work. But many of the debates have been about ideas internal to the history profession: not as their work has been used or misused in the wider society. Even at the height of the radical movement of reinterpreting African history two historians could devote a whole book to a critique of historiography of Africa, including the nationalist traditions that were emerging within it, without discussing the influence of the conflicting models on the wider society.[1]

Archaeologists too have been aware of the potential of their models and reconstructions of the past for undermining racist myths and defining new pride in African achievements. But as with historians, there have been many impacts of the political world on the operation of archaeology, but rare contexts in which archaeology had an impact on political debates and discourses, even in southern Africa where the distance between research findings and the dominant ideologies of racist societies were farthest.[2] Ideas that had the potential to undermine some of the assumptions of dominant white ideologies had only limited wider impact; 'the compelling body of archaeological work on precolonial African societies that existed by the early 1970s was bypassed almost in its entirety by liberation movements in South Africa and abroad'.[3]

THE OLD AND THE NEW

The glories of the African continent's past were reflected during the transition to post-colonial Africa. The names of Africa's ancient states were revived in several independence movements. Part of French West Africa (French Sudan) became independent in 1960

American student and Maasai child. (Paul Shaffner)

under the revival of the ancient name of Mali, the thirteenth-to-sixteenth-century empire that overlapped the boundaries of the modern state. The Gold Coast under the leadership of Kwame Nkrumah (subject of a biographical study by Basil Davidson) took the name Ghana on independence in 1957, after the state that thrived from the eighth to the eleventh century in and around Mali.

The independence movements fighting the white regime in (formerly southern) Rhodesia took the name Zimbabwe, and this was transferred to the country in 1980: it was the first country to be named after an archaeological site type. The term was used by the liberation movements as early as 1960; the foundation of the Zimbabwe African People's Union in December 1961 (with Joshua Nkomo as President and Robert Mugabe as 'Publicity and Information Secretary') adopted the name into that of the new party, which was created within ten days of the banning of its predecessor National Democratic Party.[4] The new party referred to the country as Zimbabwe in its list of goals. The name was retained by the breakaway Zimbabwe African National Union in 1963. Interestingly, the Europeanised spelling was retained rather than the Shona *Dzimba [dza]mabwe*.

In the period before democratic elections, Zimbabwe (Rhodesia) housed a movement of critical history whose mentors included British academic Terence Ranger until his expulsion in 1963. Like

Basil Davidson, 15 years his senior, Ranger's writing and career can be said to have developed through the range from radical optimism to radical pessimism, while maintaining an open self-criticism. He noted on his return to teach in Zimbabwe in 1997 that his role in creating a 'nationalist historiography' was now looked down on by university students; but that university history as a whole was being abandoned in the face of a new, selective, 'patriotic history' that suited the Mugabe regime.[5] Much of this 'patriotic history' related to the emphasis on recent and violent resistance movements. But there was a major celebration of the deep past in 2003, when an expensive ceremony was held to celebrate the return to the country from Germany of a fragment of one of the soapstone birds quoted from Great Zimbabwe. That site itself had less impact on the national consciousness given Zimbabwe's economic difficulties. With the decline of tourism for which Great Zimbabwe was a major destination, *The Standard* newspaper quoted a local comment on the ruins that 'now we see them just as another heap of stones'.[6] Meanwhile the school syllabus, which had shifted in 1991 to reflect a progressive (if simplified) nationalist historiography, was changed in 2002 to a much narrower approach that emphasised patriotic themes and the perspectives of the Mugabe government.[7]

Several of the South African liberation movements took the name Azania, from a little-used classical name for coastal regions of Africa. The first such use was early in the movement for independent African states, 'Azania' being cited at the All-Africa People's Congress in Accra in 1958. It was considered by the liberation movements as a new name for South Africa, a proposal that was not adopted by the electorally successful African National Congress. Their long-term rivals the Pan Africanist Congress of South Africa, founded in 1959 with a choice of names, none of which included 'Azania',[8] only later added 'of Azania' to its name and its military arm Poqo became 'The Azanian People's Liberation Army'. The name was used by other groups to distinguish themselves, and their 'Africanness', from the ANC. The term was used by the Azanian People's Organisation, founded in 1978, which held a seat in the post-democratisation parliament, and the Socialist Party of Azania, which emerged as a small group in 1998.

The deep history of Africa has played an occasional and eclectic role in the ideology of independent African nation states, though a number of rulers would aspire to aspects of former grandeur in their domestic arrangements. Newly democratic South Africa saw the promotion by its vice-president (and future second president) Thabo Mbeki of the idea of the 'African Renaissance', a theme formalised by a 1998 conference. This was a concept concerned with the future of Africa and South Africa in that context, with little relationship to the broad sweep of what had gone before.[9] References to history were rare in Mbeki's speeches and then only by contrast:

> As we recall with pride the African scholar and author of the Middle Ages, Sadi of Timbuktu, who had mastered such subjects as law, logic, dialectics, grammar and rhetoric, and other African intellectuals who taught at the University of Timbuktu, we must ask the question – where are Africa's intellectuals today! ... The beginning of our rebirth as a Continent must be our own rediscovery of our soul, captured and made permanently available in the great works of creativity represented by the pyramids and sphinxes of Egypt, the stone buildings of Axum and the ruins of Carthage and Zimbabwe, the rock paintings of the San, the Benin bronzes and the African masks, the carvings of the Makonde and the stone sculptures of the Shona.[10]

The 'African Renaissance' initiative ignored much of the recent radical historiography of southern African history. In the 1998 conference of 470 delegates in Johannesburg set up to define and refine the meaning of the African Renaissance, including some speakers invited from overseas, history played an ambiguous role, more as a rallying cry.[11] A thoughtful broad sweep narrative of human history by Bernard Magubane put general historical issues in a western Marxist tradition. Other papers treated the past more malleably and in exhortative mode. Dialo Diop invoked the work of Cheikh Anta Diop and his followers, while local literary academic Mbulelo Mzamane cited both Diop and Basil Davidson, listing selective achievements of the deep African past, and claimed 'African warrior nationalists, mostly kings, outmanoeuvred and out-generalled their better-armed antagonists'.[12] Guyanan Ivan van Sertima, author of a book claiming pre-Columbian African voyaging to the Americas, presented a catalogue of early African science. In general the event bypassed the critical strength of southern African historical and archaeological studies. The African Renaissance movement, being associated with Thabo Mbeki, looked unlikely to survive his own fall from grace in 2008.

TRIBALISM PAST AND PRESENT

Much of this account of approaches to the African past has described the impact of oversimplified schemas in the world of ideas. In the real world, one of the most dangerous of simplifications has been the yearning to classify into ethnic groups: often simplified in the African context as tribes and tribalism.

Categorising, classifying, naming is a prerequisite of power in many human endeavours. The scientific advances in classifying chemical substances, and in Linnaean classification of fauna and flora, underlay the advances of modern science. In colonial administration, the ability to apply both direct and indirect rule frequently relied on a 'tribal' model in which the territories and peoples in administration, under colonial rule or as 'protectorates', were given clear demarcations on a tribal basis. It was easier to understand diverse societies if they were divided into separate tribal groups with clear lines of identity, territory and often language. It was easier to apply indirect rule and manage finances, social and economic administration if there were recognised chiefs and rulers for each tribal group, even if these were societies without a longstanding tradition of chieftainship or a longstanding unity of ethnic identity.

In reality, of course, the identity of an individual always had flexibility. An ethnic identity could be changed by marriage, by willing or forced migration, by capture or enslavement, or just by acceptance; it could change voluntarily by religious conversion. Not only under European colonisation was it advantageous to belong to one ethnic group rather than another and to change tribal identity. The invention of tribal identities has been subject to many studies.[13] The role of ethnic identity in post-independent African states has underlain many of the conflicts that have beset new states. Pride in ethnic identity and the past of 'tribal' and language groups has had widely varying impacts, both positive and dangerous.

In order to make their work seem 'relevant', scholars at times used terminology of local ethnic groups in loose reference to the finds of the pre-modern past. When local communities came to claim this past as their own, the specialists were not always pleased. A post-democratisation exhibit at South Africa's National Gallery in Cape Town celebrating art presented the finds of eleventh-century Mapungubwe as the achievement of the Venda people.[14] By contrast, in the mid-1970s Zambia's major museum, the Livingstone Museum, reorganised and relabelled its displays of ethnography and traditional art, which were dominated by the creative arts of the Luvale and adjacent groups on the country's north-west, and retitled them as the art and traditions of Zambia, to give emphasis to a nation state whose borders and identity were relatively recent.

Dominance of political power by members of a particular ethnic or language group has, of course, been a feature of many modern African states. Resistance has been by revolution, by long-term interregional conflict and by secessionist movements such as that of Biafra in 1967–70. But often these reflected territorial boundaries – not necessarily hard-edged boundaries – between groups whose separated geographical areas of settlement had solidified during the colonial period. While colonial classifications might divide people, they might also unite them, as language groups consolidated under administrative arrangements. With education in a common language, ethnic identities could merge into larger units that survived the post-colonial era.

Among the greatest tragedies arising from the ideas of tribal identity is that of the conflict between 'Hutu' and 'Tutsi' in the interlacustrine region of central Africa, and especially the popular genocide of Tutsi in Rwanda during 1994, when between 800,000 and a million people were slaughtered over a three-month period. This was not a conflict between one geographic location and another: people classified as Hutu and Tutsi live patchworked across a broad region, with a woman changing tribal classification if she married into another group. In a comprehensive analysis of the Rwanda massacre Mahmood Mamdani[15] suggests that the Belgian colonial administration had constructed for their own purposes in the 1920s and 1930s the hard lines between an outsider 'Hamitic' Tutsi elite and a broadly classified indigenous Bantu Hutu, requiring all to have an identity card showing them to be Tutsi or Hutu or the minority Twa. Tutsi identity put someone closer to the centre of power. The political identity then changed as the state changed and evolved through the twentieth century. The perception of firm difference between two distinct ethnic identities solidified and turned into one of the worst episodes of contemporary history.

Thus the concept and classification of African peoples into tribes and tribal groups had moved from a partially applicable structure to convenient shorthand, to an administrative necessity to a major threat to the welfare of many parts of the continent. While the ruling groups in many nation states play down their ethnic units to maintain the solidity of the modern nation state, perceptions of tribalism remained.

The very word 'tribe" can convey to different individuals outside Africa either a sense of barbarism and backwardness, or an image of the authentic, original and unspoilt continent. 'Tribal ways', 'tribal traditions' and 'tribal art' convey a different mood from 'tribalism'.[16]

OUTSIDERS: FROM DEPENDENCY TO THE ROMANTIC PRIMITIVE WILDERNESS

Two longstanding images of the continent came to stand as contrasts in the perspective of outsiders to Africa. One could be described as romantic primitivism. The other attracted the new name 'Afropessimism'; this saw social and economic decline leading to dependency, of numerous states and societies whose future success relies on external aid.

The motivation of the Cold War, which led western and communist states to compete for support with financial aid, had ceased by the collapse of the Soviet Union in 1991. Subsequent perceptions of dependency have ranged from the generosity of individuals, to the activity of governments individually and collectively. The worse the human suffering that can be displayed, the greater the generosity of private donors.[17] For non-African governments, a mixture of motives have inspired verbal and practical commitments to African aid and development, but most aid from non-African governments is channelled through African governments, many of which the voluntary sector often describe as part of the problem rather than the solution. For all the goodwill that may underlie private and some public aid, the dependency image is of course an echo of the missionary endeavour and of the rationale declared for much of the colonial era.

The previous chapter showed a range of outsider images and a change over 50 years, from radical optimism to radical pessimism in attitudes of some progressive observers from the west. Despite wars, development challenges, and the spread of HIV infection and AIDS in many African (especially sub-Saharan African) countries, commentators would often comment on the inspiring optimism of many African people. But attempts to quantify this show differing results. In the comparative surveys summarised as the Satisfaction with Life Index, or World Happiness Index, most African counties north and south show up badly. The Human Development Index of the UN Development Programme has only Libya, Seychelles and Mauritius in the high group; 26 African countries in the medium group and 24 low or not classifiable; indeed, apart from East

Timor and Afghanistan, *all* the least developed countries are in Africa. Among other indicators, the migration of skilled African professionals away from the continent suggests a level of dissatisfaction: in 2004, it was recorded the emigration of technically skilled people has left only 20,000 engineers and scientists in Africa, servicing a population of about 600 million.[18] And as well as African professionals abandoning their own continent, some external social scientists whose career and dedication had been to the African field have retreated in despair to other areas, usually quietly, occasionally with a statement of rationale:

> While I continued to write and research on Third World development issues, I gradually became deeply disillusioned and distressed by what was going on in Africa itself. To put it simply, I thought that the people among whom I had lived in the 1970s, and whose intelligence and perseverance in adversity I had come to admire greatly, were being grossly betrayed and abused by their supposed political leaders and governors. I therefore gave up researching and writing on the continent from the early 1980s.[19]

The alternative to the dependency image of Africa is romanticisation of aspects of the continent: Africa as a context for unspoilt landscapes, exotic wildlife, rural people leading simpler and more honest lives than their national urban compatriots or the developed world. The romanticism for the supposed primitive and unspoilt in Africa is a long tradition that includes images in classical literature, pre-colonial European tales, through to the selective sponsorship of certain ethnic groups; and the development of ecotourism, including high-end wilderness holiday reserves neatly shielding the 'real' Africa.

National parks and their private equivalents originated as game parks, often initially to protect species for European hunting right. They reflect a long heritage in colonial times when the term 'game park' defined both preservation and hunting reserve for those authorised. The long-term conservation goals have at times created conflict with the traditional hunting patterns of local African peoples, although the creation and maintenance of parks is not always at the expense of local residents – there is a long and varied pattern of the emergence of conservation reserves.[20]

In all this the idea of a timeless Africa returns; romanticism and enthusiasm for the primitive and the wilderness is effectively a challenge to the passage of time and the dramatic cycles of change that have created the twenty-first-century African states. It is often effectively a denial of Africa having a dynamic past; a reassertion of the image of a timeless land with stability rather than progress, regression, challenge and change. When a South African corporation buys up a large block of grazing land, removes the sheep, buys wild animals at auction and sells American tourists the rights to shoot them, they are pretending the land is an unspoilt wilderness. In uncertain commodity markets, a national park with franchised facilities or a private reserve can bring a flow of substantial and essential foreign currency. The more the promotion pretends this is access to an unchanged ancient wilderness, the more the appeal; sometimes the more traditional-looking the buildings, the more can be charged for the authentic African experience.

Both fiction and travellers' tales in the second half of nineteenth-century Europe featured the wonders achieved with a rifle in the forests, savannahs and deserts of Africa south of the Mediterranean belt. The 'man in the wilderness' could celebrate his power with slaughter on a scale by then unavailable in Europe or America.

But new and human forms of 'the primitive' were to emerge in consciousness and admiration – first in art and later in people themselves. African objects – craft created for everyday life and ritual – turned into African art much later than the period of their collection. Their designation as art accelerated a new generation of craft made for sale to new markets of westerners, but then eventually also to the renewal of creative artistic traditions.

Objects from Africa joined curiosities of humanity, flora, fauna and geology in gentlemen's collections from the earliest time of European trade and contact with Africa. Some of these entered public collections: in the original collection donated to form the British Museum in 1753 were 29 African objects. Exploration and the beginnings of the colonial era transformed this. By the time the Berlin Museum für Völkerkunde opened in 1886 it had 10,000 African objects.[21] African art was displayed in ethnographic museums, created in the colonial era to reflect the distance between metropolis and primitive world.[22]

The transition of African sub-Saharan ethnography to 'primitive art' or *art nègre* in western ideas probably appeared first in Paris. The initial public displays of African objects reflected and celebrated the French colonial endeavour. Temporary displays from 1878 onwards led to the opening of the Musée d'Ethnographie at the

Trocadero in 1882; four years later a display of the booty from de Brazza's West African Expedition attracted 30,000 visitors.

The recognition of these ethnographic curiosities as art was not immediate. It is attributed to a group of artists around 1906, who were developing and searching for new means of expression that would go beyond the conventions of impressionism. Matisse, Derain and Vlaminck were all pioneers in an enthusiasm for what African art showed them, in the period 1906–7, but it was probably Pablo Picasso who took this furthest, declaring as a turning point a visit to the Trocadero in 1907, the year when he painted *Les Demoiselles d'Avignon*. He would later proclaim 'primitive sculpture has never been surpassed'.[23]

These artists were looking for new ideas; in the wood carvings of West and equatorial Africa they found images, especially those using and manipulating the human form, that corresponded to some of the innovations they were pursuing. It was affinities between African art and the new European art as much as influence that brought African creations, especially carvings, into the concept of 'art'. Modern art became interested in a primitive object *because* their own exploration made such objects relevant to their own work. 'Contact with African masks and sculptures ... helped European artists to modify their style of representation and experiment with a non-representational aesthetic.'[24]

But this was not universally accepted; most African art in France remained in ethnographic rather than art museums.[25] With the New York exhibition at the Museum of Modern Art in 1935, of 'African Negro Art', the *celebration* of the primitive had been advanced. The art itself had not changed its function, its nature, but its classification by some outsiders had started to transform it. The concept of timeless art from a society without history had not, however, been eroded.

Alongside enthusiasm for the natural world and now for the creative crafts from Africa, came a selective enthusiasm for 'primitive' peoples among western outsiders to the continent. There had been much less enthusiasm among travellers and writers from the Islamic world: those of whatever race who embraced Islam were fully part of the *umma*, those who had not converted were *kafir*. Ironically, many of the colonial officials from the Christian west came to feel greater empathy with the Islamic political entities within their colonies than with the pagans whose rituals, beliefs and political structures were much more enigmatic.

If some in western society found the African townspeople and villagers challenging, or unsympathetic, there developed an enthusiasm for certain societies, especially the hunter or pastoralist herder, who seemed to represent a romantic, likable Africa: 'romantic primitivism celebrates what is simple about Africa; it salutes the cattle-herder rather than the castle-builder'.[26] This did not apply when the outsider group became the enemy: the Baqqara Arabs who supported the Mahdiyya revolt experienced the force of empire when the British killed 11,000 in the 1898 Battle of Omdurman; the French Foreign Legion felt less than romantic about its continual skirmishes with desert peoples in occupied North Africa. A majority of Herero and Ovambo were killed by German arms in South-West Africa in 1904–7. But Germany would then celebrate romantic primitivism when Leni Riefenstahl, propagandist filmmaker to the Nazis, embraced and made famous the Nuba of Sudan in her post-war photographic career.

In the 1970s an image of change was brought home to a wider audience by Colin Turnbull's study of the Ik of Uganda and Kenya, former hunters who were forced to become farmers and whose society and personal relationships fell apart into a world of callous selfishness. But earlier the same author had fulfilled the romantic admiration for the equatorial pygmies with his work on the baMbuti people of the Congo region.[27]

When people were not a threat, the romantic image could remain. The nomadic Tuareg of the Sahara held such an image in the west, of the blue-veiled desert warrior, an image that long outlasted their nomadic identity. By the 1960s their nomadic lifestyle had substantially changed with the modern independent states of North and West Africa less enthused at the image of the noble savage.[28]

The Maasai of Kenya and northern Tanzania are another community much favoured by the romantic enthusiasts for the primitive. Seen as a timeless nomadic pastoralist community, with distinct dress and customs, the Maasai have long fascinated outsiders and visitors – they live conveniently close to a number of national parks. The Maasai have benefited in a number of ways from the image they hold. They are far from the oldest of East African communities, and their adoption of a purely pastoral economy seems to have been later still.[29] Many who call themselves Maasai do not pursue pastoralism and the occasional non-Maasai may dress the part and pose for tourists. Aware of their image, Maasai have been politically astute in both the later colonial period and in the modern state, with what has been described as a 'contrived ethnicity' to confirm, where appropriate, to stereotype, and appeal to enthusiasts for a 'Vanishing Africa'.

Perhaps of greatest romantic appeal are the Bushmen (San) of Southern Africa: seen as the survivors of an earlier phase of human history, that of the hunter-gatherer. Physically distinct from negro farmers of the region, the idea of the archetypal traditional Bushman has been reinforced in book, television documentary and film.[30] The popular image of the Bushman combined and conflated images of the Kalahari communities (especially the !Kung), with knowledge of the Cape Bushmen who had lived in the Western Cape until the eighteenth century.[31]

The wider awareness of Bushmen outside southern Africa can be traced to the remarkable success of the work of South African creative writer Laurens van der Post. He 'revealed' the Bushmen to the wider world in the 1950s: with a six-part British television series *Lost World of the Kalahari*, with his vastly successful book of the same title in 1958 and its successor *The Heart of the Hunter* in 1961.[32] These books created both fascination and sympathy for the isolated world of the small desert hunters with their remarkable mythologies. They inspired further popular books, while archaeologists leapt on the opportunity to use remnant 'stone age' peoples as an analogy for understanding much older prehistoric communities.

The reality of Van der Post's life and work was unveiled, with some sadness, by his biographer in 2001, some five years after his death.[33] This showed that the brilliant writer of both fiction and non-fiction extended his imagination into his supposedly factual work and indeed into his personal narratives; the boundary between reported fact and creative fiction in his work being fluid. Although Van der Post had been to the Kalahari before, his experience with 'the Bushmen' before these two books seems to have been limited to a fortnight spent with one group of 30 Bushmen on the edge of the Kalahari; much of the mythology he reported in his book was drawn from material collected from survivors of the quite distinct !Xam Cape Bushmen community and documented between 1875 and 1923. But readers of the book had believed what they chose to believe, even if the image of the absorbed Cape Bushmen has been transferred to the Kalahari. In the books themselves, which have no formal references, he does write of his 'short stay' with a 'small Bushmen clan' and mentions his use of the earlier sources. It is what he did not say that drew criticism, especially in the context of a life shown to have had many falsehoods. His work 'moves uneasily between levels – between the present and mythological times'. The

Bushmen have lived with and alongside farmers and pastoralists for centuries, and moved between hunting, herding, working for pastoralists and farmers. The 'wild' Bushman is 'largely a figment of [Van der Post's] imagination'.[34]

The image of isolated desert hunter-gatherer Bushmen, fossils from an ancient world, simplifies a complex reality. The Kalahari San (Bushmen) have long been involved in the wider economy, with social and economic ties to Tswana and other neighbouring farmers and pastoralists; the part of the economy represented by subsistence foraging may have shifted quite recently.[35] Such a critique emphasises the 'search for authenticity' and the 'invention of Bushmen', which have created the image since the mid-twentieth century.

At times it may help a community to be perceived as an authentic primitive, with a traditional way of life under threat; but such an image may also be negative and disadvantageous in a fast-changing nation.

CONCLUSIONS

Current enthusiasm for a timeless African wilderness, and for selected supposedly simpler societies within it, provides a final aspect of the simplifying narratives of the continent that this book has discussed. Models applied to large parts of the diverse continent serve the needs of those who create or use them. They rarely serve the needs of all those to whom these grand narratives are applied, irrespective of the motives of their creators.

We have seen how outsiders have created names and images for Africa past and present. Some suited political or religious needs. 'We' need both terminology and description for 'them' – whether 'them' is all of the African continent or those parts of the continent that are not us. This applies if 'we' are the pharaonic Egyptians, or the Romans colonising the Mediterranean coast, or the Islamic cultures distinguishing believer from non-believer. It applies if we are white South Africans looking north, or the modern American ecotourist or European charitable donor looking in from outside.

A harsh way to deny an identity is to deny a history. We have seen how the deep and complex history of Africa has been denied, and the risk that comes from more recent romanticism in celebrating supposedly timeless cultures. Inventing a history where outsiders are credited with African cultural developments – Mediterranean or Arabian or Indian Ocean civilisations – was taking hold of Africa's past and giving it to others.

But other threats come from creating a history when that history comes to serve a particular need. Emphasis on certain periods, certain cultures, certain racial characteristics, certain ethnic identities and 'tribes' may play a progressive role in one time and place but come to mislead in others. And in the grand sweep surveys of human origins, Africa continues to be a context for approaches and theories that may not stand the test of changing knowledge and perspectives.

The stimulus remains to develop, question and improve, but above all diversify the understanding of the many pasts of the African continent. There is little to lose by constant challenge to simplified narratives. The futures of Africa's diverse peoples have much to gain from continuing to probe, interpret and understand the continent's distant and recent past.

Notes

CHAPTER 1: THE CHANGING SHAPE AND PERCEPTION OF 'AFRICA'

1. A. Mazrui, 'The re-invention of Africa: Edward Said, V.Y. Mudimbe and beyond', *Research in African Literatures* (2005), **36**, 68–82; citing Melville Herskovits' argument that the continent is a geographical fiction.

2. See V.Y. Mudimbe, *The Idea of Africa*, Bloomington, IN: Indiana University Press & London: James Currey, 1994; V.Y. Mudimbe, *The Invention of Africa: gnosis, philosophy and the order of knowledge*, Bloomington, IN: Indiana University Press, 1988; Mazrui, 'The re-invention of Africa'. Mazrui accused Said and Mudimbe of stereotyping the west while criticising their stereotyping of others. General discussion by K.A. Appiah, *In My Father's House: Africa in the philosophy of culture*, London: Methuen, 1992; of narrower focus is A.E. Coombes, *Reinventing Africa: museums, material culture and popular imagination in late Victorian and Edwardian England*, New Haven, CT: Yale University Press, 1994.

3. Even the 53 member states of the African Union do not include the whole continent, since Morocco left in 1984, and the remaining European-controlled islands are of course excluded.

4. Scott Maceachern, 'Where in Africa does Africa start? Identity, genetics and African studies from the Sahara to Darfur', *Journal of Social Archaeology* (2007), **7**, 393–412. This article notes a particular example of this danger: the confusion outside Africa in classifying Darfur during its conflicted recent history.

5. Journals too define their interest: the *International Journal of Middle East Studies* includes 'the Arab world' broadly.

6. This classification was borrowed by others. The African literature publishing programmes of specialist imprints such as Heinemann, Longman and Three Continents Press in the USA included black and coloured South Africans but not white South Africans; white writers were published in different contexts.

7. A canal linking the Red Sea with the Nile was excavated under the sixth-to-fifth-century BC Persian ruler Darius I.

8. A. Mazrui, *The Africans: a triple heritage*, Boston: Little Brown & London: BBC Publications, 1986, 28–34.

9. Papers in E.S. Vrba, G.H. Denton, T.C. Partridge and L.H. Burckle (eds), *Paleoclimate and Evolution with Emphasis on Human Origins*, New Haven, CT: Yale University Press, 1995. Julia Lee-Thorp has suggested there is little evidence for this, and the main changes to a more open environment occurred ca. 1.7 million years ago. See C.J. Luyt and J.A. Lee-Thorp, 'Carbon isotope ratios of Sterkfontein fossils indicate a marked shift to open environments c. 1.7 Myr ago', *South African Journal of Science* (2003), **99**, 271–3 and http://gsa. confex.com/gsa/2003AM/finalprogram/abstract_65304.htm .

10. Increasingly called *Homo ergaster* in an African context.

11. C. Gamble, *Timewalkers: the prehistory of global colonisation*, Harvard, MA: Harvard University Press, 1993, 10; E. Cornelissen, 'Human responses to changing environments in Central Africa between 40,000 and 12,000 B.P.', *Journal of World Prehistory* (2002), **16**, 197–235.

12. A.B. Smith, in L. Krzyzaniak and M. Kobusiewicz (eds), *Late Prehistory of the Nile Basin and the Sahara*, Poznan: Museu Archeologiczoe w Poznanin, 1989, 68–78; S.L. Carto, A.J. Weaver, R. Hetherington, Y. Lam, and E.C. Wiebe, 'Out of Africa and into an ice age: on the role of global climate change in the late Pleistocene migration of early modern humans out of Africa', *Journal of Human Evolution* (2009), **56**, 139–51.

13. R. Derricourt, 'Getting "Out of Africa": sea crossings, land crossings and culture in the hominin migrations', *Journal of World Prehistory* (2005), **19**, 119–32.

14. Unless one accepts the argument in R. Dennell and W. Roebroeks, 'An Asian perspective on early human dispersal from Africa', *Nature* (2005), **438**, 1099–1104.

15. Derricourt, 'Getting "Out of Africa"'.

16. There has been intensive archaeological research on many of these, while others have produced no archaeological record. P.M. Mitchell, 'Towards a comparative archaeology of Africa's islands', *Journal of African Archaeology* (Frankfurt) (2004), **2**, 229–50.

17. Island settlement back goes back four to seven millennia in most island groups, two millennia earlier in larger islands with a 10,340 BP (before present) date at Akrotiri on Cyprus. There is no unambiguous evidence for Palaeolithic presence on Cyprus or Crete. The Palaeolithic evidence on Thasos in the northern Aegean is attributable to a land bridge while Sicily had a land bridge to Italy until ca. 14,000–12,000 BP. Although there is early material from Corfu, the island was linked by land to the mainland at glacial maxima. There is Upper Palaeolithic settlement in Corfu. Gamble, *Timewalkers*, 239; J.F. Cherry, 'The first colonisation of the Mediterranean islands: a review of recent research', *Journal of Mediterranean Archaeology* (1990), **3**, 145–221.

18. T.F. Strasser et al., 'Stone Age seafaring in the Mediterranean: evidence from the Plakias region for Lower Palaeolithic and Mesolithic habitation of Crete', *Hesperus* (2010), **79**, 145–90.

19. J.O. Pintado, 'Les cultures préhistoriques des îles Canaries', *L'Anthropologie* (1987), **91**, 653–78 notes the sixth-century maximum in dating but the cultural likelihood there was no settlement earlier than the second millennium BC. There are arguments that indirect evidence supports human arrivals before 5,000 BP: L. Zöller, H. Suchdolezt and N. Küster, 'Geoarchaeological and chrono-metrical evidence of early human occupation on Lanzarote (Canary Islands)', *Quaternary Science Reviews* (2003), **22**, 1299–1307. These have promptly been challenged: J.C. Carracedo, J. Meco, A. Lomoschitz, M.A. Perera, J. Mallester and J.-F. Betancor, 'Comment on "Geoarchaeological and chrono-metrical evidence of early human occupation on Lanzarote (Canary Islands)", by Zöller et al.', *Quaternary Science Reviews* (2004), **23**, 2045–8.

20. Any early settlement from the mainland is assumed to have been by a land bridge that vanished about 8,000 BP. E. Mateu, D. Comas, F. Calafell, A. Perez-Lezaun, A. Abade and J. Bertranpetit, 'A tale of two islands: population history and mitochondrial DNA sequence variation of Bioko and Sao Tome, Gulf of Guinea', *Annals of Human Genetics* (1997), **61**, 507–18; B. Clist,

'Nouvelles données archéologiques sur l'histoire ancienne de la Guinée-Equatoriale'. *L'Anthropologie* (1998), **102**, 213–17.

21.   J. Zarins, 'Obsidian in the larger context of predynastic/archaic Egyptian Red Sea trade', in J. Reade (ed.), *The Indian Ocean in Antiquity*, London: Kegan Paul International, 1996, 89–105.

22.   T. Insoll, *The Archaeology of Islam in sub-Saharan Africa*, Cambridge: Cambridge University Press, 2003, 145–9; M. Horton and J. Middleton, *The Swahili: the social landscape of a mercantile society*, Oxford: Blackwell, 2000, 26–7; F.A. Chami, 'The ancient cultural sequence for the central coast of east Africa: a new perspective', in *The Development of Urbanism from a Global Perspective*, [1993] www.arkeologi.uu.se/afr/projects/BOOK/default.htm; F.A. Chami, 'The early Iron Age on Mafia island and its relationship with the mainland', *Azania* (1999), **34**, 1–10. The African Early Iron Age is attested on the islands of Kwale and Koma and the larger island of Mafia, 20km from the mainland. An experimental crossing in a dhow took eight hours (in strong winds) to reach Mafia.

23.   Roman beads have been found in the Rufiji delta of Tanzania some 40km from the coast dated to ca. third to fifth centuries AD. More significant are recent claims for material on Juani island near Mafia, and including Greco-Roman, Syrian and Sassanian materials and settlement back to 600 BC. Early Iron Age sherds have been claimed for Zanzibar, while Later Stone Age material has been found at Pate. Horton and Middleton, *Swahili*, 31; F.A. Chami, 'Roman beads from the Rufiji Delta, Tanzania: first incontrovertible archaeological link with the Periplus', *Current Anthropology* (1999), **40**, 237–41; Chami, 'Early Iron Age'; Juani island in a preliminary report by Chami; F.A. Chami and A. Kwekason, 'Neolithic pottery traditions from the islands, the Coast and the Interior of East Africa', *African Archaeological Review* (2003), **20**, 65–80.

24.   F.A. Chami, *The Unity of African Ancient History 3000 BC to AD 500,* Dar es-Salaam: E & D, 2006, 139.

25.   P. Verin and H. Wright, 'Madagascar and Indonesia: new evidence from archaeology and linguistics', *Bulletin of the Indo-Pacific Prehistory Association* (1999), **18**, 35–41. Indirect evidence supports earlier human contact from around 350 BC. D.A. Burney, L.P. Burney, L.R. Godfrey, W.L. Jungers, S.M. Goodman, H.T. Wright and A.J.T. Jull, 'A chronology for late prehistoric Madagascar', *Journal of Human Evolution* (2004), **47**, 25–6; R.D.E. MacPhee and D.A. Burney, 'Dating of modified femora of extinct dwarf Hippopotamus from southern Madagascar', *Journal of Archaeological Science* (1991), **18**, 695–706.

26.   S. Snape, 'The emergence of Libya on the horizon of Egypt', in D. O'Connor and S. Quirke (eds), *Mysterious Lands*, London: UCL Press, 2003, 93–106.

27.   D. O'Connor and A. Reid (eds), *Ancient Egypt in Africa*, London: UCL Press, 2003, 12–13; O'Connor and Quirke, *Mysterious Lands*, 8–10.

28.   S.P. Harvey, 'Interpreting Punt: geographic, cultural and artistic landscapes', in O'Connor and Quirke, *Mysterious Lands*, 81–91; O'Connor and Reid, *Ancient Egypt*, 12–13; J. Phillips, 'Punt and Aksum: Egypt and the Horn of Africa', *Journal of African History* (1997), **38**, 423–57.

29.   D. Meeks, 'Locating Punt', in O'Connor and Quirke, *Mysterious Lands*, 53–80.

30.   Meeks, 'Locating Punt', 59–61.

31.   Herodotus, *Histories*, 4.42.

32. Discussed in M. van Wyk Smith's ambitious book *The First Ethiopians*, Johannesburg: Wits University Press, 2009, 61–72, 443.

33. See L. Thompson and J. Ferguson (eds), *Africa in Classical Antiquity*, Ibadan: Ibadan University Press, 1969.

34. Van Wyk Smith, *The First Ethiopians*, 3–4.

35. Mudimbe, *The Idea of Africa*, 71–80; Herodotus, *Histories*, 4.169–94; B. Shaw, 'Eaters of flesh, drinkers of milk', *Ancient Society* (1982/3), **13/14**, 14–15; *Aithiopians: Histories*, 2.22, 2.29, 2.30, 4.183, 7.70.

36. L. Thompson, 'Classical contacts with West Africa', in Thompson and Ferguson, *Africa*, 1–25, at 5.

37. J. Ferguson, 'Eastern Africa and the Graeco-Roman World', in Thompson and Ferguson, *Africa*, 26–61.

38. S. Raven, *Rome in Africa*, 3rd edn, London: Routledge, 1993, xxvi.

39. M. Wheeler, *Rome Beyond the Imperial Frontiers*, Harmondsworth: Penguin 1955, 129.

40. C. Daniels, 'Africa', in J. Wacher (ed.), *The Roman World*, I, London: Routledge, 1986, 223–65.

41. *Cambridge Dictionary of Classical Civilisation*, Cambridge: Cambridge University Press, 2006, 320.

42. I. de Rachewiltz, *Prester John and Europe's Discovery of East Asia*, Canberra: ANU Press, 1972, 2.

43. Osman Sid Ahmed Ismail, 'The historiographical tradition of African Islam', in T.O. Ranger (ed.), *Emerging Themes of African History*, Dar es Salaam: East African Publishing House, 1968, 7–13.

44. J.L.Triaud, 'Sudan: Bilad al-', in C.E. Bosworth et al. (eds), *The Encyclopaedia of Islam*, new edn, 9, Leiden: Brill, 1995, 754–60.

45. Umar al-Naqar, 'Takrur: the history of a name', *Journal of African History* (1969), 3, 365–74.

46. Orthographically the province should perhaps be transliterated as Ifrīkiyā for modern Africa but Ifriķiya for the early Muslim entity. B. Lewis et al. (eds), *Encyclopédie de l'Islam*, III, Leiden: Brill, 1975, 1075.

47. J.S. Trimingham, *The Influence of Islam upon Africa*, 2nd edn, London: Longman, 1980, 34.

48. S.H.T. Kimble, *Geography in the Middle Ages*, New York: Russell & Russell, 1968 [1938], 54–5.

49. Trimingham, *Influence*, 34; D. Robinson, *Muslim Societies in African History*, Cambridge: Cambridge University Press, 2004, 27.

50. J.R.S. Philips, *The Medieval Expansion of Europe*, Oxford: Oxford University Press, 1998, 135–53.

51. Annette Kierkegaard questions the boundary between medieval Europe and the Islamic world in the medieval period when, of course, Islam dominated south-west Europe. She sees the non-racial perspective of Islam extended into Europe at this time. See A. Kierkegaard, 'Questioning the origins of the negative image of Africa in Medieval Europe', in M. Palmberg (ed.), *Encounter Images in the Meetings between Africa and Europe*, Uppsala: Nordiska Afrikainstitutet, 2001, 20–36.

52. The gold trade from West Africa pre-dated the Muslim traders – see T.F. Garrard, 'Myth and metrology: the early trans-Saharan gold trade', *Journal of African History* (1982), **23**, 443–61.

53. Philips, *Medieval Expansion of Europe*, 141; Kimble, *Geography*, 100–1; P.D. Curtin, *The Image of Africa: British ideas and action 1780–1850*, Madison, WI: University of Wisconsin Press, 1964, 11.

54. Kimble, *Geography*, 119, 193 ff.

55. Ibid., 109–11.

56. W. MacGaffey, 'Dialogues of the deaf: Europeans on the Atlantic coast of Africa', in S.B. Schwartz (ed.), *Implicit Understandings*, Cambridge: Cambridge University Press, 1994, 249–67.

57. E. Sanceau, *Portugal in Quest of Prester John*, London: Hutchinson [1943], 78; de Rachewiltz, *Prester John*, 2.

58. De Rachewiltz, *Prester John*, 56; L.N. Gumilev, *Searches for an Imaginary Kingdom: the legend of the kingdom of Prester John*, Cambridge: Cambridge University Press, 1987, 4–7, 362–6.

59. Sanceau, *Portugal in Quest*, 11–12.

60. B.W. Diffie and G.D. Winius, *Foundations of the Portuguese Empire*, 1, Minneapolis, MN: University of Minnesota Press, 1977, 159.

61. C.F. Beckingham and G.W.B. Huntingford (eds), *The Prester John of the Indies*, Cambridge: Cambridge University Press for Hakluyt Society, 2 vols, 1961; this uses the 1881 translation by Stanley.

62. Sanceau, *Portugal in Quest*, 50; E. Sanceau, *The Land of Prester John: a chronicle of Portuguese exploration*, New York: Knopf, 1944, 70, 79.

63. The story of Prester John was re-echoed in fiction when John Buchan's 1910 novel presents a Zulu clergyman who makes claims to be the inheritor of Prester John's spiritual role.

64. J.M. Massing, 'The image of Africa and the iconography of lip-plated African in Pierre Desceliers's world map of 1550', in T.F. Earle and K.J.P. Lowe (eds), *Black Africans in Renaissance Europe*, Cambridge: Cambridge University Press, 2005, 48–69.

65. Edited by Filippo Pigafetta and translated into English 1597 by Abraham Hartwell.

66. E.g. Duarte Pacheco Pereira, *Esmeraldo de situ Orbis,* written ca. 1505–8; English edn edited by G.H.T. Kimble, London: Hakluyt Society, 1937.

67. Earle and Lowe, *Black Africans*, 43–4; B. Davidson, *The Search for Africa*, London: James Currey & New York: Crown, 1994, 43; José Lingna Nafafé, *Colonial Encounters: issues of culture, hybridity and creolisation. Portuguese mercantile settlers in West Africa*, Frankfurt: Peter Lang, 2007, gives a nuanced account of these relations, augmented by an interesting record of Europeans who settled into African societies.

68. J. Lawrence, 'Black Africans in Renaissance Spanish literature', in Earle and Lowe, *Black Africans*, 70–93.

69. James Walvin quotes 3,000 slaves in fifteenth-century Venice; 9,500 slaves in 1550 Lisbon and 14,500 slaves in the diocese of Seville by 1565: J. Walvin, *Making the Black Atlantic: Britain and the African diaspora*, London: Cassell, 2000, 1–3.

70. Earle and Lowe, *Black Africans*, xvi, 20.

71. A. Korhonen, 'Washing the Ethiopian white: conceptualising black skin in Renaissance England', in Earle and Lowe, *Black Africans*, 94–112.

72. 9.56 million, according to P.D Curtin, *The Atlantic Slave Trade: a census*, Madison, WI: University of Wisconsin Press, 1969, 268; closer to 17 million, according to P.G. Lovejoy, *Transformations in Slavery*, Cambridge: Cambridge

University Press, 1983, 45, 137. Many variant calculations exist. In addition to perhaps another 25 per cent who died on voyage were the deaths both direct and indirect from the slave raiding in Africa.

73. Curtin, *Atlantic Slave Trade*, 265; Walvin, *Making*, 20–2.
74. Curtin, *Image of Africa*, 320; T.J. Bassett, 'Cartography and empire building in nineteenth-century West Africa', *Geographical Review* (1994), **84**, 316–35.
75. Curtin, *Image of Africa*, vi, 480.
76. The Anglo-Egyptian Sudan dates from 1899; Nigeria had formal status as a colony in 1900; the South African Republics acknowledged British sovereignty in 1902; the transformation of the Congo from crown property to Belgian colony was as late as 1908.
77. P.S. Zachernuk, 'African history and imperial culture in colonial Nigerian schools', *Africa* (1998), **68**, 484–505. This article surveys the range of views on history teaching.
78. A.V. Murray, *The School in the Bush: a critical study of the theory and practice of native education*, 2nd edn, London: Longman, 1938, 19.
79. Ibid., 203–4, 317–19.

CHAPTER 2: MYTHIC AND MYSTIC AFRICA

1. Herodotus, *Histories*, 3,113; 3,101; 4,168–310.
2. P.D. Curtin, *The Image of Africa: British ideas and action 1780–1850*, Madison, WI: University of Wisconsin Press, 1964, 205 notes the assumptions of James MacQueen, *Geographical and Commercial View of Northern and Central Africa*, Edinburgh: William Blackwood, 1821, that the Muslim states of West Africa must be ruled by white North Africans. The ideas are still promulgated – e.g. http://phoenicia.org/zimbabwe.html.
3. P. Garlake, *Great Zimbabwe*, London: Thames & Hudson, 1973, 51–62.
4. J. Campbell, *Travels in South Africa*, London: Westley, 2 vols, 1822; M. Wilson and L. Thompson (eds), *The Oxford History of South Africa*, 1, Oxford: Oxford University Press, 1969, 139–40.
5. H.M. Walmsley, *The Ruined Cities of Zulu Land*, 2 vols, London: Chapman & Hall, 1869, esp. 162–76; reissued as *Wild Sports and Savage Life in Zululand*. The author's brother served on the Zulu frontier and is acknowledged in the novel and a source of the narrative; see N. Etherington, *Rider Haggard*, Boston: Twayne, 1984, 39; G. Monsman (ed.), *King Solomon's Mines* by H. Rider Haggard, Toronto: Broadview, 2002, 290 ff.
6. D. Hammond and A. Jablow, *The Africa that Never Was: four centuries of British writing about Africa*, New York: Twayne, 1970, 66 ff.
7. Ibid., 13, 197.
8. In later novels can be found Maasai with Roman ancestry and Nigerians with Chinese forebears – ibid., 129.
9. Garlake, *Great Zimbabwe*, 64; E.E. Burke (ed.), *The Journals of Carl Mauch*, Salisbury: National Archives of Rhodesia, 1969.
10. R.N. Hall and W.G. Neal, *The Ancient Ruins of Rhodesia: Monomotapae imperium*, 2nd edn, London: Methuen, 1904, 244.
11. *Illustrated London News*, 11 January 1873, quoted in Monsman, *King Solomon's Mines*, 289–90.
12. P. Mitchell, 'Andrew Anderson and the nineteenth century origins of southern African archaeology', *Southern African Humanities* (2001), **13**, 37–60.

13. In the 1905 edition (London: Cassell), 8 he identifies the Kukuanas with the Matabele (Ndebele). This Zulu-related community was necessary to the story so that the Zulu-speaking characters from Natal could communicate with and understand the Kukuanas, though of course the Ndebele language was only introduced to the area in the earlier nineteenth century.

14. Though in his youth he repeated the view that the Zulu might be of Arab stock and have Jewish traditions! – Lilias Rider Haggard, *The Cloak that I Left: a biography of the author Henry Rider Haggard K.B.E.*, Ipswich: Boydell Press, 1976, 36.

15. Quoted in ibid., 122–3; in Haggard's *Days of My Life* he says it was 'a work of pure imagination'. But Etherington, *Rider Haggard*, 39 notes that the Zimbabwe ruins already appeared on Jeppe's map of the Transvaal.

16. Haggard, *Cloak that I Left*, 231.

17. R. Summers, *Ancient Mining in Rhodesia and Adjacent Areas*, Salisbury: National Museums of Rhodesia, 1969.

18. *The Church Quarterly Review*, 1888, reprinted in Monsman, *King Solomon's Mines*, 251.

19. A.M. Stauffer (ed.), *She* by H. Rider Haggard, Toronto: Broadview, 2006, 29. This edition reproduced the serialised version.

20. *Pall Mall Gazette*, 4 January 1887, reprinted in Stauffer, *She*, 281–2.

21. V.L. Cameron, *The Queen's Land, or, Ard al Malakat*, London: Swan Sonnenschein, 1886. See also http://www.violetbooks.com/lostrace-check-guide.html.

22. K. Tidrick, *Heart-Beguiling Araby*, Cambridge: Cambridge University Press, 1981; see also R. Irwin, *For Lust of Knowing: the orientalists and their enemies*, London: Allen Lane, 2006.

23. Haggard, *Cloak that I Left*, 231–3.

24. The RGS talk was published as J.T. Bent, 'The Ruins of Mashonaland, and explorations in the country', *Proceedings of the Royal Geographical Society* (1892), **14**, 273–98. His book is J.T. Bent, *The Ruined Cities of Mashonaland*, London: Longmans, 1892; 3rd edn 1896 (reprinted Bulawayo: Books of Rhodesia, 1969); Garlake, *Great Zimbabwe*, 66–9.

25. Bent, *Ruined Cities*, 64.

26. Ibid., 121, 204–5, 214–15, 228, 336–7; Garlake, *Great Zimbabwe*, 66.

27. Bent, *Ruined Cities*, 176.

28. Bent, 'Ruins', 273, 288–9.

29. Bent, *Ruined Cities*, 220–2, 227–9.

30. Ibid., ix, xiv.

31. D. Killick, 'Cairo to Cape: the spread of metallurgy through eastern and southern Africa', *Journal of World Prehistory* (2009), **22**, 399–414.

32. A. Wilmot, *Monomotapa (Rhodesia): its monuments, and its history from the most ancient times to the present century*, London: T.F. Unwin, 1896. Introduction reprinted in Stauffer, *She*, 307 11.

33. Haggard in Wilmot, *Monomotapa*, xv. At the same time that Rhodes sponsored Wilmot's book he sponsored Haggard's brother in a prospecting company, which may have influenced Haggard's cooperation in the book. See W.H. Worger, 'Southern and Central Africa', in R.W. Winks (ed.), *Historiography*, volume 5 of *The Oxford History of the British Empire*, Oxford: Oxford University Press, 2001, 515.

34. There are numerous references to Solomon in the Qur'an, as also to Sheba, but not Ophir. This makes it unlikely that the Portuguese derived the Ophir identification from Muslim traders, as suggested by S.T. Carroll, 'Solomonic legend: the Muslims and the Great Zimbabwe', *International Journal of African Historical Studies* (1988), **24**, 233–47.

35. A.E. Coombes, *Reinventing Africa: museums, material culture and popular imagination in late Victorian and Edwardian England*, New Haven, CT: Yale University Press, 1994, 141; see also A.H. Keane, *Ethnology*, Cambridge: Cambridge University Press, 1895.

36. A.H. Keane, *The Gold of Ophir: whence brought and by whom?*, London: Stanford, 1901.

37. Ibid., ix–xiii, 5, 57–8.

38. R. Gayre of Gayre and R. Nigg, *The Origin of the Zimbabwean Civilisation*, Salisbury: Galaxie Press, 1972.

39. K. Peters, *Im Goldland des Altertums*, München: J.F. Lehmann, 1902.

40. Hall and Neal, *Ancient Ruins*, 56, 98, 168–72.

41. Sir John Willoughby of the BSAC undertook some quick, destructive excavations a year after Bent.

42. R.N. Hall, *Great Zimbabwe, Mashonaland, Rhodesia*, London: Methuen, 1905, xxvi; Garlake, *Great Zimbabwe*, 71–6; 'at every corner one might expect to come face with Rider Haggard's She' (29).

43. Hall, *Great Zimbabwe*, 13. He also noted parallels with ancient Jewish customs in the modern peoples of the area and endorsed Bent's affiliation to ancient Sabaeans of Arabia (190–3).

44. B.G. Trigger, *A History of Archaeological Thought*, Cambridge: Cambridge University Press, 1989, 131–5; Bent, *Ruined Cities*; M. Hall, 'Hidden history: Iron Age archaeology in Southern Africa', in P. Robertshaw (ed.), *A History of African Archaeology*, London: James Currey & Portsmouth, NH: Heinemann, 1990, 59–77.

45. D.R. MacIver, *Medieval Rhodesia*, London: Macmillan, 1906; R.N. Hall, *Prehistoric Rhodesia*, London: Fisher Unwin, 1909.

46. G. Caton-Thompson, *The Zimbabwe Culture: ruins and reactions*, Oxford: Clarendon Press, 1931. She acknowledged the many correspondents on the site whom she had filed under 'Insane' – viii.

47. Ibid., 9.

48. MacIver, *Medieval Rhodesia*, 85.

49. G. Caton-Thompson, *Mixed Memoirs*, Gateshead: Paradigm, 1983, 131.

50. S. Marchand, 'Leo Frobenius and the revolt against the West', *Journal of Contemporary History* (1997), **32**, 153–70. The most contentious views on African history were omitted from the centenary selection in English translation published as *Leo Frobenius 1873–1973: eine anthologie*, Wiesbaden: Franz Steiner, 1973.

51. L. Frobenius, *Und Afrika Sprach*, 2 vols, Berlin: Vita, 1912–13; L. Frobenius, *Atlantis: Volksmirchen und Volksdichtungen Afrikas*, 12 vols, Jena: Diederichs, 1921–28.

52. Caton-Thompson, *Mixed Memoirs*, 133–4; N. Schlanger, 'The Burkitt affair revisited: colonial implications and identity politics in early South African prehistoric research', *Archaeological Dialogues* (2003), **10**, 5–26, esp. 21–3.

53. St C.A. Wallace, *The Great Zimbabwe Ruins, Mashonaland, Southern Rhodesia* [London, printed by Hazell, Watson & Viney], 1934, 10. Ironically it was

'Weary' Wallace who organised the logistics and labour of Caton-Thompson's excavations: see Caton-Thompson, *Mixed Memoirs*, 117 ff.

54. R.J. Fothergill (ed.), *The Monuments of Southern Rhodesia*, [Bulawayo:] Commission for the Preservation of Natural and Historical Monuments and Relics, 1953, 68–74; C.K. Cooke, *A Guide to the Historic and Pre-historic Monuments of Rhodesia*, Bulawayo: Historical Monuments Commission, 1972; T.N. Huffman, *Guide to the Great Zimbabwe Ruins*, Salisbury: Trustees of the National Museums & Monuments of Rhodesia, 1976; reviewed R. Derricourt, *African Book Publishing Record* (1979), 5, 20–1.

55. H. Kuklick, 'Contested monuments: the politics of archeology in Southern Africa', in G.W. Stocking (ed.), *Colonial Situations: essays on the contextualization of ethnographic knowledge*, Madison, WI: University of Wisconsin Press, 1991, 135–69, see esp. 158–62.

56. Summers, *Ancient Mining*, 6–7.

57. Hall and Neal, *Ancient Ruins*.

58. C.A. Hromnik, *Indo-Africa: towards a new understanding of Sub-saharan Africa*, Cape Town: Juta, 1981.

59. M. Hall and C.H. Borland, 'The Indian connection: an assessment of Hromnik's "Indo-Africa"', *South African Archaeological Bulletin* (1982), 37, 75–80.

60. In a book published locally in 2006 Tanzanian professional archaeologist Felix A. Chami has advanced a grand sweep of theories linking ancient Egypt to southern and eastern Africa, with a 'Libyco–Berber–Khoisan corridor' bringing peoples from North to South Africa *after* the main migrations of black African people; F.A. Chami, *The Unity of African Ancient History 3000 BC to AD 500*, Dar es-Salaam: E & D, 2006.

61. A.J. Clement, *The Kalahari and its Lost City*, Cape Town: Longmans, 1967; list on 195–6.

62. There is considerable ambiguity over when and for how long he travelled. Clement, *Lost City*, 79–86.

63. *Cape Argus*, 22 July 1885, reprinted in Clement, *Lost City*, 162–4.

64. G.A. Farini, 'A recent journey in the Kalahari', *Proceedings of the Royal Geographical Society and Monthly Record of Geography* (1886), 8, 437–53.

65. Ibid., 447.

66. G.A. Farini [W.L. Hunt], *Through the Kalahari Desert*, London: Sampson Low, Marston, Searle & Rivington, 1886; New York: Scribner & Welford (reprinted Cape Town: Struik, 1973); Clement, *Lost City*, 67–9.

67. Farini, *Through the Kalahari Desert*, vi–vii; Clement, *Lost City*, 67–9.

68. Farini, *Through the Kalahari Desert*, 269.

69. Clement, *Lost City*, 24, 28.

70. A. Paton (ed. Hermann Wittenberg), *Lost City of the Kalahari*, Scottsville: University of KwaZulu-Natal Press, 2005. Paton's biographer Peter Alexander (pers. comm.) confirmed that Paton was talked into participating in (and eventually paying for) the expedition by a friend, Sailor Ibbotson, at a time when Paton was in a period of personal stress. The manuscript was rediscovered in Paton's papers.

71. *Rand Daily Mail*, 1 August 1964, quoted in Clement, *Lost City*, 35–6.

72. Clement, *Lost City*, 145–51.

73. http://www.wilbursmithbooks.com/novels/the_sunbird.html.

74. Martin Hall has drawn links between myths of the lost cities of Africa, Wilbur Smith's writing and the huge 1990s resort development The Lost City, in M.

Hall, 'The legend of the lost city; or, the man with golden balls', *Journal of Southern African Studies* (1995), **21**, 179–99.

75. http://credomutwa.com/about/.

76. Mutwa, *My People*, Harmondsworth: Penguin, 1971, 222–4.

77. D. Chidester, 'Credo Mutwa, Zulu shaman: the invention and appropriation of indigenous authenticity in African folk religion', *Journal for the Study of Religion* (2002), **15**, 65–85.

78. Since the 1980s it has been translated into a number of African languages – http://198.54.80.51/search/amutwa/amutwa/1%2C4%2C26%2CB/frameset &FF=amutwa+credo+vusamazulu+1921&5%2C%2C23.

79. V.C. Mutwa, *Song of the Stars: the lore of a Zulu shaman*, Barrytown, NY: Barrytown Ltd, 1996. Reissued ca. 2003 by Destiny Books of Rochester as *Zulu Shaman: dreams, prophecies, and mysteries*.

80. Mutwa, *My People*, 56–63, 69 ff, 96, 119–20, 123, 136–7, 145, 156.

81. Ibid., 9.

82. Chidester, 'Credo Mutwa, Zulu shaman'.

83. C.P. Blakeney, 'Review of *Indaba My Children*', *African Historical Studies* (1968), **1**, 122–5.

84. *Times Literary Supplement*, 15 December 1966, 1166 [anonymous review].

85. K.P. Kent, 'Review of *Indaba, My Children*', *Africa Today* (1968), **15**, 35.

86. B. Rose, 'Review of *Indaba, My Children*', *Journal of Modern African Studies* (1965), **3**, 471–2.

87. P. Carstens, 'Vusamazulu Credo Mutwa, *Indaba My Children*: African tribal history, legends, customs and religious beliefs', *African and Asian Studies* (1968), **3**, 146–7.

88. P.L. van den Berghe, 'Credo Vusa'mazulu Mutwa, *My People, My Africa*', *African and Asian Studies* (1972), **7**, 140–1.

89. B. Davidson, 'Review of *My people, My Africa*', *Saturday Review* (1969), **52**, 13 September, 32.

90. C.P. Blakeney, 'Review of *Indaba My Children*', *African Historical Studies* (1968), **1**, 122–5.

91. Chidester, 'Credo Mutwa, Zulu shaman', 67, 72–3, 82.

92. http://www.livevideo.com/video/urnow/115AA93BA5DF4624A87D78EBD19 43B91/credo-mutwa-reveals-the-reptil.aspx.

93. Chidester's thoughtful analysis is a rare example of scholars seeking to understand Mutwa's life and work.

94. Mutwa, *My People*, 163, 165–6.

95. L. Watson, *Lightning Bird: the story of one man's journey into Africa's past* (also *Lightning Bird: an African adventure*), London: Hodder & Stoughton, 1982, reprinted in paperback in 1983, is an account of Adrian Boshier, with a publisher's puff 'how a lone Englishman survived unarmed in the African jungle and was instructed in the secrets of a witch doctor'.

96. Watson, *Lightning Bird*, 1983 edn, 143 ff.

CHAPTER 3: LOOKING BOTH WAYS

1. A longer version of this chapter appeared as R. Derricourt, 'The enigma of Raymond Dart', *International Journal of African Historical Studies* (2009) **42**, 257–82. See also R. Derricourt, 'Raymond Dart and the danger of mentors', *Antiquity* (2010), **84**, 230–5.

2. A. Keith, 'The Taungs skull', *Nature* (1925), **116**, 11.

3. A detailed, but uncritical and hagiographical, narrative biography of Dart was published as F. Wheelhouse and K.S. Smithford, *Dart: scientist and man of grit*, Sydney: Transpareon Press, 2001, complementing Dart's own memoir, R.A. Dart and D. Craig, *Adventures with the Missing Link*, London: Hamish Hamilton, 1959 and other sources (P.V. Tobias, *Dart, Taung and the Missing Link*, Johannesburg: Witwatersrand University Press, 1984). Critical assessments appeared as S. Dubow, 'Human origins, race typology and the other Raymond Dart', *African Studies* (1996), **55**, 1–30, and S. Dubow, *Scientific Racism in Modern South Africa*, Cambridge: Cambridge University Press, 1995.

4. S. Marchand, 'Leo Frobenius and the revolt against the West', *Journal of Contemporary History* (1997), **32**, 153–70.

5. Wheelhouse and Smithford, *Dart*.

6. G. Elliot Smith, *The Ancient Egyptians and the Origin of Civilization*, London & New York: Harper, 1911; G. Daniel, *The Idea of Prehistory*, Harmondsworth: Penguin, 1964.

7. R.A. Dart, 'The South African Negro', *American Journal of Physical Anthropology* (1929), **13**, 309–18, at 315.

8. Dart's publications are listed in Wheelhouse and Smithford, *Dart*, 331–43; M. Dart, 'Raymond A. Dart – list of publications 1920–1967', *South African Journal of Science* (1968), **64**, 134–40; I. Fischer, *Professor Raymond Arthur Dart: a bibliography of his works*, Johannesburg: University of the Witwatersrand, Department of Bibliography, Librarianship and Typography (cyclostyled), 1969.

9. Wheelhouse and Smithford, *Dart*, 58.

10. R.A. Dart, 'Associations with and impressions of Sir Grafton Elliot Smith', *Mankind* (1972), **8**, 171–5.

11. The timetable of events has been reconstructed by Tobias, *Dart, Taung*, 16–34, correcting some errors by Dart and Craig, *Adventures*.

12. R.A. Dart, 'Australopithecus africanus: The Man-Ape of South Africa', *Nature* (1925), **115**, 2884, 195–9, reprinted *South African Journal of Science* (1968), **64**, 51–7.

13. Dart and Craig, *Adventures*, 50–1; R.A. Dart, 'The status of Australopithecus', *American Journal of Physical Anthropology* (1940), **26**, 167–86.

14. A. Keith et al., 'The fossil anthropoid ape from Taungs', *Nature* (1925), **115**, 234–6.

15. Keith, 'The Taungs skull', 11.

16. P.V. Tobias, 'Piltdown: an appraisal of the case against Sir Arthur Keith', *Current Anthropology* (1992), **33**, 243–93; Dart and Craig, *Adventures*, 64.

17. A. Keith, 'Australopithecenae or Dartians', *Nature* (1947), **159**, 377.

18. R.A. Dart, 'A note on Makapansgat: a site of early human occupation', *South African Journal of Science* (1925), **22**, 454.

19 R Derricourt, 'Patenting hominins: taxonomies, fossils and egos', *Critique of Anthropology* (2009), **29**, 193–204.

20. P. Tobias, *Into the Past: a memoir*, Johannesburg: Picador Africa, 2005, 218.

21. R.A. Dart, 'The Makapansgat proto-human Australopithecus Prometheus', *American Journal of Physical Anthropology* (1948), **6**, 259–83, at 275.

22. B. Wood, 'An interview with Phillip Tobias', *Current Anthropology* (1989), **30**, 215–24, at 216.

23. S. James, 'Hominid use of fire in the Lower and Middle Pleistocene: a review of the evidence', *Current Anthropology* (1989), **30**, 1–26.

24. Dart and Craig, *Adventures*, 157–8.

25. Wood, 'An interview', 215–16.

26. R.A. Dart, *The Osteodontokeratic Culture of Australopithecus prometheus*, Pretoria: Transvaal Museum Memoir 7, 1957.

27. R.A. Dart, 'Further light on australopithecine humeral and femoral weapons', *American Journal of Physical Anthropology* (1959), **17**, 87–94.

28. R.A. Dart, 'From cannon-bone scoops to skull bowls at Makapansgat', *American Journal of Physical Anthropology* (1962), **20**, 287–95.

29. Dart and Craig, *Adventures*, 114, 201.

30. R. Ardrey, *African Genesis*, New York: Athaneum, 1961.

31. R.K. Brain, *The Hunters or the Hunted?*, Chicago: Chicago University Press, 1981; D.L. Wolberg, 'The hypothesized Osteodontokeratic Culture of the Australopithecines', *Current Anthropology* (1970), **11**, 23–37; P. Shipman and J.E. Phillips, 'On scavenging by hominids and other carnivores', *Current Anthropology* (1976), **17**, 170–2.

32. R.A. Dart, 'Boskop remains from the South-east African Coast', *Nature* (1923), **112**, 623–5.

33. Ibid.; Wheelhouse and Smithford, *Dart*, 57.

34. R.A. Dart, 'Recent discoveries bearing on human history in Southern Africa', *Journal of the Royal Anthropological Institute* (1940), **70**, 13–27.

35. R. Singer, 'The Boskop "race" problem', *Man* (1958), **58**, 173–8.

36. R.A. Dart and N. del Grande, 'The ancient iron-smelting cavern at Mumbwa', *Transactions of the Royal Society of South Africa* (1931), **19**, 379–427, at 421.

37. R.A. Dart, 'Three strandlopers from the Kaokaoveld Coast', *South African Journal of Science* (1955), **51**, 175–9.

38. Dart, 'Recent discoveries', 22.

39. R.A. Dart, 'Racial origins', in I. Schapera, ed., *Bantu-speaking Tribes of South Africa: an ethnographic survey*, London: Routledge, 1937, 1–37.

40. P.V. Tobias, 'The biology of the Southern African Negro', in W.D Hammond-Tooke, ed., *The Bantu-speaking Peoples of Southern Africa*, London: Routledge, 1974, 3–45, at 11.

41. Dart and Craig, *Adventures*, 71–2; Wheelhouse and Smithford, *Dart*, 184–5; see also Dubow, 'Human origins', 16–19; R.A. Dart, 'A Hottentot from Hong Kong: pre-Bantu population exchanges between Africa and Asia', *South African Journal of Medical Science* (1952), **17**, 117–42, at 125–6.

42. R.A. Dart, 'The historical succession of cultural impacts upon South Africa', *Nature* (1925), **115**, 425–9.

43. M. Burkitt, *South Africa's Past in Stone and Paint*, Cambridge: Cambridge University Press, 1928; A.J.H. Goodwin and C. van Riet Lowe, *The Stone Age Cultures of South Africa*, Annals of the South African Museum 27, Cape Town: South African Museum, 1929.

44. Dart and del Grande, 'Ancient iron smelting', 403.

45. R.A. Dart, 'Phallic objects in Southern Africa', *South African Journal of Science* (1929), **26**, 553–62; R.A. Dart, 'A Chinese character as a wall motive in Rhodesia', *South African Journal of Science* (1939), **36**, 74–6; R.A. Dart, 'The ritual employment of bored stones by Transvaal Bantu tribes', *South African Archaeological Bulletin* (1948), **3**, 61–6.

46. R.A. Dart, 'Rhodesian engravers, painters and pigment miners of the fifth millennium', *South African Archaeological Bulletin* (1953), **8**, 91–6, at 94; R.A. Dart, 'Further data on the origin and phallic character of conical and perforated stones', *South African Journal of Science* (1932), **29**, 731–41, at 737.

47. R.A. Dart, 'Paintings that link south with north Africa', *South African Archaeological Bulletin* (1963), **18**, 29–30.

48. Dart, 'Historical succession', 426.

49. Dart, 'A Chinese character'.

50. Dubow, 'Human origins', 99; *Cape Times*, quoted in G. Caton-Thompson, *Mixed Memoirs*, Gateshead: Paradigm Press, 1983, 130–6.

51. Dart and Craig, *Adventures*, 68–71; Wheelhouse and Smithford, *Dart*, 118, 203.

52. R.A. Dart, 'A polished stone pendant from Makapansgat valley', *South African Archaeological Bulletin* (1949), **4**, 83–6.

53. Dart, 'Rhodesian engravers'.

54. Dart, 'South African Negro', 315.

55. R.A. Dart, 'Population fluctuation over 7000 years in Egypt', *Transactions of the Royal Society of South Africa* (1940), **27**, 95–145.

56. Ibid., 96–7.

57. R.A. Dart, *African Serological Patterns and Human Migrations*, Claremont: South African Archaeological Society, 1951.

58. Dart, 'Hottentot from Hong Kong', 136–8.

59. R.A. Dart, 'Death ships in South West Africa and South-East Asia', *South African Archaeological Bulletin* (1962), **17**, 231-3.

60. Dart, 'Historical succession'; Dart and Craig, *Adventures*, 74.

61. R.A. Dart, 'Nickel in ancient bronzes', *Nature* (1924), **113**, 888.

62. R.A. Dart, 'The Bronze Age in southern Africa', *Nature* (1929), **123**, 495–6.

63. Dart and del Grande, 'Ancient iron smelting'; Wheelhouse and Smithford, *Dart*, 145.

64. Dart and del Grande, 'Ancient iron smelting', 419.

65. Ibid., 382; Wheelhouse and Smithford, *Dart*, 188.

66. R.A. Dart, 'The discovery of a stone age manganese mine at Chowa, Northern Rhodesia', *Transactions of the Royal Society of South Africa* (1934), **22**, 55–70.

67. Dart and del Grande, 'Ancient iron smelting', 400, 423.

68. R.A. Dart, 'The birth of symbology', *African Studies* (1968), **27**, 15–27.

69. Wheelhouse and Smithford, *Dart*, 189–91.

70. Ibid., 266–70.

71. R.A. Dart, 'The antiquity of mining in Southern Africa', *South African Journal of Science* (1967), **63**, 264–7; R.A. Dart and P. Beaumont, 'Amazing antiquity of mining in Southern Africa', *Nature* (1967), **216**, 407–8; R.A. Dart and P. Beaumont, 'Evidence of Iron Age mining in Southern Africa in the Middle Stone Age', *Current Anthropology* (1969), **10**, 127–8; R.A. Dart and P. Beaumont, 'On a further radiocarbon date for ancient mining in Southern Africa', *South African Journal of Science* (1971), **67**, 10–11.

72. Dart and Beaumont, 'Amazing antiquity'.

73. R.A. Dart and P.B. Beaumont, 'Iron Age radiocarbon dates from western Swaziland', *South African Archaeological Bulletin* (1969), **24**, 71.

74. Dubow, *Scientific Racism*, 287.

75. Tobias, *Dart, Taung*, 14; Dubow, *Scientific Racism*, 45–6; Dubow, 'Human origins', 11–12; F. Wheelhouse, *Raymond Arthur Dart: a pictorial profile*.

Professor Dart's discovery of 'The Missing Link', Sydney: Transpareon Press, 1983, 18; Dart, 'Note on Makapansgat', 79.

76. S. Dubow, *A Commonwealth of Knowledge: science, sensibility and White South Africa 1820–2000*, Oxford: Oxford University Press, 2006; Dubow, 'Human origins', 6–7.

77. Dubow, *Commonwealth of Knowledge*, 207.

78. Dart and Craig, *Adventures*, 241–2.

79. Quoted in ibid., 31.

80. Tobias, *Into the Past*, 216–17.

81. Daniel, *Idea of Prehistory*, 88–107.

82. Dart, 'Associations'.

83. Tobias, *Into the Past*, 68; P.V. Tobias, 'Homage to Emeritus Professor R A Dart on his 75th birthday', *South African Journal of Science* (1968), **64**, 42–50; P.V. Tobias, 'Raymond Arthur Dart (1893–1988)', *Nature* (1989), **337**, 211.

84. Tobias, *Into the Past*, 24.

CHAPTER 4: EGOS AND FOSSILS

1. Henry Morton Stanley was able to choose the European members of the Emin Pasha relief expedition of 1886–9 from over 400 applicants.

2. Clark Howell, cited in R. Lewin, *Bones of Contention*, London: Penguin, 1989, 25.

3. For example, the announcement in *Nature* (2004), **431** of the Flores 'Hobbit' hominid associated with Mike Morwood appeared in the name of 14 authors from eight institutions and the accompanying description associated with Peter Brown appeared in the name of seven authors from two institutions.

4. Most literature referred to the search for *hominids*, but current practice applies 'hominids' to both humans and the great apes and the term 'hominins' is now used for the lineage separate from that which led to the great apes. Until recently literature wrote of 'fossil man', but this has changed to a less gendered terminology.

5. R. Derricourt, 'Patenting hominins: taxonomies, fossils and egos', *Critique of Anthropology* (2009), **29**, 193–204.

6. R. Foley, 'Species diversity in human evolution: challenges and opportunities', *Transactions of the Royal Society of South Africa* (2005), **60**, 67–72. A new australopithecine species was proposed in 2010 for a find in South Africa: L.R. Berger et al., '*Australopithecus sediba*: a new species of *Homo*-like Australopith from South Africa', *Science* (2010), **328**, 195–204.

7. The requirements of international taxonomic nomenclature are to give species names italicised in context are followed by originator and date unitalicised.

8. *Obituary Notices of Fellows of the Royal Society* (1952), **8**, 36–70.

9. There have been numerous narrative accounts in print of Louis Leakey and the Leakey family. These includes Leakey's own autobiographical books, *White African*, London: Hodder & Stoughton, 1937, and *By the Evidence: memoirs 1932–1951*, New York: Harcourt Brace Jovanovich, 1974; a biography by friend Sonia Cole, written at the invitation of Mary Leakey: S. Cole, *Leakey's Luck: the life of Louis Seymour Bazett Leakey 1903–1972*, London: Collins, 1975; and a more thorough and less inhibited account of the whole family and their relations by Virginia Morell, *Ancestral Passions: the Leakey family and the quest for humankind's beginnings*, New York: Simon & Schuster, 1995.

10. Morell, *Ancestral Passions*, 80–93; Cole, *Leakey's Luck*, 90–104. He had announced a new species at a 1933 conference.

11. Morell, *Ancestral Passions*, 69, 73, 91, 118, 187–94; Cole, *Leakey's Luck*, 16, 210–11, 231.

12. Morell, *Ancestral Passions*, 205–7, 225–36.

13. Ibid., 292.

14. J.E.G. Sutton, 'Archaeology and reconstructing history in the Southern Highlands: the intellectual legacies of G.W.B. Huntingford and Louis S.B. Leakey', *History in Africa* (2006), **33**, 297–320.

15. E.g. Morell, *Ancestral Passions*, 65, 83–4, 99.

16. Ibid., 39, 68, 105, 178, 184.

17. Louis was 29, Mary was 20. See Cole, *Leakey's Luck*, 106 and Morell, *Ancestral Passions*, 68 ff.

18. Fifty-five was a common retirement age for British staff appointed to the colonial civil service.

19. M Posnansky, *Africa and Archaeology: empowering an expatriate life*, London: The Radcliffe Press, 2009, 98, 126, 209–10.

20. Morell, *Ancestral Passions*, 265.

21. Ibid., 31, 55, 89, 126, 150, 210, 272, 307–8, 331–2, 369–71.

22. Ibid., 181 ff.

23. L.S.B. Leakey, 'A new fossil skull from Olduvai', *Nature* (1959), **184**, 491–3, dated 15 August 1959, though the issue was actually published the following month.

24. Morell, *Ancestral Passions*, 316 ff; Cole, *Leakey's Luck*, 305–23.

25. Cole, *Leakey's Luck*, 351–67; Morell, *Ancestral Passions*, 362–71.

26. Morell, *Ancestral Passions*, 536.

27. Ibid., 450–2.

28. Popular accounts of Johanson's work appear in the co-authored D.C. Johanson and M.A. Edey, *Lucy: the beginnings of humankind*, New York: Simon & Schuster, 1981; and D.C. Johanson and J. Shreeve, *Lucy's Child,* New York: Morrow, 1989.

29. Morell, *Ancestral Passions*, 529, 533, 537. This controversy was at its most public in a television appearance on the US Walter Cronkite show; see the appropriately named *Bones of Contention* by Roger Lewin, London: Penguin, 1989, 13ff.

30. Lewin, *Bones of Contention*, 168 quotes Johanson: 'There I was, the son of a Swedish immigrant who was a cleaning lady. And I had been invited ... to participate in a Nobel Symposium.'

CHAPTER 5: STIRRING THE GENE POOL

1. R.G. Klein, *The Human Career: human biological and cultural origins*, 2nd edn, Chicago: University of Chicago Press, 1999, 514 ff.

2. Recently specialists have moved to referring to the African specimens of *H. erectus* under the species name *H. ergaster*.

3. P. Villa, 'Early Italy and the colonization of Western Europe', *Quaternary International* (2001), **75**, 113–30.

4. C. Finlayson et al., 'Late survival of Neanderthals at the southernmost extreme of Europe', *Nature* (2006), **443**, 850–3.

5. J. Agustí, H.-A. Blain, G. Cuenca-Bescós and S. Bailon Agusti, 'Forcing of first hominid dispersal in Western Europe', *Journal of Human Evolution* (2009), 57, 815–21.

6. R. Derricourt, 'Getting "Out of Africa": sea crossings, land crossings and culture in the hominin migrations', *Journal of World Prehistory* (2005), 19, 119–32; P. Vermeersch, '"Out of Africa" from an Egyptian point of view', *Quaternary International* (2001), 75, 1030–1112; R. Said, *The River Nile: geology, hydrology and utilization*, Oxford: Pergamon, 1993. However, if the Nile did dry up at 1.8 million years ago this could have been an incentive for the first migrations out of Africa; if it ran again at 800,000 years ago this would coincide with the dramatic spread of Acheulian culture into Eurasia.

7. R. Dennell, *The Palaeolithic Settlement of Asia*, Cambridge: Cambridge University Press, 2009, 333.

8. Ibid.; R. Dennell and W. Roebroeks, 'An Asian perspective on early human dispersal from Africa', *Nature* (2005), 438, 1099–1104.

9. M.J. Morwood and W.J. Jungers, 'Conclusions: implications of the Liang Bua excavations for hominin evolution and biogeography', *Journal of Human Evolution* (2009), 57, 640–8.

10. M. Morwood and I. Davidson, 'Out of ancient disasters, forebears may have colonised new lands', *Sydney Morning Herald*, 14 January 2004. The concept of rafting is discussed in more detail by J.M.B. Smith, 'Did early hominids cross sea gaps on natural rafts?', in M.I. Metcalf et al. (eds), *Faunal and Floral Migrations and Evolution in SE Asia–Australasia*, Lisse: Swets & Zeitlinger, 2001, 409–16.

11. C.B.M. McBurney, *The Stone Age of North Africa*, Harmondsworth: Penguin, 1960, 191–2.

12. J.D. Clark, *The Prehistory of Southern Africa*, Harmondsworth: Penguin, 1959, 155 etc.

13. S. Cole, *The Prehistory of East Africa*, 2nd edn, London: Weidenfeld & Nicolson, 1964.

14. J.D. Clark, *The Prehistory of Africa*, London: Thames & Hudson, 1970, 105 ff.

15. Ibid., 120.

16. Still up to ca. 80,000 in C.G. Sampson, *The Stone Age Archaeology of Southern Africa*, New York: Academic Press, 1974.

17. D.W. Phillipson, *African Archaeology*, Cambridge: Cambridge University Press, 1985, 60–3.

18. Summaries in Klein, *Human Career*, 503–4; G.C. Conroy, *Reconstructing Human Origins: a modern synthesis*, New York: Norton, 1997, 385–6; M. Cartmill and F.H. Smith, *The Human Lineage*, Hoboken, NJ: Wiley-Blackwell, 2009, 299–300; key arguments: D.W. Frayer, M.H. Wolpoff, A.G. Thorne, F.H. Smith and G.G. Pope, 'Theories of modern human origins: the paleontological test', *American Anthropologist* (1993), 95, 14–50; M.H. Wolpoff et al., 'Multiregional evolution: a world-wide source for modern human populations', in M.H. Nitecki and D.V. Nitecki (eds), *Origins of Anatomically Modern Humans*, New York: Plenum Press, 1994, 175–99.

19. Dennell, *Palaeolithic Settlement*, 333.

20. M.H. Wolpoff et al., 'Modern human ancestry at the peripheries: a test of the replacement theory', *Science* (2001), 291, 293–7; V. Eswaran, H. Harpending and A.R. Rogers, 'Genomics refutes an exclusively African origin of humans', *Journal of Human Evolution* (2005), 49, 1–18.

21. Derricourt, 'Patenting hominins', 201; Dennell *Palaeolithic Settlement*, 456.
22. R.E. Green et al., 'Analysis of one million base pairs of Neanderthal DNA', *Nature* (2006), **444**, 330; J.P. Noonan et al., 'Sequencing and analysis of Neanderthal genomic DNA', *Science* (2006), **314**, 1113–18.
23. R. Leakey, 'Early *Homo sapiens* remains from the Omo valley region of south-west Ethiopia', *Nature* (1969), 222, 1132–3; M.H. Day, 'Early *Homo sapiens* remains from the Omo River Region of South-west Ethiopia: Omo human skeletal remains', *Nature* (1969), **222**, 1135–8; I. McDougall, F.H. Brown and J.G. Fleagle, 'Stratigraphic placement and age of modern humans from Kibish, Ethiopia', *Nature* (2005), **433**, 733–6.
24. J.D. Clark, et al., 'Stratigraphic, chronological and behavioural contexts of Pleistocene *Homo sapiens* from Middle Awash, Ethiopia', *Nature* (2003), **423**, 747–52; T.D. White, B. Asfaw, D. DeGusta, H. Tilbert, G.D. Richards, G. Suwa and F.C. Howell, 'Pleistocene *Homo sapiens* from Middle Awash, Ethiopia', *Nature* (2003), **423**, 742–7.
25. E.g. R.L. Cann et al., 'Mitochondrial DNA and human evolution', *Nature* (1987), **329**, 111–12; L. Vigilant et al., 'African populations and the evolution of human mitochondrial DNA', *Science* (1991), **253**, 1503–7; a useful summary of the methodology and arguments is in Conroy, *Reconstructing Human Origins*, 387–401.
26. M. Ingman, H. Kaessmann, S. Pääbo and U. Gyllensten, 'Mitochondrial genome variation and the origin of modern humans', *Nature* (2000), **408**, 709–13.
27. E.g. M.K. Gonder, H.M. Mortensen, F.A. Reed, A. de Sousa and S.A. Tishkoff, 'Whole-mtDNA genome sequence analysis of ancient African lineages', *Molecular Biology and Evolution* (2007), **24**, 757–68.
28. Cartmill and Smith, *Human Lineage*, 436.
29. Klein, *Human Career*, 515; R. Klein, 'Anatomy, behaviour and modern human origins', *Journal of World Prehistory* (1995), **9**, 167–98.
30. W. Noble and I. Davidson, *Human Evolution, Language and Mind: a psychological and archaeological inquiry*, Cambridge: Cambridge University Press, 1996.
31. Ibid., 214.
32. Klein, *Human Career*, 454–9.
33. Ibid., 467–70.
34. Cartmill and Smith, *Human Lineage*, 392–6.
35. Klein, *Human Career*, 512.
36. Ibid., 589.
37. Noble and Davidson, *Human Evolution*, 206–7.
38. C. Henshilwood and J. Sealy, 'Bone artefacts from the Middle Stone Age at Blombos Cave, Southern Cape, South Africa', *Current Anthropology* (1997), **38**, 890–5.
39. F. d'Errico, C. Henshilwood, M. Vanhaeren and K. van Niekerk, '*Nassarius kraussianus* shell beads from Blombos Cave: evidence for symbolic behaviour in the Middle Stone Age', *Journal of Human Evolution* (2005), **48**, 3–24; C.S. Henshilwood, F. d'Errico and I. Watts, 'Engraved ochres from the Middle Stone Age levels at Blombos Cave, South Africa', *Journal of Human Evolution* (2009), **57**, 27–47.
40. K.S. Brown et al., 'Fire as an engineering tool of early modern humans', *Science* (2009), **325**, 859–62; C.W. Marean et al., 'Early human use of marine resources

and pigment in South Africa during the Middle Pleistocene', *Nature* (2007), **449**, 905–8.

41. J. Parkington, 'The archaeology of Late Pleistocene encephalisation in the Cape, Southern Africa', in H. Soodyall (ed.), *The Prehistory of Africa*, Johannesburg: Jonathan Ball, 2006, 64–75; C.L. Broadhurst, Y. Wang, M.A. Crawford, S.C. Cunnane, J.E. Parkington and W.F. Schmidt, 'Brain-specific lipids from marine, lacustrine, or terrestrial food resources: potential impact on early *Homo sapiens*', *Comparative Biochemistry and Physiology, Part B* (2002), **131**, 653–73.

42. I. Tattersall, 'Human origins: out of Africa', *Proceedings of the National Academy of Sciences* (2009), **106**, 16018–21, presents the rather curious argument that the human brain early had the potential for symbolic cognition but this was unexploited until discovered through the invention of language.

43. Noble and Davidson, *Human Evolution*, 184.

44. T.F. Strasser et al., 'Stone Age seafaring in the Mediterranean: evidence from the Plakias region for Lower Palaeolithic and Mesolithic habitation of Crete', *Hesperus* (2010), **79**, 145–90.

45. Q.D. Atkinson, R.D. Gray and A.J. Drummond, 'Bayesian coalescent inference of major human mitochondrial DNA haplogroup expansions in Africa', *Proceedings of the Royal Society B* (2009), **276**, 367–73.

46. Klein, *Human Career*, 402–4, 487–9; Conroy, *Reconstructing Human Origins*, 439–45.

47. In Marine Isotope Stage (MIS) 5e; A. Vaks et al., 'Desert speleotherms reveal climatic window for African exodus of early modern humans', *Geology* (2007), **35**, 831–4; A.H. Osborne et al., 'A humid corridor across the Sahara for the migration of early modern humans out of Africa 120,000 years ago', *Proceedings of the National Academy of Sciences* (2008), **105**, 16444–7.

48. In geological timescale, Dennell sees the movement of modern humans from Africa into Asia as most likely in a warm, moist interglacial, probably MIS 5, which is bracketed between 130,000 and 71,000 years ago, and climate studies show wide variability in the period 145,000–75,000 years ago, but this would relate to the early movement, which did not lead to the Eurasian dispersal. Dennell, *Palaeolithic Settlement*, 462 etc.; S.L. Carto et al., 'Out of Africa and into an ice age: on the role of global climate change in the late Pleistocene migration of early modern humans out of Africa', *Journal of Human Evolution* (2009), **56**, 139–51.

49. J.F. O'Connell and F.J. Allen, 'Dating the colonization of Sahul (Pleistocene Australia–New Guinea): a review of recent research', *Journal of Archaeological Science* (2004), **31**, 835–53.

50. J. Mulvaney and J. Kamminga, *Prehistory of Australia*, Sydney: Allen & Unwin, 1999, 103–12.

51. A. Beyin, 'The Bab al Mandab vs the Nile–Levant: an appraisal of the two dispersal routes for early modern humans out of Africa', *African Archaeological Review* (2006), **23**, 5–30.

52. The glacial MIS 4; P. Soares, et al., 'Correcting for purifying selection: an improved human mitochondrial molecular clock', *American Journal of Human Genetics* (2009), **84**, 740–59; Ingman, 'Mitochondrial genome variation'.

53. P. Mellars, 'Why did modern human populations disperse from Africa *ca.* 60,000 years ago? A new model', *Proceedings of the National Academy of Sciences* (2006), **103**, 9381–6; P. Forster and S. Matsumura, 'Did early humans go north or south?', *Science* (2005), **308**, 965–6.

54. Carto, 'Out of Africa'.
55. Mellars, 'Why did modern'.
56. Z. Jacobs et al., 'Ages for the Middle Stone Age of Southern Africa: implications for human behaviour and dispersal', *Science* (2008) **322**, 733–5.
57. D.M. Behar et al., 'The dawn of human matrilineal diversity', *American Journal of Human Genetics* (2008), **82**, 1130–40.
58. E.g. C. Stringer, 'Coasting out of Africa', *Nature* (2000), **405**, 24–6.
59. M.D. Petraglia, 'The Lower Palaeolithic of the Arabian Peninsula: occupations, adaptations, and dispersals', *Journal of World Prehistory* (2003), **17**, 141–78.
60. J. Rose, 'The Arabian corridor migration model: archaeological evidence for hominin dispersals into Oman during the Middle and Upper Pleistocene', *Proceedings of the Seminar for Arabian Studies* (2007), **37**, 1–19.
61. M.D. Petraglia and J.I. Rose (eds), *The Evolution of Human Populations in Arabia: paleoenvironments, prehistory and genetics*, Dordrecht: Springer, 2009.
62. R. Crassard, 'The Middle Paleolithic of Arabia', in Petraglia and Rose, *Evolution*, 151–68.
63. All within MIS 5. A.G. Parker, 'Pleistocene climate change in Arabia: developing a framework for hominin dispersal over the last 350 ka', in Petraglia and Rose, *Evolution*, 39–49.
64. V.M. Cabrera et al., 'The Arabian peninsula: gate for human migrations out of Africa or cul-de-sac? A mitochondrial DNA phylogeographic perspective', in Petraglia and Rose, *Evolution*, 79–87.
65. J.S. Field and M.M. Lahr, 'Assessment of the southern dispersal: GIS-based analyses of potential routes at Oxygen Isotope Stage 4', *Journal of World Prehistory* (2005), **19**, 1–45; Forster, 'Did early humans'; P. Mellars, 'Going East: new genetic and archaeological perspectives on the modern human colonization of Eurasia', *Science* (2006), **313**, 796–800; V. Macaulay et al., 'Single, rapid coastal settlement of Asia revealed by analysis of complete mitochondrial genomes', *Science* (2005), **308**, 1034–6 continues to indicate an out-of-Africa dispersal at around 55,000–70,000 years ago, 5,000–20,000 years before any clear archaeological record, suggesting the need for archaeological research efforts focusing on this time window.
66. Soares, 'Correcting for purifying selection'.

CHAPTER 6: ANCIENT EGYPT AND AFRICAN SOURCES OF CIVILISATION

1. C.G. Seligman, *Races of Africa*, London: Thornton Butterworth, 1930; 4th edn London: Oxford University Press, 1966, 61–2.
2. Ibid., 96; still retained in the 4th edn, 61–2.
3. E.R. Sanders, 'The Hamitic hypothesis: its origin and functions in time perspective', *Journal of African History* (1969), **10**, 521–32; Stephen Howe, *Afrocentrism: mythical pasts and imagined homes*, London: Verso, 1998, 115–16.
4. M. Mamdani, *When Victims Become Killers: colonialism, nativism, and the genocide in Rwanda*, Princeton: Princeton University Press, 2001.
5. W.R. Dawson (ed.), *Sir Grafton Elliot Smith: a biographical record by his colleagues*, London: Jonathan Cape, 1938.
6. Some 434 publications are listed in Dawson, *Smith*, 219–56.

7. F.W. Jones, 'In Egypt and Nubia', in ibid., 139–50.
8. Dawson, *Smith*, 54.
9. G.E. Smith, *Ancient Egyptians and the Origin of Civilization*, London: Harper & Bros, 1911, with 2nd expanded edition 1923.
10. Ibid., 2nd edn, 79, 91–2.
11. Introduction to ibid., 2nd edn.
12. Ibid., 2nd edn, 185.
13. D. O'Connor, 'Egypt and Greece: the Bronze Age evidence', in M. Lefkowitz and G.M. Rogers (eds), *Black Athena Revisited*, Chapel Hill, NC: University of North Carolina Press, 1996, 49–61, notes (54) that Egypt was unlikely to have spread their maritime activities even to the Mediterranean.
14. Smith, *Ancient Egyptians*, 2nd edn, 196–200.
15. Dawson, *Smith*, 69.
16. M.S. Drower, *Flinders Petrie*, Madison, WI: University of Wisconsin Press & London: Gollancz, 1985, 345–7.
17. Dawson, *Smith*, from different contributors.
18. Smith, *Ancient Egyptians*, 2nd edn, vii.
19. G.E. Smith, *The Migrations of Early Culture*, Manchester: Manchester University Press & London: Longmans Green, 1915; 2nd edn 1929; *On the Significance of the Geographical Distribution of the Practice of Mummification: a study of the migrations of peoples and the spread of certain customs and beliefs*, Manchester: Manchester Literary and Philosophical Society, 1915; *The Evolution of the Dragon*, Manchester: Manchester University Press, 1919; *The Evolution of Man: essays*, London: Humphrey Milford, 1924; 2nd edn 1927; *In the Beginning: the origin of civilisation*, London: Howe, 1928; new edn 1932, London: Watts (Thinkers Library); *Human History*, 1930, London: Cape; rev. edn 1934; *Early Man: his origin, development and culture*, London: Benn, 1931; *The Diffusion of Culture*, London: Watts, 1933.
20. Smith, *Human History*, 49, fig. 13; 89, fig. 29.
21. Ibid., 122 ff.
22. V.G. Childe, *The Most Ancient East: the oriental prelude to European prehistory*, London: Kegan Paul, Trench, Trubner, 1928.
23. Smith, *Human History*, 345, 439.
24. Smith, *The Diffusion of Culture*, 209.
25. Wang Gung-wu noted with surprising civility Smith's views that Chinese civilisation owed its origins to ancient Egypt; 'Chinese civilization and the diffusion of culture', in A.P. Elkin and N.W.G. Macintosh (eds), *Grafton Elliot Smith: the man and his work*, Sydney: Sydney University Press, 1974, 197–209.
26. R.A. Dart, 'Cultural diffusion from, in and to Africa', in Elkin and Macintosh, *Smith*, 160–74.
27. A thorough and thoughtful analysis of Diop in context is Howe, *Afrocentrism*, 163–92; see also M. Hughes-Warrington, *Fifty Key Thinkers on History*, London: Routledge, 2007, 74–82; K.C. MacDonald, 'Cheikh Anta Diop and Ancient Egypt in Africa', in D. O'Connor and A. Reid (eds), *Ancient Egypt in Africa*, London: UCL Press, 2003, 93–106.
28. F.-X. Fauvelle, *L'Afrique de Cheikh Anta Diop: histoire et idéologie*, Paris: Éditions Karthala, 1996, 181–3 for a brief biographical note; 215–19 for a bibliography of Diop's published work.
29. A. Ba Konaré (ed.), *Petit précis de remise à niveau sur l'histoire africaine à l'usage du president Sarkozy*, Paris: La Découverte, 2008, 12, 99, 113–24.

30. C.A. Diop, *The African Origins of Civilization: myth or reality*, Westport, CT: Laurence Hill, 1974 [translations of chapters from the 1955 and 1967 books].

31. T. Obenga, *Cheikh Anta Diop: Volney et le Sphinx*, Paris: Présence Africaine, 1995.

32. Fauvelle, *L'Afrique*, 10.

33. Ibid., 19, 172–4.

34. Ba Konaré, *Petit précis*, 15.

35. Diop, *African Origins*, 43.

36. F. Livingstone, 'On the non-existence of human races', *Current Anthropology* (1962), **3**, 279–81.

37. A detailed analysis of why 'black or white?' is a false question, and a reflection of current social and political perspectives, is in C.L. Brace, 'Clines and clusters versus "Race": a test in ancient Egypt and the case of a death on the Nile', in Lefkowitz and Rogers, *Black Athena Revisited*, 129–64, reprinted from *Yearbook of Physical Anthropology* (1993) **36**, 1–31.

38. Diop, *African Origins*, 53.

39. Ibid., 114, 183.

40. Ibid., 113.

41. C.A. Diop, *L'unité culturelle de l'Afrique noire: domaines du patriarcat et du matriarcat dans l'antiquité classique*, Paris: Présence africaine, 1959; C.A. Diop, *Alerte sous les Tropiques*, Paris: Présence Africaine, 1990.

42. Diop, *African Origins*, 103 ff.

43. Ibid., xvii.

44. MacDonald, 'Cheikh Anta Diop', 101.

45. Brace, 'Clines', 162.

46. Diop, *African Origins*, xv.

47. Howe, *Afrocentrism*, 35; A. Isaacman, 'Legacies of engagement', *African Studies Review* (2003), **46**, 1–41, esp. 8–14.

48. Howe, *Afrocentrism*, 213–17.

49. A.M. Roth, 'Ancient Egypt in America: claiming the riches', in L. Meskell (ed.), *Archaeology Under Fire: nationalism, politics and heritage in the Eastern Mediterranean and Middle East*, London: Routledge, 1998, 217–29.

50. Howe, *Afrocentrism*, 177. Students of African history have considered the Afrocentrist movement with different reactions, many choosing to ignore it. Stephen Howe's critique of the whole movement from the progressive non-American angle has itself been criticised by Dutch scholar Wim van Binsbergen in *Politique africaine* (2000), **79**, 175–80, with a longer version at http://www.shikanda.net/afrocentrism/defence.htm. Bimsbergen has been a voice defending the role in African historiography of a further important figure: Martin Bernal.

51. A. Mazrui, 'The re-invention of Africa: Edward Said, V.Y. Mudimbe and beyond', *Research in African Literatures* (2005), **36**, 68–82, at 77.

52. M. Bernal, 'Basil Davidson: a personal appreciation', *Race and Class* (1994), **32**, 101–3.

53. Martin Bernal, *Black Athena: Afroasiatic Roots of Classical Civilization*, Volume I: *The Fabrication of Ancient Greece, 1785–1985*, London: Free Association Books & New Brunswick, NJ: Rutgers University Press, 1987; Volume II: *The Archaeological and Documentary Evidence*, 1991; Volume III: *The Linguistic Evidence*, 2006.

54. E.g. Lefkowitz and Rogers, *Black Athena Revisited*; M. Lefkowitz, *Not Out of Africa: how Afrocentrism became an excuse to teach myth as history*, New York: Basic Books, 1996; M. Bernal, *Black Athena Writes Back: Martin Bernal responds to his critics*, Durham, NC: Duke University Press, 2001 (ironically, five years before the appearance of Volume III).

55. The composite catalogue of British academic library holdings in late 2009 suggested 46 library holdings of Volume I, 29 of Volume II and only 3 of Volume III. The Australian equivalent holdings are even more biased to the first two volumes.

56. Bernal, *Black Athena*, III, 10–11, 583–4.

57. Ibid., I, 401–2, 435 ff.

58. M.K. Asante and A. Mazama (eds), *Encyclopedia of Black Studies*, Thousand Oaks, CA: Sage, 2005, 145.

59. Bernal, *Black Athena*, I, 17, 73.

60. Ibid., I, xiv.

61. Bernal, *Black Athena Writes Back*, 154–5.

62. Bernal, *Black Athena*, II, 355–8.

63. G.G.M. James, *Stolen Legacy: the Greeks were not the authors of Greek philosophy, but the people of North Africa, commonly called the Egyptians*, New York: Philosophical Library, 1954. See Bernal, *Black Africa Writes Back*, 373–95.

64. Bernal, *Black Athena*, I, 15, 51–2.

65. Ibid., I, 242; II, 268.

66. Lefkowitz, *Not Out of Africa*, 52.

67. J.A. North, 'Attributing colour to the ancient Egyptians: reflections on *Black Athena*', in O'Connor and Reid, *Ancient Egypt*, 31–8.

68. Bernal, *Black Athena*, III, 48 ff.

69. Ibid., III, 88–9.

CHAPTER 7: OLD STATES GOOD, NEW STATES BAD

1. His influence and importance are noted in A. Isaacman, 'Legacies of engagement', *African Studies Review* (2003), **46**, 1–41.

2. E.g. A. Mazrui, *The Africans: a triple heritage*, Boston: Little Brown & London: BBC Publications, 1986, 73–5; A. Mazrui, 'The re-invention of Africa: Edward Said, V.Y. Mudimbe and beyond', *Research in African Literatures* (2005), **36**, 68–82.

3. B. Davidson, *Old Africa Rediscovered*, London: Gollancz, 1959; *The Black Man's Burden: Africa and the curse of the nation state*, London: James Currey & New York: Times Books, 1992.

4. A. Temu and B. Swai, *Historians and Africanist History: a critique*, London: Zed Press, 1981, 63–4.

5. See, for example, *Northern Rhodesia Journal* from 1950, dominated by accounts of the European colony, which began only 60 years earlier.

6. R. Hunt Davis, Jr, 'Teaching African history in an era of globalization', *History Compass* (2005), 3, 1–5.

7. P.D. Curtin, 'African Studies: a personal assessment', *African Studies Review* (1971), **14**, 357–68.

8. The US Peace Corps was founded in 1961; of 195,000 volunteers since then a significant number have worked in African countries

9. M.K. Asante and A. Mazama (eds), *Encyclopedia of Black Studies*, Thousand Oaks, CA: Sage, 2005, 148.

10. F. Rojas, *From Black Power to Black Studies: how a radical social movement became an academic discipline*, Baltimore, MD: Johns Hopkins University Press, 2007, 22.

11. A.L. Smith, 'Editor's message', *Journal of Black History* (1970), **1**, 3–4. Some 40 years later the same journal would be running a special issue on the Barack Obama phenomenon.

12. Rojas, *From Black Power*, 112. In due course the field developed into a solid if specialised academic discipline, though a review of its future distinguishes the committed teachers and scholars from less qualified 'opportunists'. See M. Christian, 'Black Studies in the 21st century', *Journal of Black Studies* (2006), **36**, 698–719.

13. A useful summary of Davidson's life is in a special issue of *Race and Class* devoted to him on his 80th birthday; B. Munslow, 'Basil Davidson and Africa: a biographical essay', *Race and Class* (1994), **36**, 1–18; and B. Munslow, 'Books by Basil Davidson: a chronology of original editions', *Race and Class* (1994), **36**, 105–6. Munslow notes Davidson was offered a safe parliamentary seat by the post-war Labour Party but declined.

14. V. Brittain, 'Obituaries: Basil Davidson', *The Guardian*, 10 July 2010, 37. See also 'Basil Davidson', *The Daily Telegraph*, 19 July 2010.

15. http://www.hull.ac.uk/arc/downloads/DDCcatalogue.pdf catalogues UDC papers, which include pamphlets by Davidson on Germany (ca. 1949, 1950, 1952, 1955 and 1958), Berlin (1961), Spain (1951), Japan (1951), China (1953), South Africa (1953), NATO (1954), Hungary (1956), the Arab World (1956) disarmament (1960), Angola (1961) and Africa (1962).

16. Brief summary by T. Falola and J.E. Tishken, 'Basil Davidson', in K. Boyd (ed.), *Encyclopedia of Historians and Historical Writing*, Chicago: Fitzroy Dearborn, 1999, 286–7, who note his work is seen as 'biased and selective' and that his works have been translated into 17 languages.

17. Davidson, *Black Man's Burden*, 5–6.

18. B. Davidson, *Report on Southern Africa*, London: Cape, 1952.

19. [P.S.], *African Affairs* (1953), 82–3.

20. B. Davidson and A. Ademola (eds), *The New West Africa: problems of independence*, London: Allen & Unwin, 1953 & New York: Macmillan, 1954.

21. B. Davidson, *The Search for Africa*, London: James Currey & New York: Crown, 1994, 99.

22. B. Davidson. *The African Awakening*, London: Jonathan Cape, 1955.

23. Davidson, *Search for Africa*, 180.

24. B. Davidson, *The Story of Africa*, London: Mitchell Beazley, 1984.

25. Munslow, 'Basil Davidson and Africa', 8–10.

26. B. Davidson, *The People's Cause: a history of guerrillas in Africa*, London: Longman, 1981.

27. S. Howe, 'The interpreter: Basil Davidson as public intellectual', *Race and Class* (1994), **36**, 19–43.

28. *The Millennium Development Goals Report 2005*, New York: United Nations Department of Public Information DPI/2390, May 2005.

29. *The Millennium Development Goals Report 2009*, New York: United Nations, 2009.

30. Davidson, *Black Man's Burden*.

31. Howe, 'The interpreter', 25.
32. O. Patterson, 'Rethinking black history', *Harvard Educational Review* (1971), **41**, 297–315.
33. B. Davidson, *Old Africa Rediscovered*, London: Gollancz, 1959; 2nd edn London: Longman, 1970.
34. Davidson, *Old Africa Rediscovered*, 2nd edn, 266-8.
35. Ibid., 2nd edn, 16.
36. B. Davidson, *African Kingdoms* [Netherlands]: TimeLife International 1967.
37. Oliver in Davidson, *African Kingdoms*, 7.
38. B. Davidson, *Black Mother*, 2nd edn, London: Longman, 1970, 35, 47, 96.
39. Ibid., 196.
40. Ibid., 208.
41. Ibid., 247.
42. B. Davidson, *Africa: history of a continent*, London: Weidenfeld & Nicolson, 1966; new edition, *Africa in History: themes and outlines*, New York: Collier, 1991.
43. Davidson, *Africa in History* (1991), 66, 71, 180.
44. Ibid., 91.
45. Ibid., 151.
46. Ibid., 277.
47. Ibid., 100.
48. Ibid., 310–14.
49. Ibid., 311.
50. B. Davidson, *Africa in History*, St Albans: Granada (Paladin), 1974.
51. Ibid., 326.
52. Davidson, *Africa in History* (1991), 351.
53. Ibid., 371.
54. Ibid., xxi.
55. B. Davidson, *Africa in History*, London: Orion, 2001.
56. B. Davidson *Africa in Modern History*, London: Allen Lane, 1978.
57. B. Davidson, 'The search for Africa's past', reprinted in Davidson, *Search for Africa*, 21.
58. Davidson, *Search for Africa*, 247–8.

CHAPTER 8: THE PRESENT OF THE PAST

1. A. Temu and B. Swai, *Historians and Africanist History: a critique*, London: Zed Press, 1981.
2. N. Shepherd, 'The politics of archaeology in Africa', *Annual Review of Anthropology*, (2002), **31**, 189–209; N. Shepherd, 'State of the discipline: science, culture and identity in South African archaeology, 1870–2003', *Journal of Southern African Studies* (2003), **29**, 823–44.
3. Shepherd, 'Politics', 197.
4. E.M. Sibanda, *The Zimbabwe African People's Union 1961-87: a political history of insurgency in Southern Rhodesia*, Trenton, NJ: Africa World Press, 2005, 91–3.
5. T. Ranger, 'Nationalist historiography, patriotic history and the history of the nation: the struggle over the past in Zimbabwe', *Journal of Southern African Studies* (2004), **30**, 215–34. Ironically, the Mugabe senior team included a

former historian of repute, Stan Mudenge, as minister of foreign affairs then minister of higher education.

6. Ranger, 'Nationalist historiography', 231. As with many countries holding a distinguished deep past, echoes of the prehistoric stone-building tradition have been used in modern architecture: see I. Pikirayi, 'The kingdom, the power and forevermore: Zimbabwe culture in contemporary art and architecture', *Journal of Southern African Studies* (2006), **32**, 755–70.

7. T. Barnes, '"History has to play its role": constructions of race and reconciliation in secondary school historiography in Zimbabwe 1980–2002', *Journal of Southern African Studies* (2007), **33**, 633–51.

8. G.M. Gerhart, *Black Power in South Africa: the evolution of an ideology*, Berkeley: University of California Press, 1978, 207.

9. M. Gevisser, *A Legacy of Liberation: Thabo Mbeki and the future of the South African dream*, New York: Palgrave Macmillan, 2009, 220–2; T. Mbeki, *Africa Define Yourself*, Cape Town: Tafelberg, 2002; here (91) he does define palaeontology and archaeology as a resource emerging from its narrower relevance to scientists and museum staff.

10. T. Mbeki, 13 August 1998, on http://www.anc.org.za/ancdocs/history/mbeki/1998/tm0813.htm.

11. M.W. Makgoba (ed.), *African Renaissance: the new struggle*, Sandton: Mafube & Cape Town: Tafelberg, 1999 presents the edited papers, including those by Magubane, Diop, Mzamane and Sertima.

12. M. Mzamane in Makgoba, *African Renaissance*, 183.

13. L. Vail (ed.), *The Creation of Tribalism in Southern Africa*, London: James Currey & Berkeley: University of California Press, 1989.

14. Shepherd, 'State of the discipline', 824–5.

15. M. Mamdani, *When Victims Become Killers: colonialism, nativism, and the genocide in Rwanda*, Princeton: Princeton University Press, 2001. See especially 16, 34–5, 51, 73–87, 99–100.

16. See W. Rubin (ed.), *Primitivism in 20th Century Art*, 2 vols, New York: Museum of Modern Art, 1984, Rubin, 74 note 1 for a discussion of the term 'tribal art'.

17. The name of the major 1994 fundraising event Band-Aid, which started the modern era of mass donations for Africa, was of course a pun on the short-term medical supply item.

18. *The Use of Science in UK International Development Policy*, House of Commons Science & Technology Select Committee, 2004.

19. Gavin Kitching at http://www.gavinkitching.com/africa.htm and links – see his article 'Why I gave up African Studies', *African Studies Review & Newsletter [Australia]* (2000), **22**, 21–6, reprinted in *Mots Pluriels* (December 2000), **16**.

20. B. Child, 'The emergence of parks and conservation narratives in southern Africa', in H. Suich and B. Child (eds), *Evolution and Innovation in Wildlife Conservation*, London: Earthscan, 2009, 19–33.

21. Jean-Louis Paudrat, 'From Africa', in Rubin, *Primitivism*, 125–75, esp. 125–37.

22. A.E. Coombes, *Reinventing Africa: museums, material culture and popular imagination in late Victorian and Edwardian England*, New Haven, CT: Yale University Press, 1994 details the British engagement with African images and objects at the height of imperial expansion.

23. To Jaime Sebartés in 1940. See Rubin, *Primitivism*. Picasso's own collection of African objects was unexceptional: 'you don't need a masterpiece to get the idea', Rubin, *Primitivism*, 14.

24. S. Lemke, *Primitive Modernism: black culture and the origins of transatlantic modernism*, New York: Oxford University Press, 1998, 6–7; Rubin, *Primitivism*, 11.

25. D. Touré, 'Taxonomy of African arts in France 1900–1999', *Mots Pluriels* (December 1999), **12**.

26. A. Mazrui, 'The re-invention of Africa: Edward Said, V.Y. Mudimbe and beyond', *Research in African Literatures* (2005), **36**, 68–82, at 77.

27. C. Turnbull, *The Mountain People*, London: Jonathan Cape, 1972; C. Turnbull, *The Forest People*, London: Chatto & Windus, 1961.

28. J. Keenan, *The Tuareg: people of the Ahaggar*, London: Allen Lane, 1977, 4, 7, 312.

29. T. Spear and R. Waller (eds), *Being Maasai: ethnicity and identity in East Africa*, Oxford: James Currey, 1993, 1–2, 14, 290–2.

30. John Marshall's documentary film *The Hunters* was released in 1957. The 1980 feature film *The Gods Must be Crazy* by Jamie Uys was the most successful South African film for many years.

31. A. Barnard, *Hunters and Herders of Southern Africa: a comparative ethnography of the Khoisan peoples*, Cambridge: Cambridge University Press, 1992.

32. First publications were L. van der Post, *The Lost World of the Kalahari*, London: Hogarth Press, 1958; *The Heart of the Hunter*, London: Hogarth Press, 1961.

33. J.D.F. Jones, *Storyteller: the many lives of Laurens van der Post*, London: John Murray 2001, esp. 210–39.

34. A. Barnard, 'The lost world of Laurens van der Post', *Current Anthropology* (1989), **30**, 104–14.

35. Ibid., 109–11; E.N. Wilmsen, *Land Filled with Flies: a political economy of the Kalahari*, Chicago: Chicago University Press, 1989.

Index